HAMMOND PUBLIC LIBRARY

3 1161 00875 8750

W9-BXW-044

Carey, Mike, 1959-
The unwritten 3, Dead
man's knock
TEEN FICTION CAREY
GN

APR 3 0 2013

HPL

WITHDRAWN

Nominated for 3 E[...]
Best New Series a[...]

"A wish-I'd-thought-of-it premise, b[...]
the very best work of their lives. [...]
more tha[...]

-Brian K. Vaug[...]

"A High-Min[...]
-PORTLAND MERCURY

"A taut thriller that slyly plays off the real-world mania for imaginary ones . . .
Carey has not only created a brisk and addictive story, sketched with crafty allusions to
classic literature, but also neatly subverted the celebrity-worship manias of fantasy fandom
and questioned the very nature of storytelling itself."

-PUBLISHERS WEEKLY

"Casually literate and intelligent, engrossing from the first page, THE UNWRITTEN is a gem
of a conspiracy story with enough metafictional layers to launch a thesis or two."

-SCRIPPS HOWARD NEWS SERVICE

"Incredibly fun and ridiculously addictive... A roller-coaster ride through a library, weaving famous
authors and characters into a tale of mystery that is, at once, oddly familiar yet highly original."

-USA TODAY

"Favorite book of the year."

- NEWSARAMA

"By the first page of the first issue of THE UNWRITTEN I was intrigued. By page 3 I knew I'd
be finishing the issue. Two pages later and I knew I'd be a fan and loyal reader of this new series
for its entire run (however long that may last - though I hope it is for many years to come). I
have been fans of Mike Carey and Peter Gross' comics work separately for many years. Now
I get to enjoy their work together in a comic series that I wish I had created. It's obvious that
the adult adventures of (possible) child star Tommy Taylor were written specifically for my
enjoyment, but I suppose they won't mind if you read along as well."

- Bill Willingham (Eisner-winning writer of *Fables*)

"Fascinating."

- BOSTON HERALD

the
unwritten
DEAD MAN'S KNOCK

Hammond Public Library
Hammond, IN

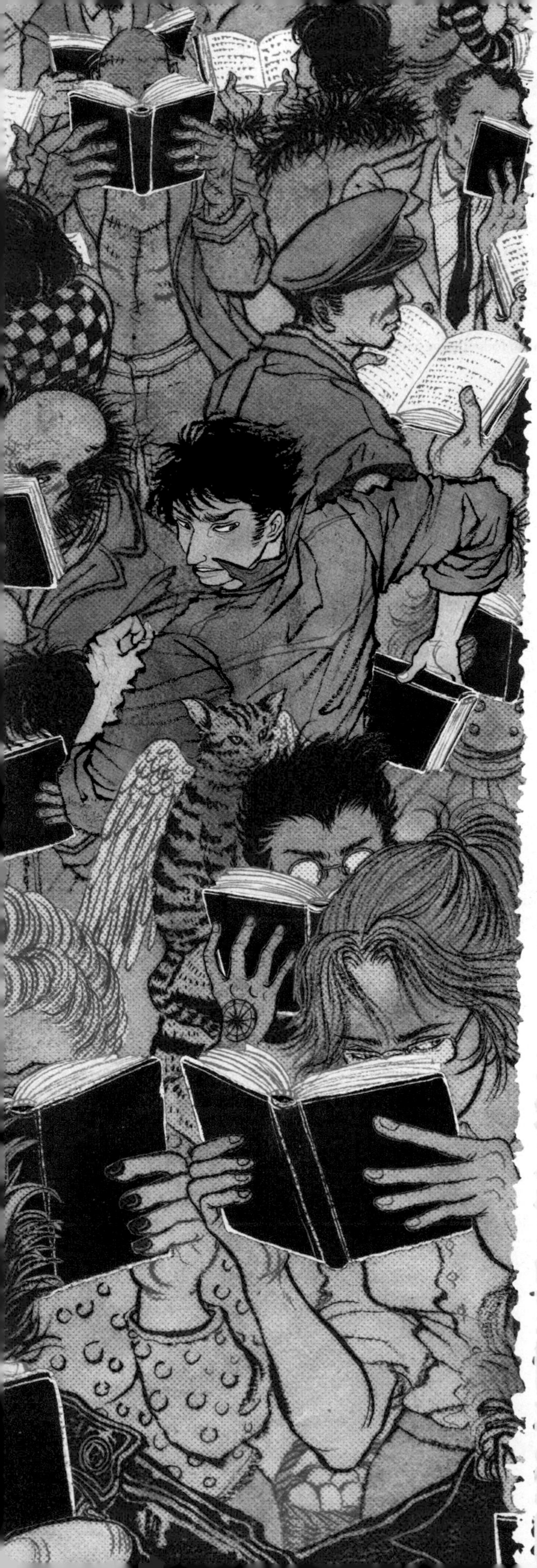

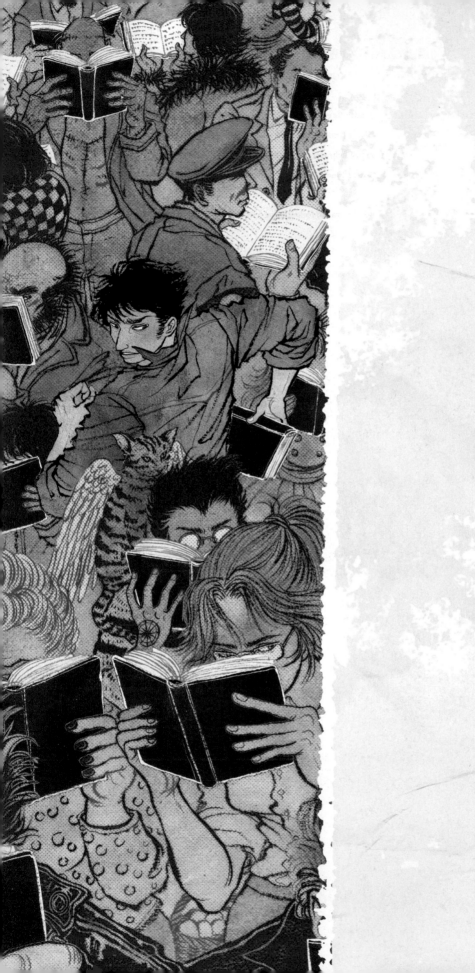

the Unwritten

DEAD MAN'S KNOCK

Mike Carey & Peter Gross Script – Story – Art

Ryan Kelly Finishes – The Many Lives of Lizzie Hexam

Chris Chuckry Jeanne McGee Colorists

Todd Klein Letterer Yuko Shimizu Cover Artist

THE UNWRITTEN created by Gross and Carey

nothing as mundane as revenge

Hammond Public Library
Hammond, IN

14.99

Karen Berger SVP-Executive Editor
Pornsak Pichetshote Editor-Original Series
Bob Harras Group Editor-Collected Editions
Robbin Brosterman Design Director-Books
Louis Prandi Art Director

DC COMICS
Diane Nelson President
Dan DiDio and Jim Lee Co-Publishers
Geoff Johns Chief Creative Officer
Patrick Caldon EVP-Finance and Administration
John Rood EVP-Sales, Marketing and Business Development
Amy Genkins SVP-Business and Legal Affairs
Steve Rotterdam SVP-Sales and Marketing
John Cunningham VP-Marketing
Terri Cunningham VP-Managing Editor
Alison Gill VP-Manufacturing
David Hyde VP-Publicity
Sue Pohja VP-Book Trade Sales
Alysse Soll VP-Advertising and Custom Publishing
Bob Wayne VP-Sales
Mark Chiarello Art Director

THE UNWRITTEN: DEAD MAN'S KNOCK
Published by DC Comics. Cover and compilation
Copyright © 2011 Mike Carey and Peter Gross.
All Rights Reserved. Originally published in single
magazine form as THE UNWRITTEN 13-18. Copyright
© 2011 Mike Carey and Peter Gross. All Rights
Reserved. VERTIGO and all characters, their distinctive
likenesses and related elements featured in this
publication are trademarks of DC Comics. The stories,
characters and incidents featured in this publication are
entirely fictional. DC Comics does not read or accept
unsolicited submissions of ideas, stories or artwork.
DC Comics, 1700 Broadway, New York, NY 10019
A Warner Bros. Entertainment Company.
Printed in the USA. First Printing.
ISBN: 978-1-4012-3046-3

SUSTAINABLE
FORESTRY
INITIATIVE
Certified Chain of Custody
Promoting Sustainable
Forest Management
www.sfiprogram.org
Fiber used in this product line meets the
sourcing requirements of the SFI program.
www.sfiprogram.org SGS-SFICOC-0130

TEEN
FICTION
CAREY

Introduction

Most people don't have the first idea about the true power of stories. I'm sure you know this. I'm sure you do, because you're a reader – you're reading this book right now. You're bound to know a thing or two about it.

Maybe you're the woman on the train who doesn't ever let the raised eyebrows of grey-looking office workers put her off her comic books. Maybe you're the kid at high school who gets teased for always having his nose buried in a Stephen King. Maybe you're a writer, like me, who was always being told, "When are you going to grow up and do something useful with your life?"

It doesn't matter which one you are, just that you're one of us. You're clued in. You know what they don't. You know how it all works. Or at least, you will soon, if you keep reading this book.

It's a sad fact that most people can't even spot a story when they see one. Most people don't know that stories aren't confined by the covers of books or by half-hour slots on TV. The world is made of stories. The world is driven by stories. When a sunburned friend tells you about their holiday, it's not a straight list of everything that happened to them – it's a story, an anecdote with a plot, a beginning, a middle and an end. Each one of their holiday snaps is a story too. When you're making a decision, and you imagine the possible outcomes – what are you doing if not telling yourself a story? History is a story. Society is a story. Countries are stories. Your plans are stories. Your desires are stories. Your own memories are stories – narratives selected, trimmed and packaged by the hidden machinery in your mind. Human beings are story engines. We have to be – to understand stories is to understand the world.

Enter THE UNWRITTEN.

Mike Carey and Peter Gross's wonderful book manages to be both a fast, engaging adventure, a huge, ambitious labyrinth of forking paths, and a thoughtful exploration of the very nature of stories both on the page and in the wider world – as the very fabric that holds society together and drives it forward. This is a brave, bold and epic book. The sheer scale of what Carey and Gross have set out to achieve here, and the risks they are willing to take while doing it, fills me with all the admiration in the world (and a little bit of envy too). This, my story-loving friends, is the real deal.

I hope you'll be as delighted and dazzled by this latest collection as I have been, and, if someone should try to interrupt you while you're reading it, if someone should try to tell you to *get your head out of the clouds*, or to *stop filling your time with silly stories*, just remember this:

Without a story there is no meaning.
And the nature of the meaning depends on the nature of the story.
To understand this is to understand the true power of stories.
And so, to control the stories, to be the one doing the telling…
Well now, wouldn't that be quite a thing…?

For everyone's sake, let's hope that Mr. Carey and Mr. Gross continue to use their considerable powers wisely…

Steven Hall
2010

Steven Hall's first novel, The Raw Shark Texts, *won the Borders Original Voices Award, the Somerset Maugham Award, and was shortlisted for the Arthur C. Clarke Award. The book has been translated into thirty languages, and a film adaptation is currently in development.*

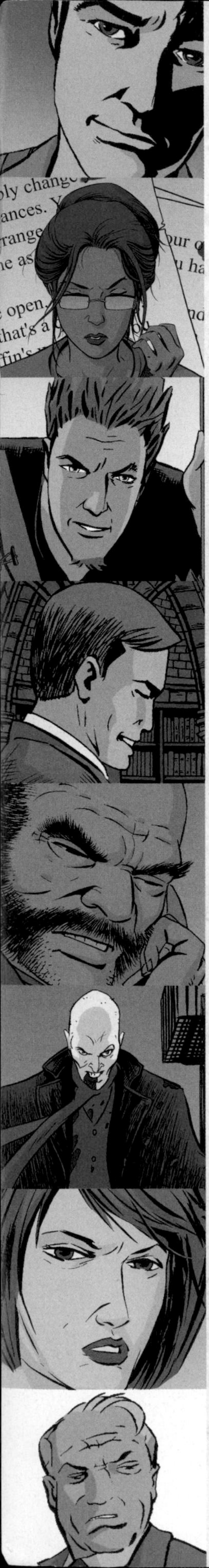

DRAMATIS PERSONAE

TOM TAYLOR

"They don't know me, because I'm not Tommy. It's more like I'm the test tube where my dad did his experiments."
Tom Taylor was the inspiration for his father's Tommy Taylor novels – the hit series of children's books starring the adventures of a boy wizard. But now he's framed for murder and on the run from the law – all courtesy of a mysterious cabal that manipulates the world's stories to strengthen their own power.

LIZZIE HEXAM

"I learn about how stories work for the same reason that soldiers learn how to strip a rifle."
Lizzie Hexam believes Tom *is* the character from the books made flesh. Sent by Wilson Taylor to protect Tom, how much more does she know than she lets on?

RICHIE SAVOY

"I'm a journalist, man. And you're the story."
The exclusive of a lifetime, that's what Richie Savoy is looking for – if he can stay alive long enough by Tom's side.

CALLENDAR

"So we've dedicated our lives to building this mansion, and now we're in the process of giving away the fucking key."
The leader of the mysterious cabal that's trying to destroy Tom's life, Callendar will stop at nothing to prevent Tom from fulfilling whatever it is that Wilson has planned for him.

PULLMAN

"Fear is a serviceable tool, I suppose... Close your eyes. I'll make this quick."
The cabal's mysterious enforcer, Pullman turns whatever he touches into fiction, but he's been alive a very long time and that life comes with vicious secrets of its own.

AMBROSIO

"You thought I was dead, Tommy Taylor. But you should have known Ambrosio always finds a way."
Tommy Taylor's nemesis in the novels, the immortal Ambrosio has taken control of prison warden Claude Chadron after the man's grief over his children's deaths opened a way for Ambrosio to enter the real world.

SUE MORGENSTERN

"Don't worry, Tom. We all got our turn at being abandoned."
Wilson Taylor's mistress, Sue Morgenstern has always carried the blame for Wilson's absences and remoteness during Tom's childhood.

WILSON TAYLOR

"All the worlds anyone ever dreamed up... they're right here."
Tom's mysterious father, Wilson Taylor has waged a one-man war against the shadowy cabal that seeks to manipulate stories for their own gain. Missing for years, he's now sent a copy of his latest Tommy Taylor novel to his editor Ernie Cole, and his plans are finally beginning to bear fruit...

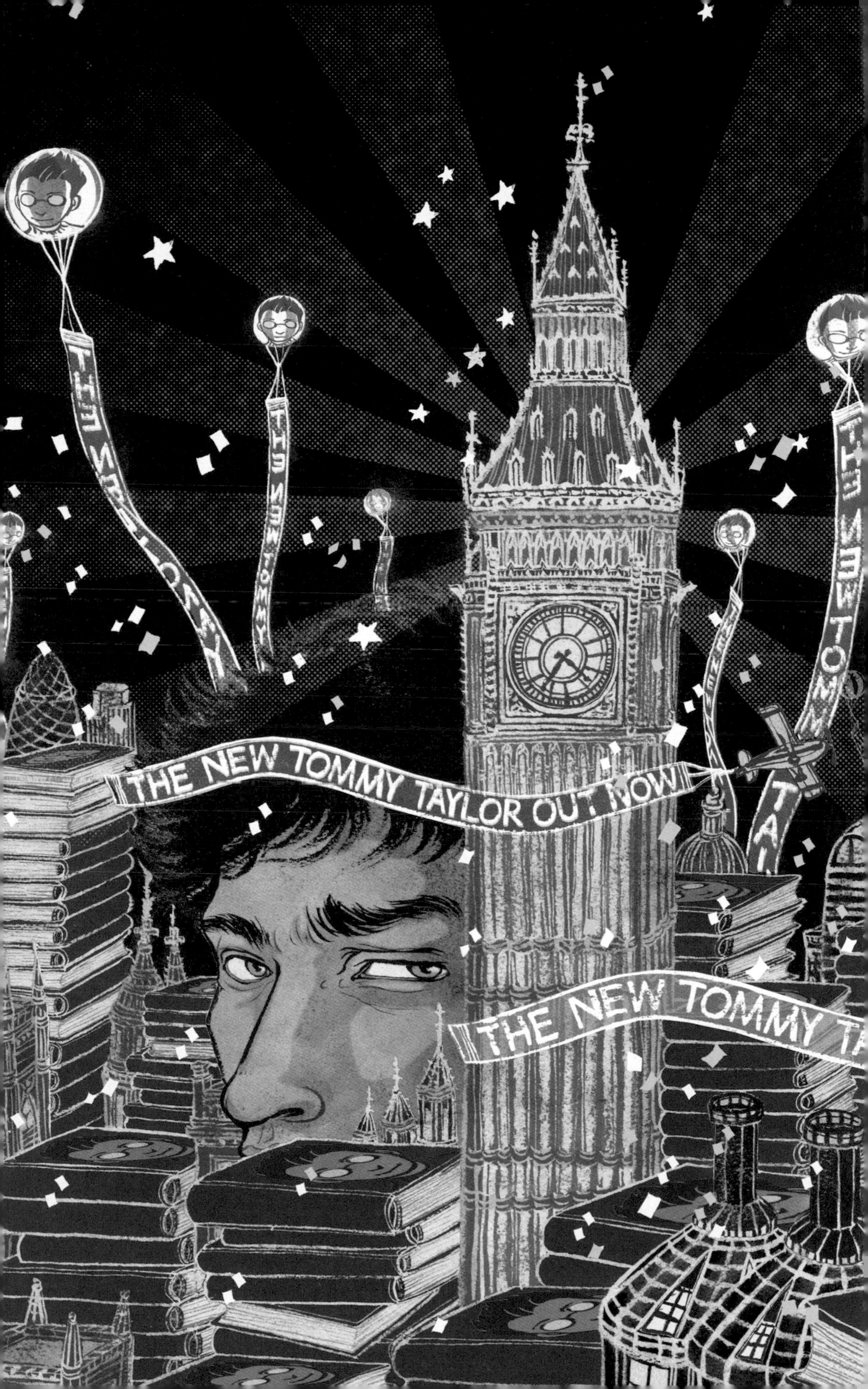
THE NEW TOMMY TAYLOR OUT NOW
THE NEW TOMMY

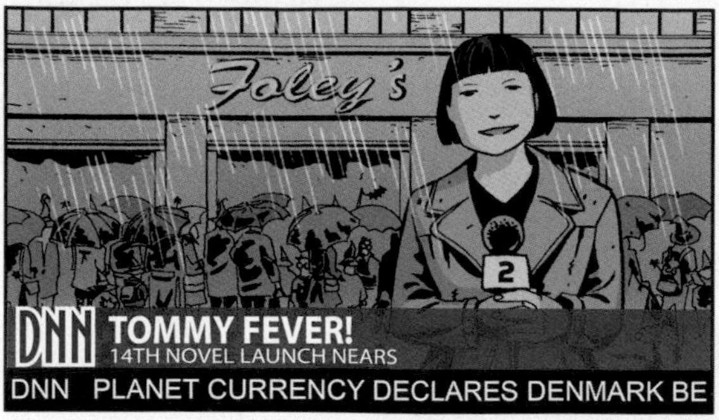
Foley's
DNN TOMMY FEVER!
14TH NOVEL LAUNCH NEARS
DNN PLANET CURRENCY DECLARES DENMARK BE

IT'S STILL ***TWO DAYS*** TO THE OFFICIAL LAUNCH OF THE FOURTEENTH TOMMY TAYLOR NOVEL, AND DESPITE HEAVY RAINS, THE LINE AT ***FOLEY'S*** IN CHARING CROSS ROAD IS THREE-QUARTERS OF A MILE LONG... SARAH?

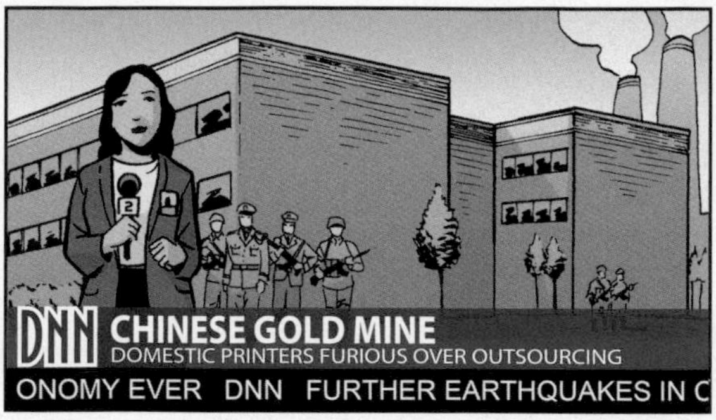
DNN CHINESE GOLD MINE
DOMESTIC PRINTERS FURIOUS OVER OUTSOURCING
ONOMY EVER DNN FURTHER EARTHQUAKES IN C

THANKS, EILEEN. CHINESE OFFICIALS CONTINUE TO DENY THAT THE ENTIRE PRINT RUN IS BEING PRODUCED ***HERE,*** AT THIS PRINTING PLANT IN XIU-TAN.

BUT THE TIGHT SECURITY CERTAINLY ***SEEMS*** TO SUPPORT THAT THEORY.

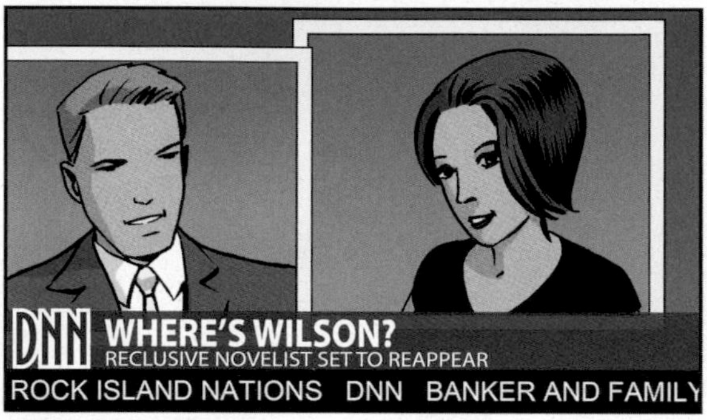
DNN WHERE'S WILSON?
RECLUSIVE NOVELIST SET TO REAPPEAR
ROCK ISLAND NATIONS DNN BANKER AND FAMILY

AND WHAT ABOUT THOSE RUMORS THAT ***WILSON TAYLOR*** HIMSELF MIGHT BE TURNING UP FOR A SIGNING?

WELL, THAT'S ALL THEY ARE RIGHT NOW. RUMORS. BUT THEY'RE CERTAINLY ***ADDING*** TO THAT FEVER-PITCH EXCITEMENT.

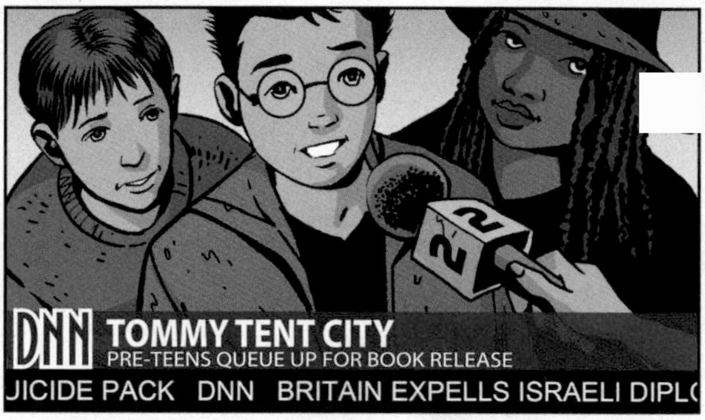
DNN TOMMY TENT CITY
PRE-TEENS QUEUE UP FOR BOOK RELEASE
UICIDE PACK DNN BRITAIN EXPELLS ISRAELI DIPL

WE'VE BEEN HERE SINCE, LIKE, ***TUESDAY.***

WE TAKE IT IN TURNS TO SLEEP, SO NO ONE CAN SLIP IN FRONT OF US.

IT'S SO COOL! IT'S LIKE WE'RE ALL PREGNANT WITH THE SAME BABY. AND NOW WE'RE ABOUT TO GIVE BIRTH!

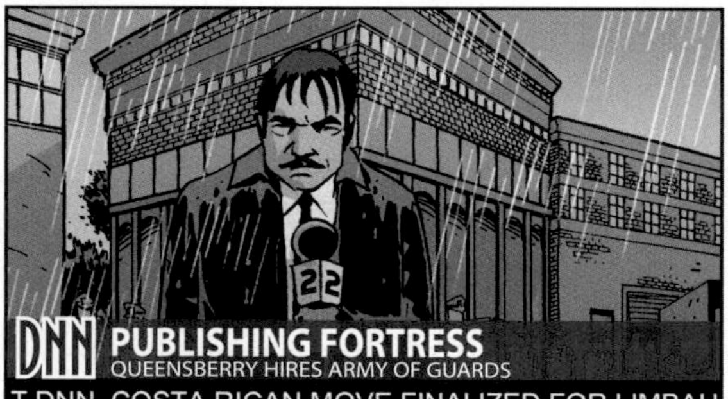
DNN PUBLISHING FORTRESS
QUEENSBERRY HIRES ARMY OF GUARDS
T DNN COSTA RICAN MOVE FINALIZED FOR LIMBAU

PUBLISHERS QUEENSBERRY HAVE HIRED TWELVE THOUSAND SECURITY GUARDS TO SAFEGUARD AGAINST POSSIBLE PIRACY--AND ALL DELIVERIES OF THE NOVEL WILL REMAIN UNDER GUARD UNTIL ***7:00 A.M.*** ON THE MORNING OF THE ACTUAL LAUNCH.

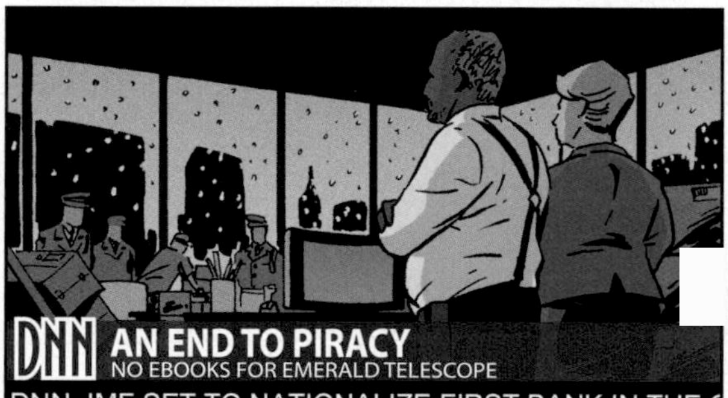
DNN AN END TO PIRACY
NO EBOOKS FOR EMERALD TELESCOPE
DNN IMF SET TO NATIONALIZE FIRST BANK IN THE C

ERNEST COLE, THE BOOK'S EDITOR, CLAIMS THERE IS NO ELECTRONIC VERSION OF THE TEXT, SO HACKERS NEEDN'T WASTE THEIR TIME ATTACKING QUEENSBERRY'S MAIL SERVER--ALTHOUGH THAT HASN'T STOPPED THEM FROM TRYING.

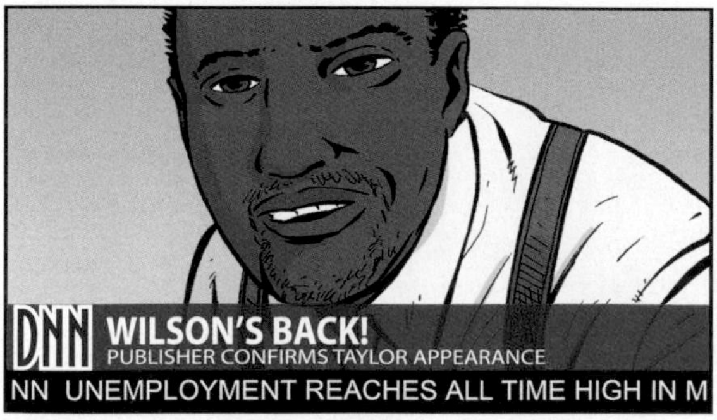
DNN WILSON'S BACK!
PUBLISHER CONFIRMS TAYLOR APPEARANCE
NN UNEMPLOYMENT REACHES ALL TIME HIGH IN M

WE WERE STUNG BEFORE, ON BOOK SIX. WILSON WILL HAVE WORDS TO SAY TO ME IF THERE'S A LEAK THIS TIME AROUND.

UMM...I MEAN, ***IF*** HE'S SHOWING. ***I'M NOT CONFIRMING THAT.***

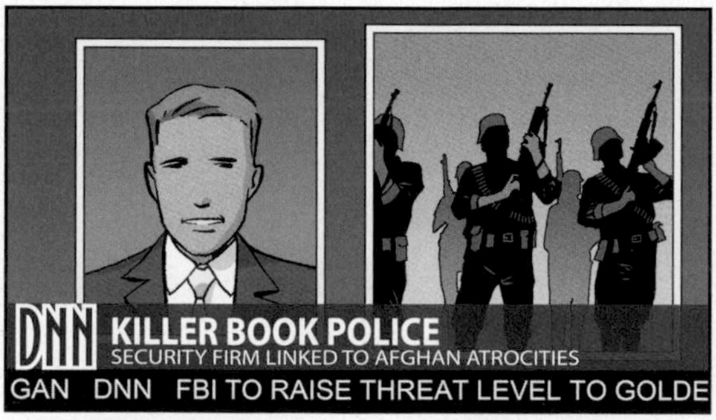
DNN KILLER BOOK POLICE
SECURITY FIRM LINKED TO AFGHAN ATROCITIES
GAN DNN FBI TO RAISE THREAT LEVEL TO GOLDE

AT 9:00 P.M.: THE PRIVATE SECURITY FIRMS HIRED BY QUEENSBERRY--WHO ARE THEY, AND WHERE HAVE THEY WORKED BEFORE? THE ANSWERS MAY SHOCK YOU.

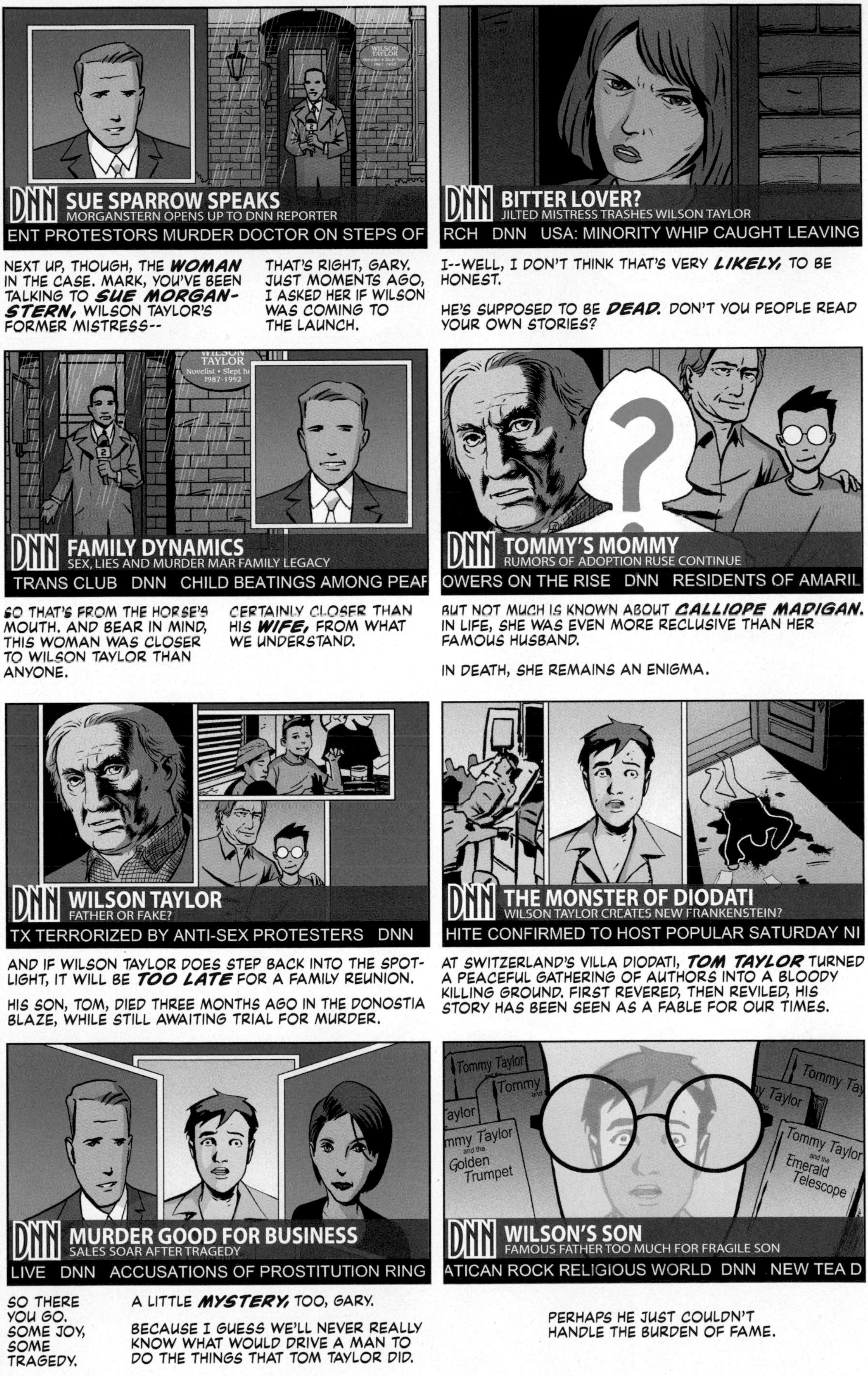
DNN SUE SPARROW SPEAKS
MORGANSTERN OPENS UP TO DNN REPORTER
ENT PROTESTORS MURDER DOCTOR ON STEPS OF
WILSON TAYLOR Novelist • Slept here 1987-1992
NEXT UP, THOUGH, THE WOMAN IN THE CASE. MARK, YOU'VE BEEN TALKING TO SUE MORGAN-STERN, WILSON TAYLOR'S FORMER MISTRESS--
THAT'S RIGHT, GARY. JUST MOMENTS AGO, I ASKED HER IF WILSON WAS COMING TO THE LAUNCH.
DNN BITTER LOVER?
JILTED MISTRESS TRASHES WILSON TAYLOR
RCH DNN USA: MINORITY WHIP CAUGHT LEAVING
I--WELL, I DON'T THINK THAT'S VERY LIKELY, TO BE HONEST.
HE'S SUPPOSED TO BE DEAD. DON'T YOU PEOPLE READ YOUR OWN STORIES?
DNN FAMILY DYNAMICS
SEX, LIES AND MURDER MAR FAMILY LEGACY
TRANS CLUB DNN CHILD BEATINGS AMONG PEAF
SO THAT'S FROM THE HORSE'S MOUTH. AND BEAR IN MIND, THIS WOMAN WAS CLOSER TO WILSON TAYLOR THAN ANYONE.
CERTAINLY CLOSER THAN HIS WIFE, FROM WHAT WE UNDERSTAND.
?
DNN TOMMY'S MOMMY
RUMORS OF ADOPTION RUSE CONTINUE
OWERS ON THE RISE DNN RESIDENTS OF AMARIL
BUT NOT MUCH IS KNOWN ABOUT CALLIOPE MADIGAN. IN LIFE, SHE WAS EVEN MORE RECLUSIVE THAN HER FAMOUS HUSBAND.
IN DEATH, SHE REMAINS AN ENIGMA.
DNN WILSON TAYLOR
FATHER OR FAKE?
TX TERRORIZED BY ANTI-SEX PROTESTERS DNN
AND IF WILSON TAYLOR DOES STEP BACK INTO THE SPOT-LIGHT, IT WILL BE TOO LATE FOR A FAMILY REUNION.
HIS SON, TOM, DIED THREE MONTHS AGO IN THE DONOSTIA BLAZE, WHILE STILL AWAITING TRIAL FOR MURDER.
DNN THE MONSTER OF DIODATI
WILSON TAYLOR CREATES NEW FRANKENSTEIN?
HITE CONFIRMED TO HOST POPULAR SATURDAY NI
AT SWITZERLAND'S VILLA DIODATI, TOM TAYLOR TURNED A PEACEFUL GATHERING OF AUTHORS INTO A BLOODY KILLING GROUND. FIRST REVERED, THEN REVILED, HIS STORY HAS BEEN SEEN AS A FABLE FOR OUR TIMES.
DNN MURDER GOOD FOR BUSINESS
SALES SOAR AFTER TRAGEDY
LIVE DNN ACCUSATIONS OF PROSTITUTION RING
SO THERE YOU GO. SOME JOY, SOME TRAGEDY.
A LITTLE MYSTERY, TOO, GARY.
BECAUSE I GUESS WE'LL NEVER REALLY KNOW WHAT WOULD DRIVE A MAN TO DO THE THINGS THAT TOM TAYLOR DID.
Tommy Taylor
Tommy Taylor and the Golden Trumpet
Tommy Taylor and the Emerald Telescope
DNN WILSON'S SON
FAMOUS FATHER TOO MUCH FOR FRAGILE SON
ATICAN ROCK RELIGIOUS WORLD DNN NEW TEA D
PERHAPS HE JUST COULDN'T HANDLE THE BURDEN OF FAME.

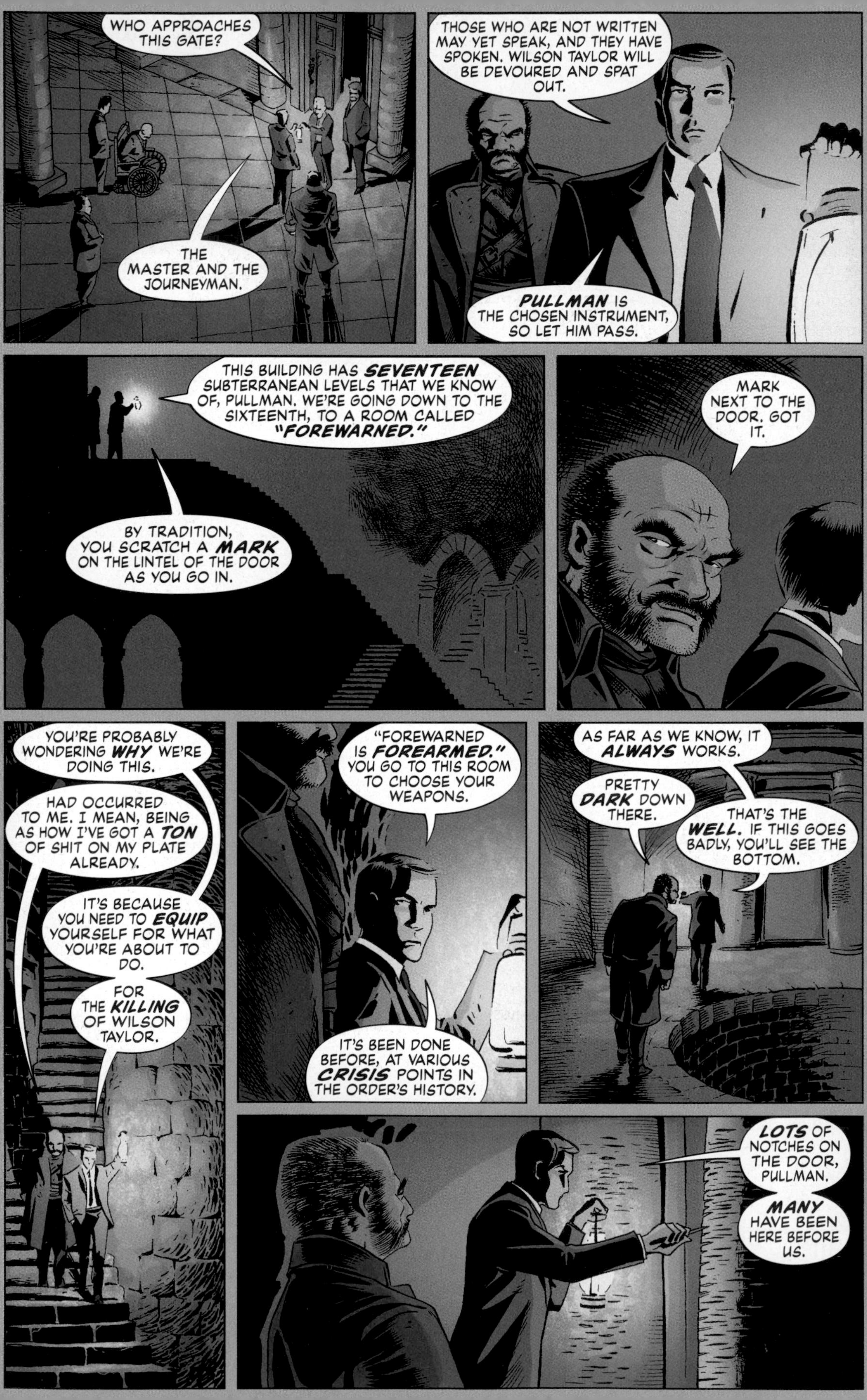
WHO APPROACHES THIS GATE?
THE MASTER AND THE JOURNEYMAN.
THOSE WHO ARE NOT WRITTEN MAY YET SPEAK, AND THEY HAVE SPOKEN. WILSON TAYLOR WILL BE DEVOURED AND SPAT OUT.
PULLMAN IS THE CHOSEN INSTRUMENT, SO LET HIM PASS.
THIS BUILDING HAS SEVENTEEN SUBTERRANEAN LEVELS THAT WE KNOW OF, PULLMAN. WE'RE GOING DOWN TO THE SIXTEENTH, TO A ROOM CALLED "FOREWARNED."
BY TRADITION, YOU SCRATCH A MARK ON THE LINTEL OF THE DOOR AS YOU GO IN.
MARK NEXT TO THE DOOR. GOT IT.
YOU'RE PROBABLY WONDERING WHY WE'RE DOING THIS.
HAD OCCURRED TO ME. I MEAN, BEING AS HOW I'VE GOT A TON OF SHIT ON MY PLATE ALREADY.
IT'S BECAUSE YOU NEED TO EQUIP YOURSELF FOR WHAT YOU'RE ABOUT TO DO.
FOR THE KILLING OF WILSON TAYLOR.
"FOREWARNED IS FOREARMED." YOU GO TO THIS ROOM TO CHOOSE YOUR WEAPONS.
IT'S BEEN DONE BEFORE, AT VARIOUS CRISIS POINTS IN THE ORDER'S HISTORY.
AS FAR AS WE KNOW, IT ALWAYS WORKS.
PRETTY DARK DOWN THERE.
THAT'S THE WELL. IF THIS GOES BADLY, YOU'LL SEE THE BOTTOM.
LOTS OF NOTCHES ON THE DOOR, PULLMAN.
MANY HAVE BEEN HERE BEFORE US.

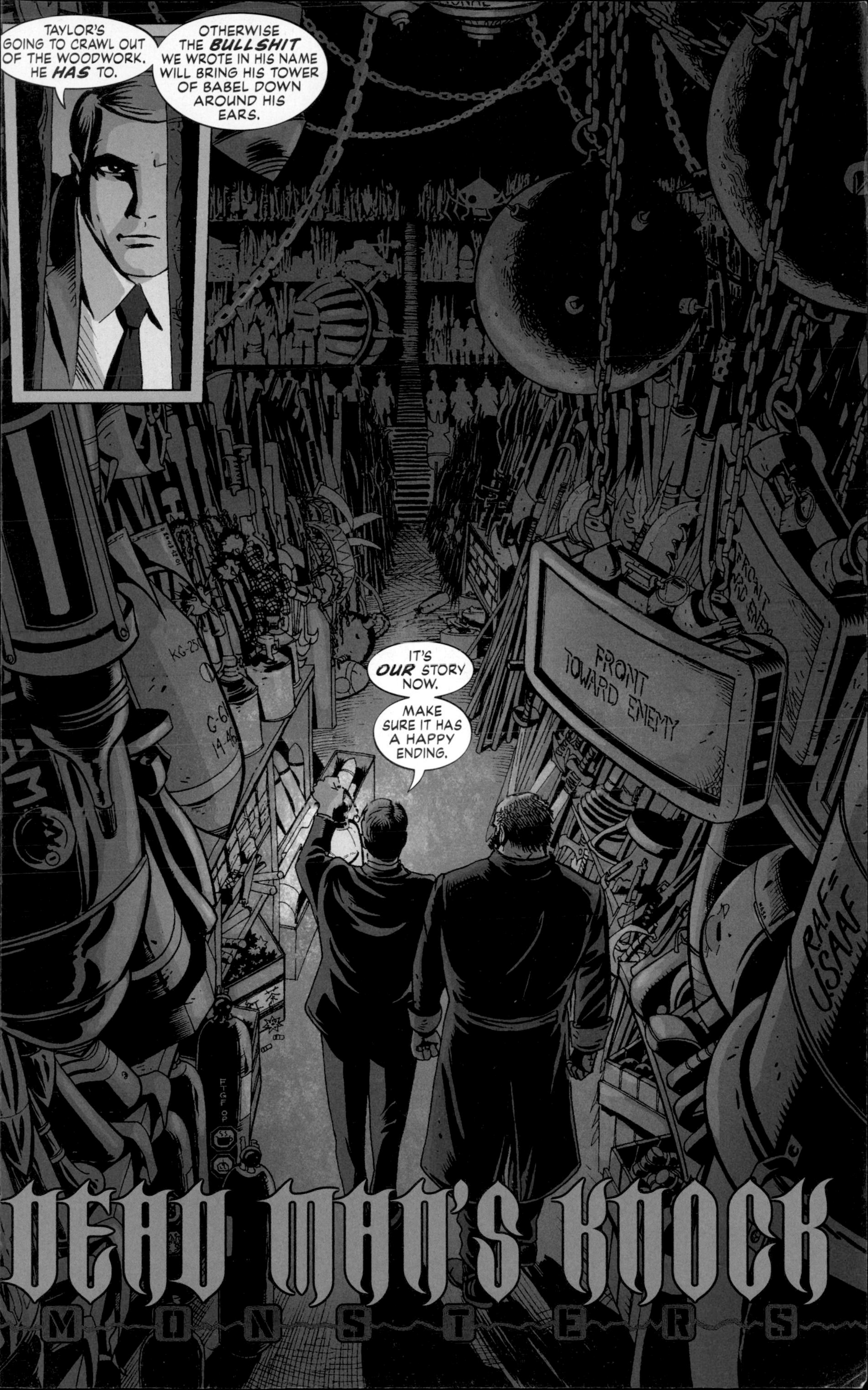
TAYLOR'S GOING TO CRAWL OUT OF THE WOODWORK. HE HAS TO.
OTHERWISE THE BULLSHIT WE WROTE IN HIS NAME WILL BRING HIS TOWER OF BABEL DOWN AROUND HIS EARS.
IT'S OUR STORY NOW.
MAKE SURE IT HAS A HAPPY ENDING.
FRONT TOWARD ENEMY
KG-250
RAF USAAF
DEAD MAN'S KNOCK
MONSTERS

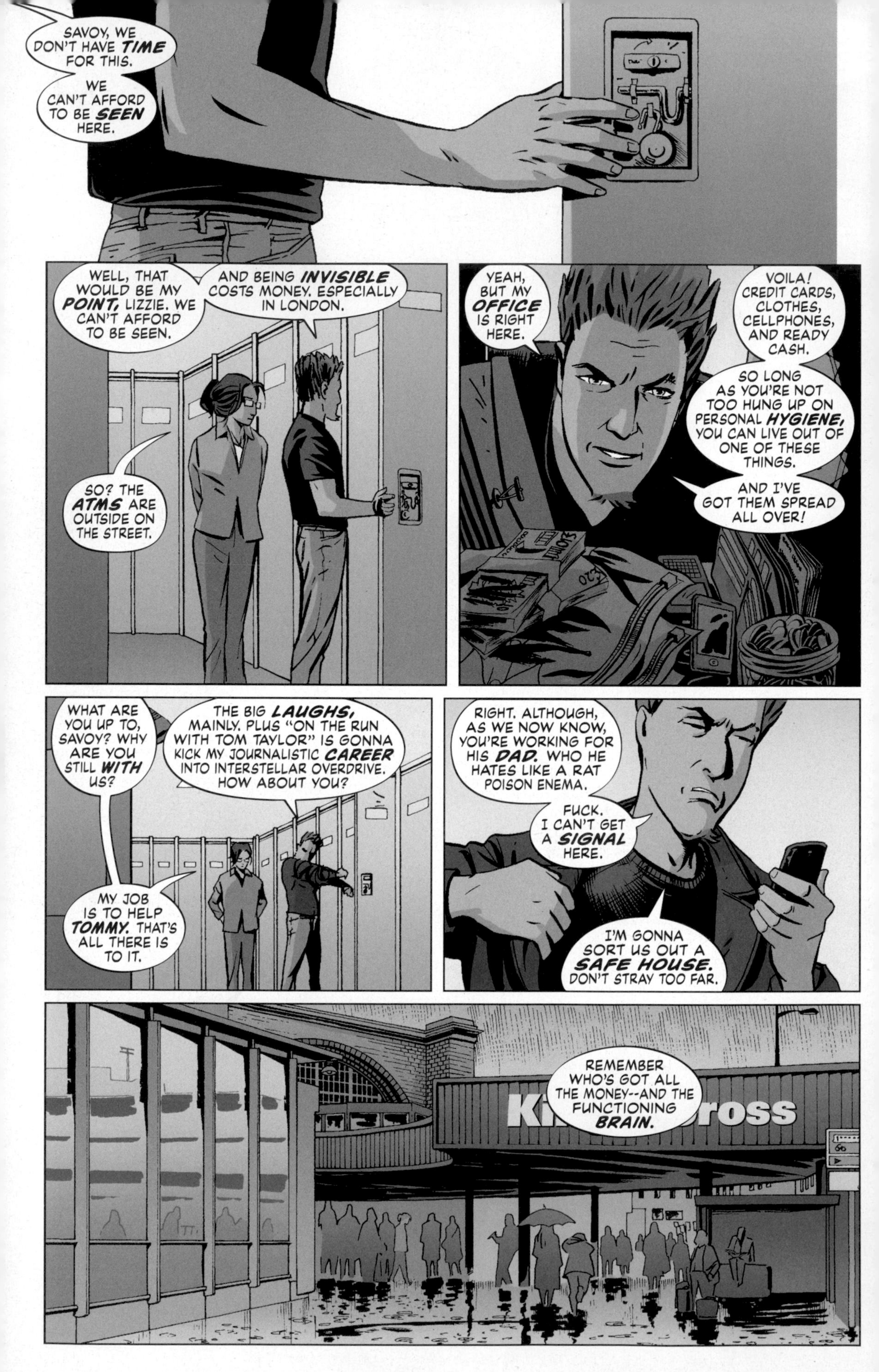
SAVOY, WE DON'T HAVE TIME FOR THIS.
WE CAN'T AFFORD TO BE SEEN HERE.
WELL, THAT WOULD BE MY POINT, LIZZIE. WE CAN'T AFFORD TO BE SEEN.
AND BEING INVISIBLE COSTS MONEY. ESPECIALLY IN LONDON.
SO? THE ATMS ARE OUTSIDE ON THE STREET.
YEAH, BUT MY OFFICE IS RIGHT HERE.
VOILA! CREDIT CARDS, CLOTHES, CELLPHONES, AND READY CASH.
SO LONG AS YOU'RE NOT TOO HUNG UP ON PERSONAL HYGIENE, YOU CAN LIVE OUT OF ONE OF THESE THINGS.
AND I'VE GOT THEM SPREAD ALL OVER!
WHAT ARE YOU UP TO, SAVOY? WHY ARE YOU STILL WITH US?
THE BIG LAUGHS, MAINLY. PLUS "ON THE RUN WITH TOM TAYLOR" IS GONNA KICK MY JOURNALISTIC CAREER INTO INTERSTELLAR OVERDRIVE. HOW ABOUT YOU?
MY JOB IS TO HELP TOMMY. THAT'S ALL THERE IS TO IT.
RIGHT. ALTHOUGH, AS WE NOW KNOW, YOU'RE WORKING FOR HIS DAD. WHO HE HATES LIKE A RAT POISON ENEMA.
FUCK. I CAN'T GET A SIGNAL HERE.
I'M GONNA SORT US OUT A SAFE HOUSE. DON'T STRAY TOO FAR.
REMEMBER WHO'S GOT ALL THE MONEY--AND THE FUNCTIONING BRAIN.

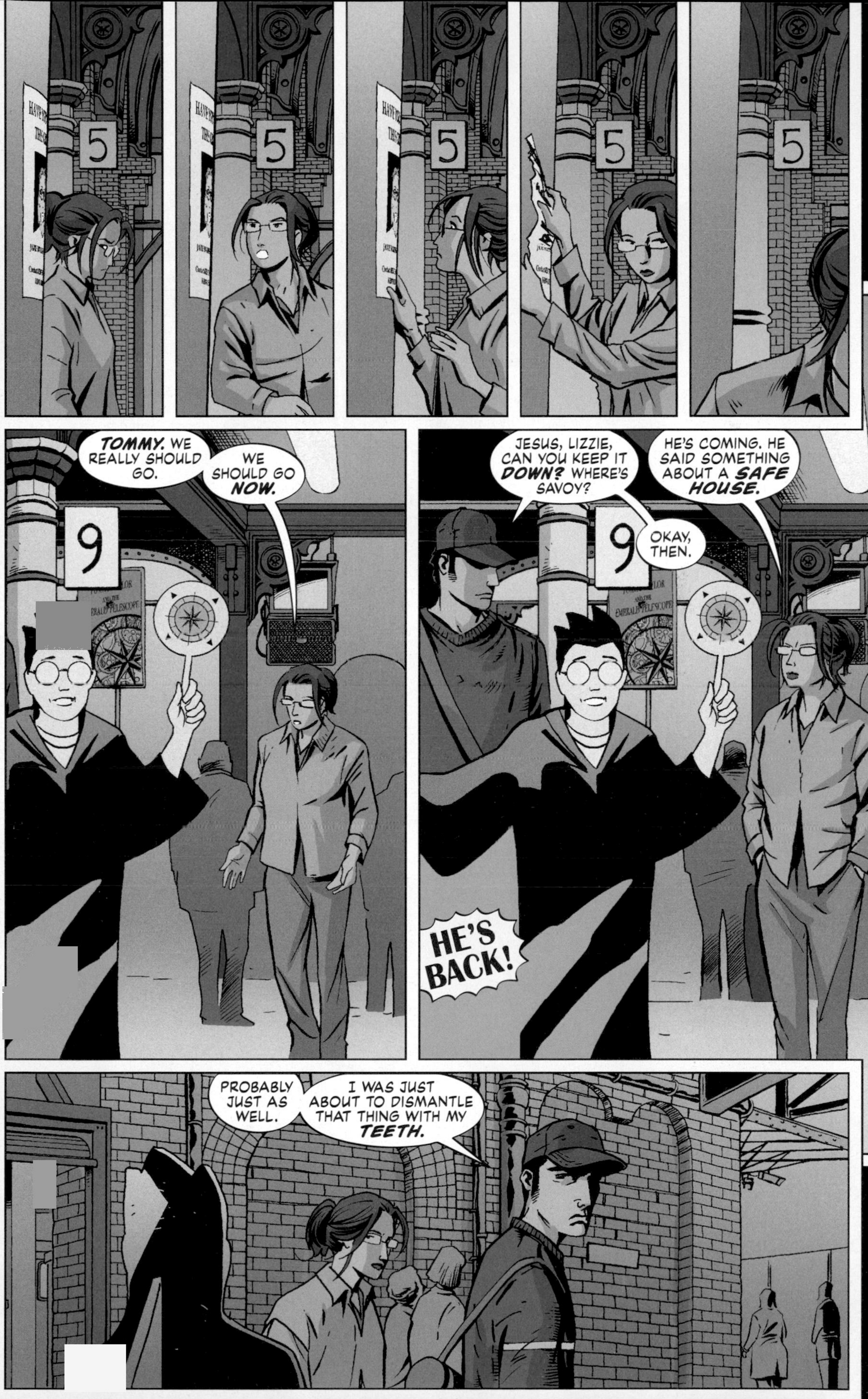

5
TOMMY. WE REALLY SHOULD GO.
WE SHOULD GO NOW.
9
JESUS, LIZZIE, CAN YOU KEEP IT DOWN? WHERE'S SAVOY?
HE'S COMING. HE SAID SOMETHING ABOUT A SAFE HOUSE.
OKAY, THEN.
HE'S BACK!
PROBABLY JUST AS WELL.
I WAS JUST ABOUT TO DISMANTLE THAT THING WITH MY TEETH.

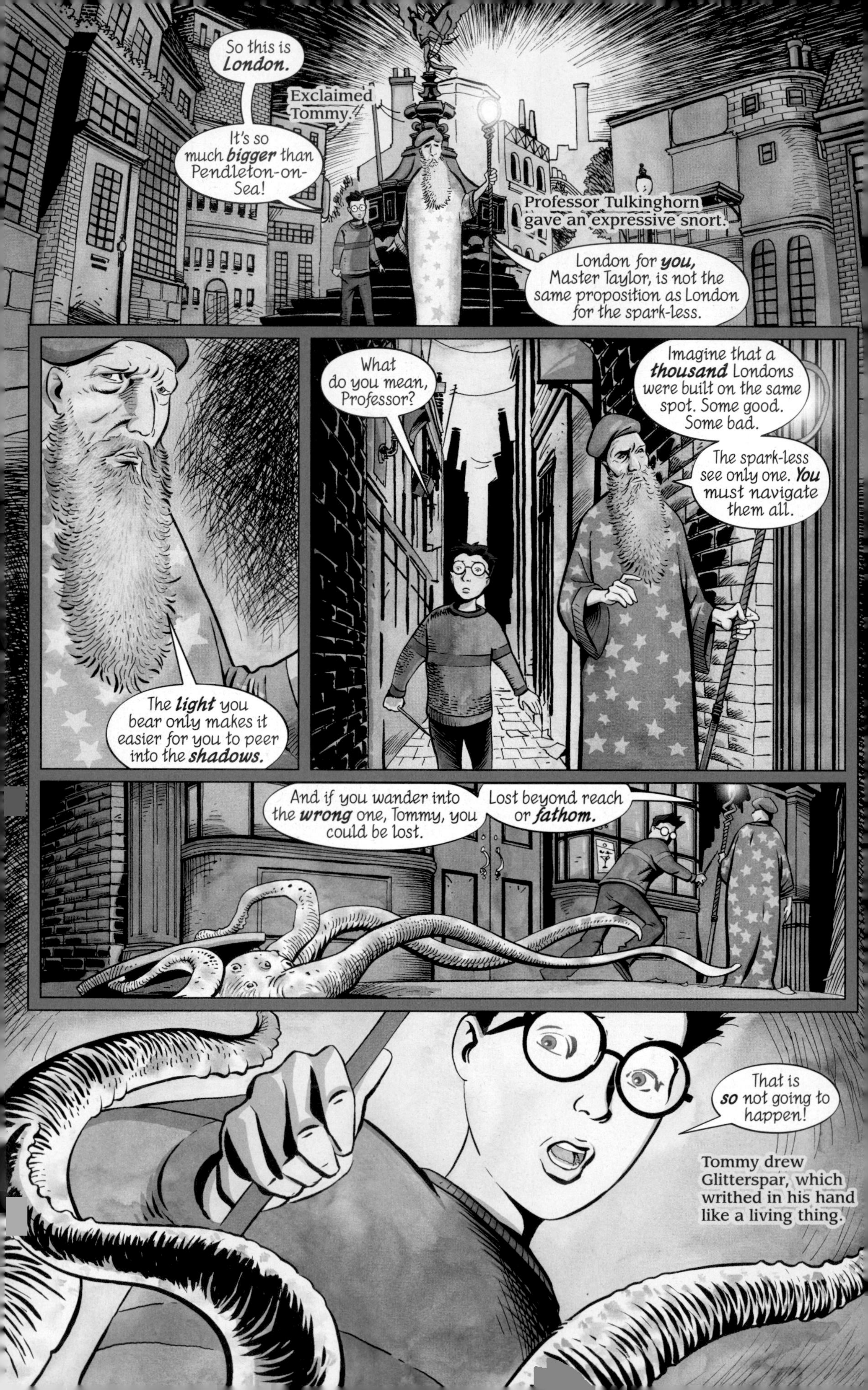
So this is *London.*
Exclaimed Tommy.
It's so much *bigger* than Pendleton-on-Sea!
Professor Tulkinghorn gave an expressive snort.
London for *you,* Master Taylor, is not the same proposition as London for the spark-less.
The *light* you bear only makes it easier for you to peer into the *shadows.*
What do you mean, Professor?
Imagine that a *thousand* Londons were built on the same spot. Some good. Some bad.
The spark-less see only one. *You* must navigate them all.
And if you wander into the *wrong* one, Tommy, you could be lost.
Lost beyond reach or *fathom.*
That is *so* not going to happen!
Tommy drew Glitterspar, which writhed in his hand like a living thing.

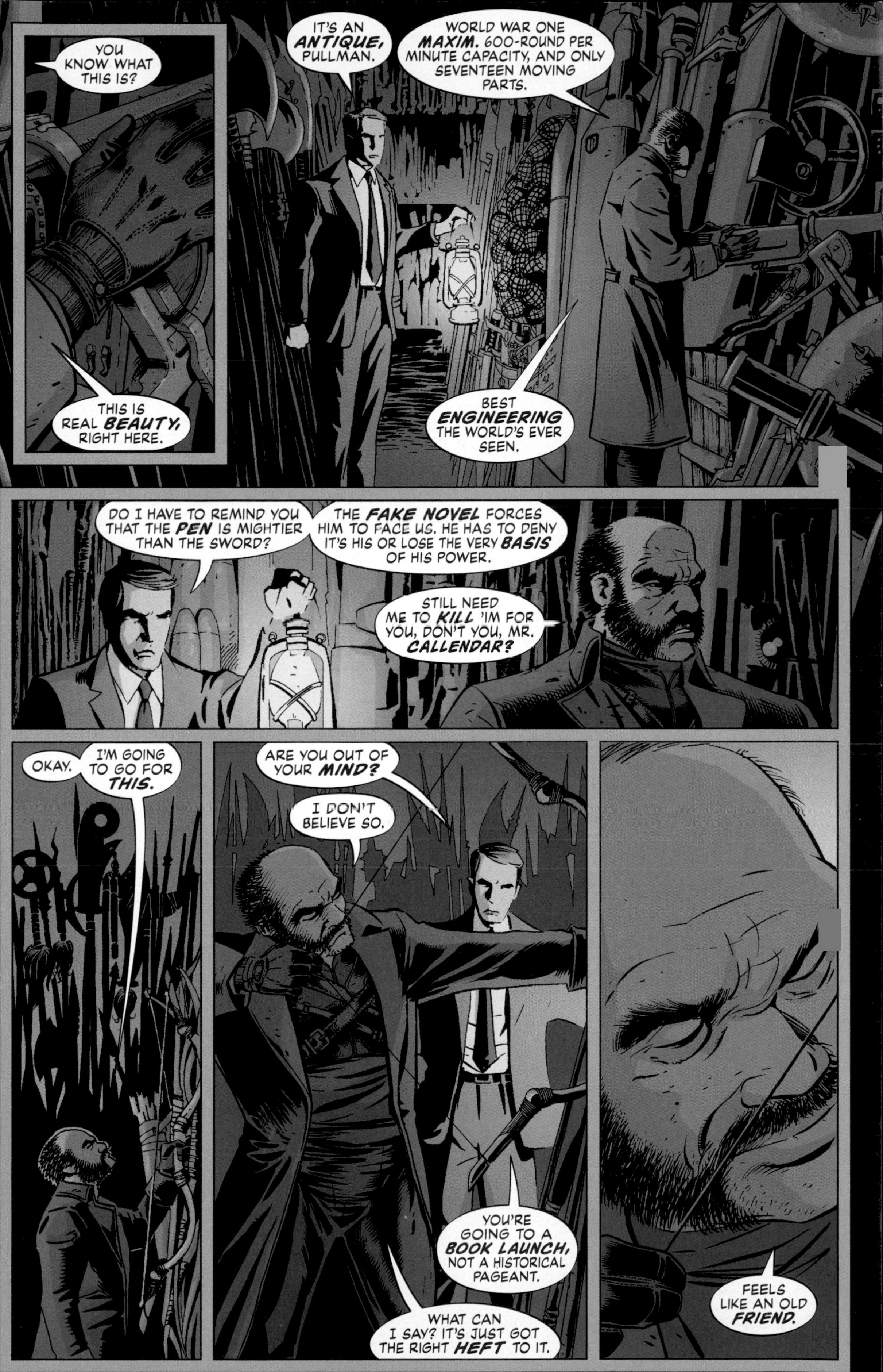
YOU KNOW WHAT THIS IS?
IT'S AN ANTIQUE, PULLMAN.
WORLD WAR ONE MAXIM. 600-ROUND PER MINUTE CAPACITY, AND ONLY SEVENTEEN MOVING PARTS.
THIS IS REAL BEAUTY, RIGHT HERE.
BEST ENGINEERING THE WORLD'S EVER SEEN.
DO I HAVE TO REMIND YOU THAT THE PEN IS MIGHTIER THAN THE SWORD?
THE FAKE NOVEL FORCES HIM TO FACE US. HE HAS TO DENY IT'S HIS OR LOSE THE VERY BASIS OF HIS POWER.
STILL NEED ME TO KILL 'IM FOR YOU, DON'T YOU, MR. CALLENDAR?
OKAY.
I'M GOING TO GO FOR THIS.
ARE YOU OUT OF YOUR MIND?
I DON'T BELIEVE SO.
YOU'RE GOING TO A BOOK LAUNCH, NOT A HISTORICAL PAGEANT.
WHAT CAN I SAY? IT'S JUST GOT THE RIGHT HEFT TO IT.
FEELS LIKE AN OLD FRIEND.

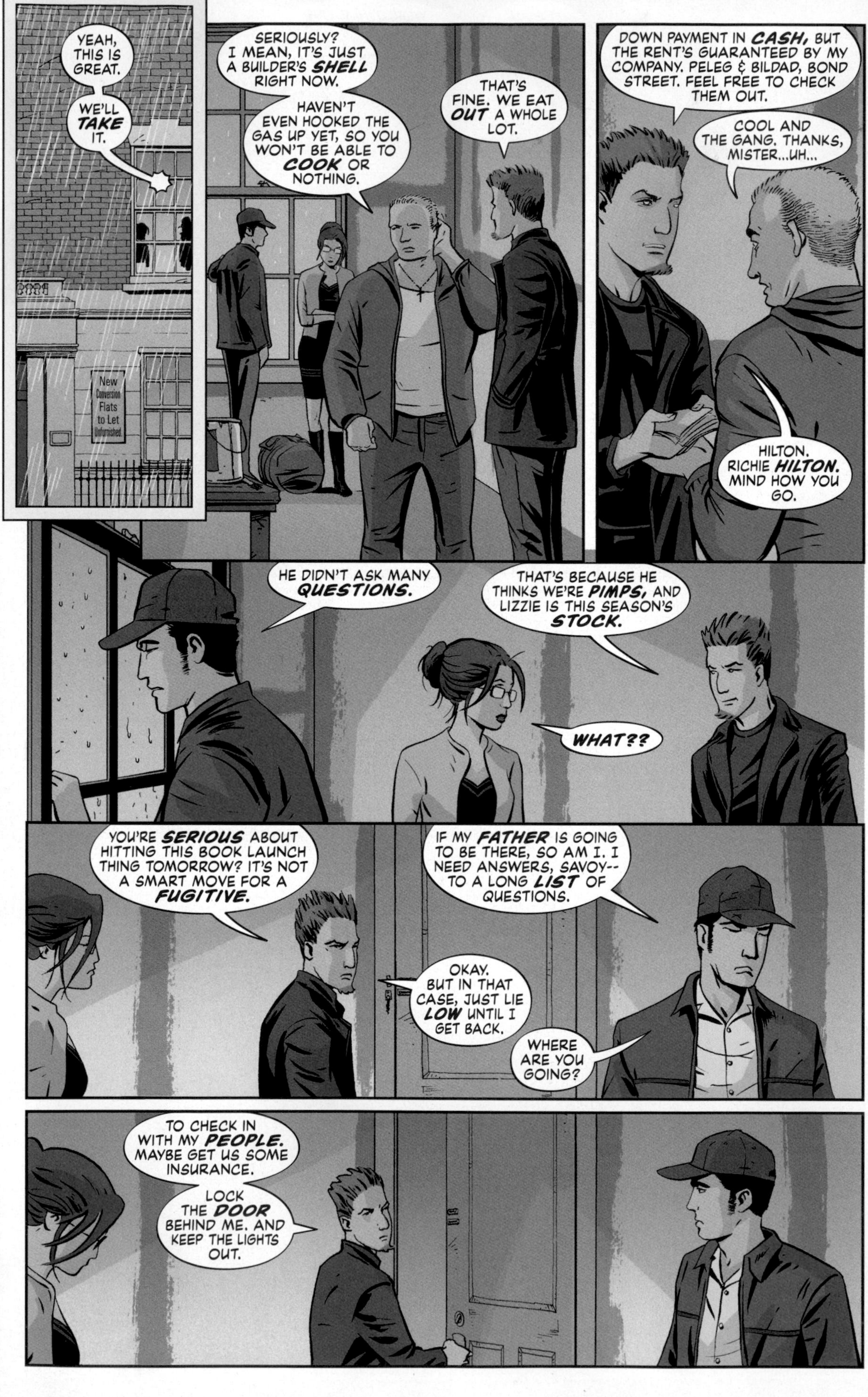

YEAH, THIS IS GREAT.
WE'LL TAKE IT.
New Conversion Flats to Let Unfurnished.
SERIOUSLY? I MEAN, IT'S JUST A BUILDER'S SHELL RIGHT NOW.
HAVEN'T EVEN HOOKED THE GAS UP YET, SO YOU WON'T BE ABLE TO COOK OR NOTHING.
THAT'S FINE. WE EAT OUT A WHOLE LOT.
DOWN PAYMENT IN CASH, BUT THE RENT'S GUARANTEED BY MY COMPANY. PELEG & BILDAD, BOND STREET. FEEL FREE TO CHECK THEM OUT.
COOL AND THE GANG. THANKS, MISTER...UH...
HILTON. RICHIE HILTON. MIND HOW YOU GO.
HE DIDN'T ASK MANY QUESTIONS.
THAT'S BECAUSE HE THINKS WE'RE PIMPS, AND LIZZIE IS THIS SEASON'S STOCK.
WHAT??
YOU'RE SERIOUS ABOUT HITTING THIS BOOK LAUNCH THING TOMORROW? IT'S NOT A SMART MOVE FOR A FUGITIVE.
IF MY FATHER IS GOING TO BE THERE, SO AM I. I NEED ANSWERS, SAVOY-- TO A LONG LIST OF QUESTIONS.
OKAY. BUT IN THAT CASE, JUST LIE LOW UNTIL I GET BACK.
WHERE ARE YOU GOING?
TO CHECK IN WITH MY PEOPLE. MAYBE GET US SOME INSURANCE.
LOCK THE DOOR BEHIND ME. AND KEEP THE LIGHTS OUT.

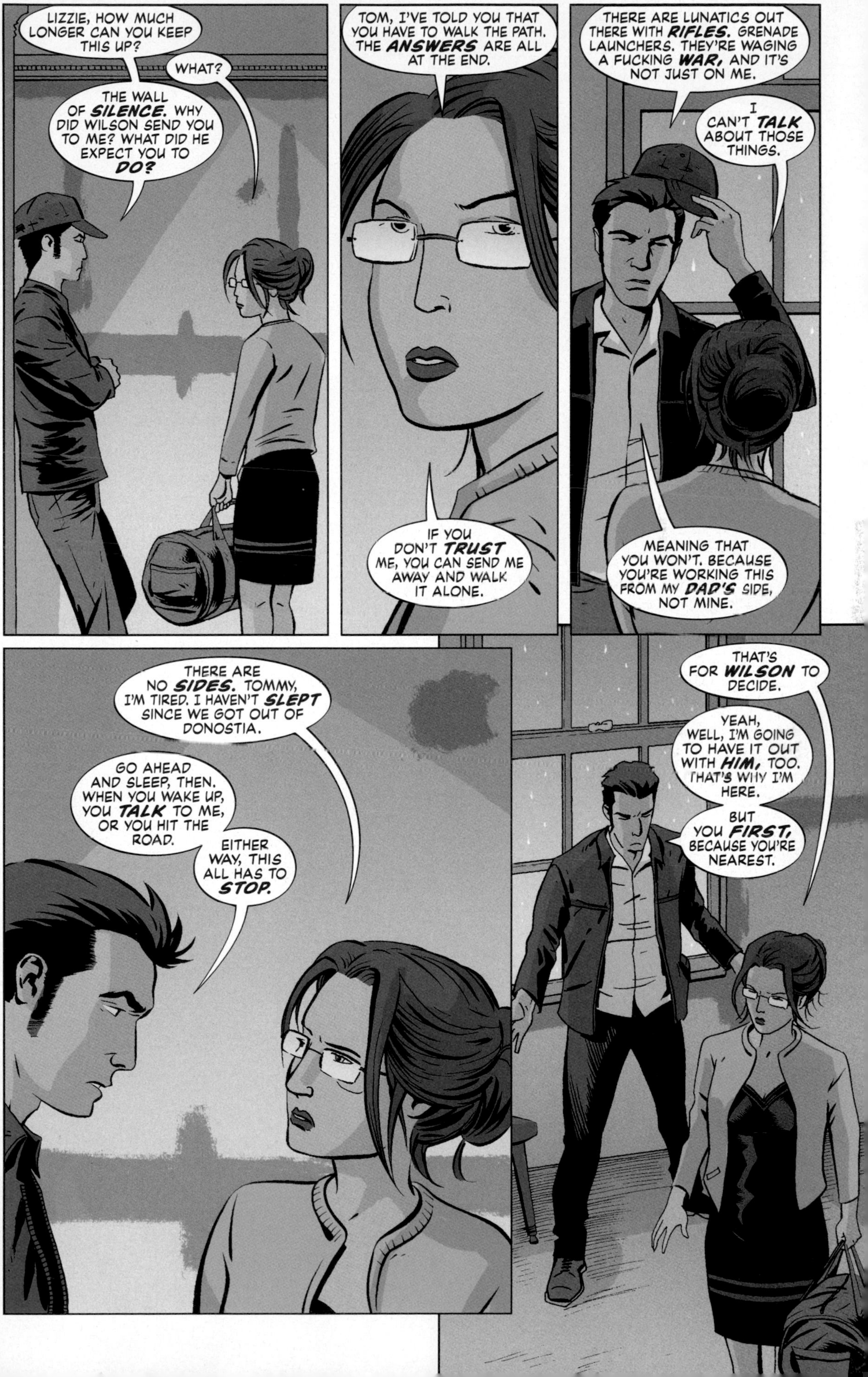
LIZZIE, HOW MUCH LONGER CAN YOU KEEP THIS UP?
WHAT?
THE WALL OF SILENCE. WHY DID WILSON SEND YOU TO ME? WHAT DID HE EXPECT YOU TO DO?
TOM, I'VE TOLD YOU THAT YOU HAVE TO WALK THE PATH. THE ANSWERS ARE ALL AT THE END.
IF YOU DON'T TRUST ME, YOU CAN SEND ME AWAY AND WALK IT ALONE.
THERE ARE LUNATICS OUT THERE WITH RIFLES. GRENADE LAUNCHERS. THEY'RE WAGING A FUCKING WAR, AND IT'S NOT JUST ON ME.
I CAN'T TALK ABOUT THOSE THINGS.
MEANING THAT YOU WON'T. BECAUSE YOU'RE WORKING THIS FROM MY DAD'S SIDE, NOT MINE.
THERE ARE NO SIDES. TOMMY, I'M TIRED. I HAVEN'T SLEPT SINCE WE GOT OUT OF DONOSTIA.
GO AHEAD AND SLEEP, THEN. WHEN YOU WAKE UP, YOU TALK TO ME, OR YOU HIT THE ROAD.
EITHER WAY, THIS ALL HAS TO STOP.
THAT'S FOR WILSON TO DECIDE.
YEAH, WELL, I'M GOING TO HAVE IT OUT WITH HIM, TOO. THAT'S WHY I'M HERE.
BUT YOU FIRST, BECAUSE YOU'RE NEAREST.

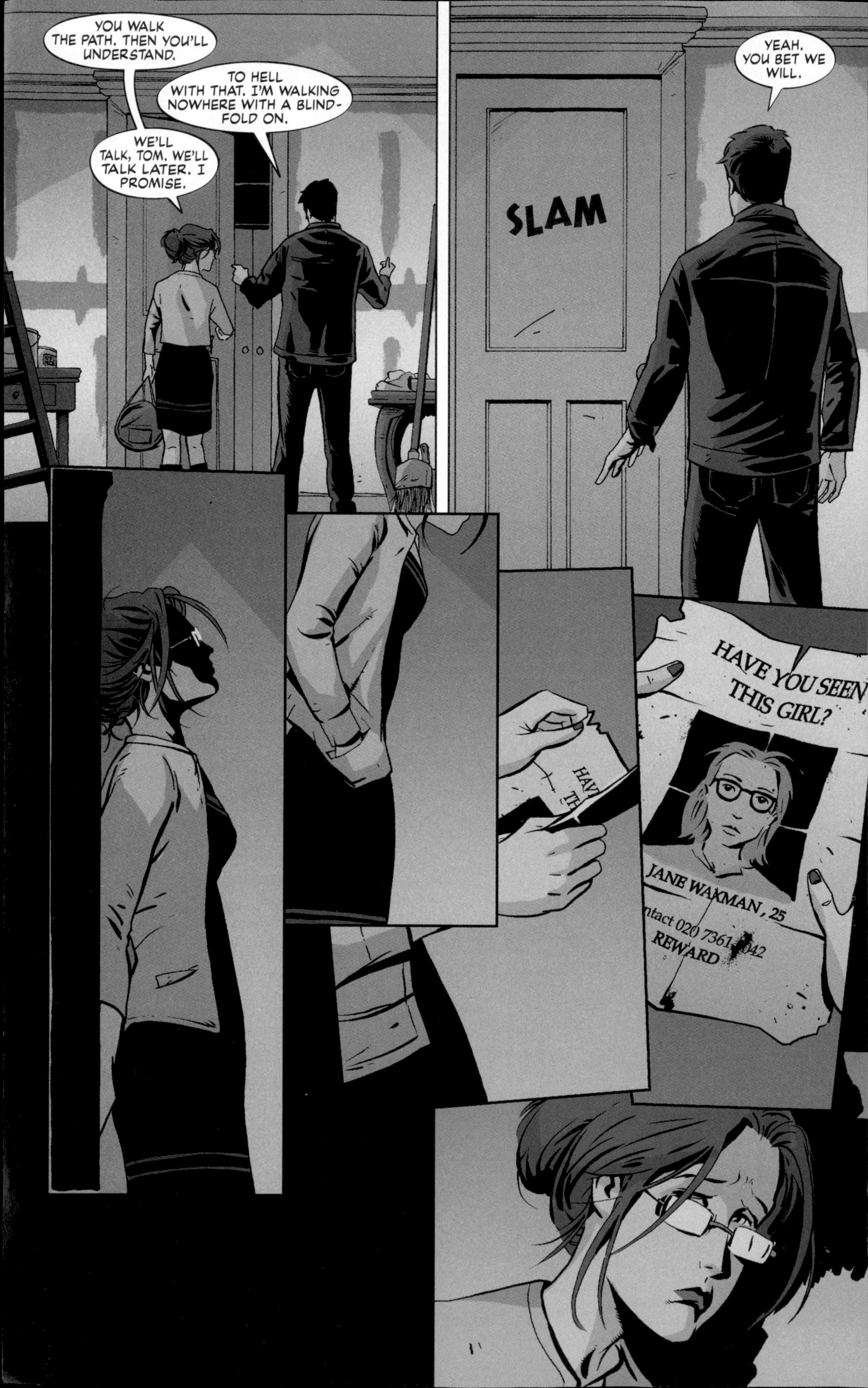
YOU WALK THE PATH. THEN YOU'LL UNDERSTAND.
TO HELL WITH THAT. I'M WALKING NOWHERE WITH A BLIND-FOLD ON.
WE'LL TALK, TOM. WE'LL TALK LATER. I PROMISE.
SLAM
YEAH. YOU BET WE WILL.
HAVE YOU SEEN THIS GIRL?
JANE WAXMAN, 25
REWARD

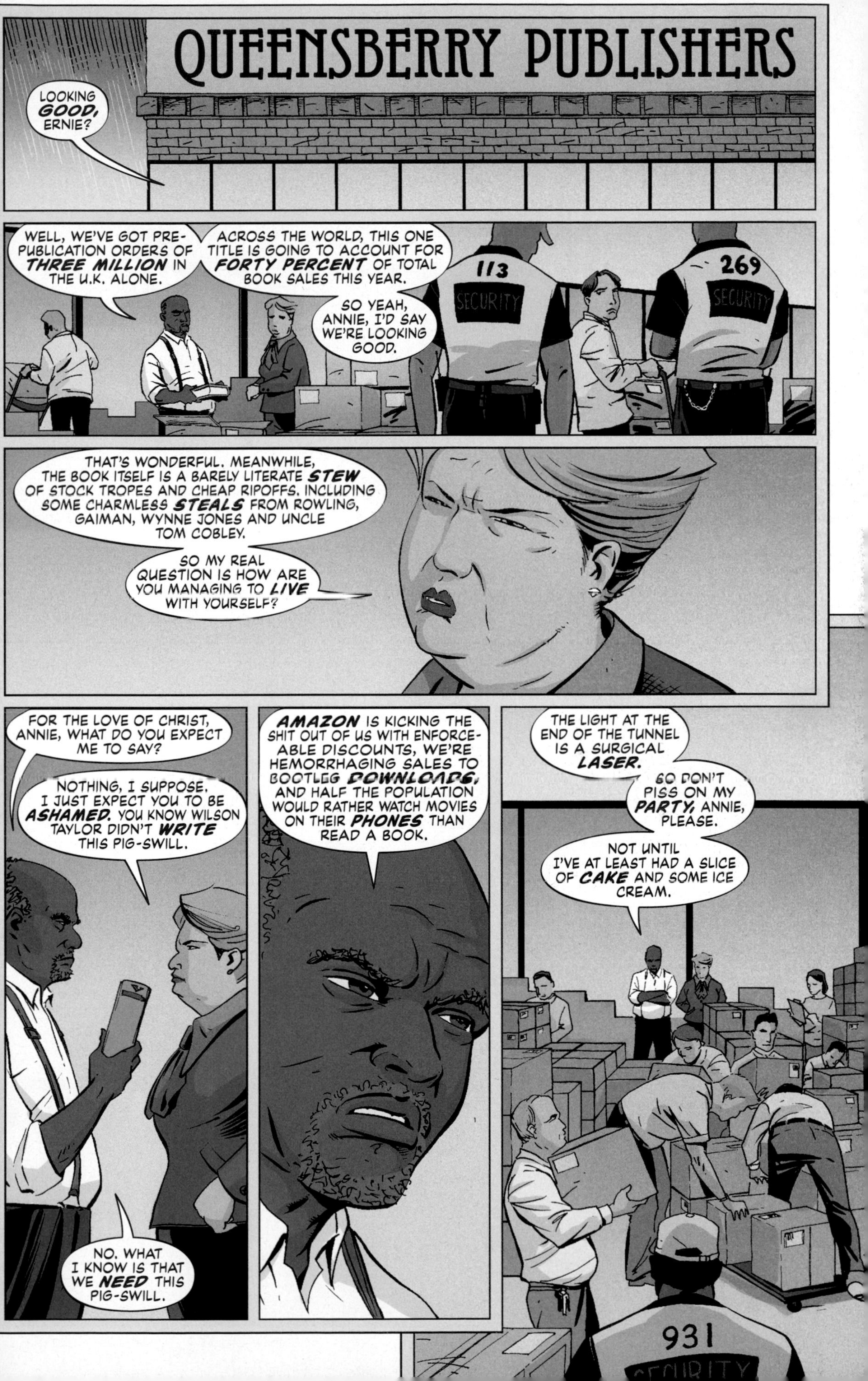
QUEENSBERRY PUBLISHERS
LOOKING GOOD, ERNIE?
WELL, WE'VE GOT PRE-PUBLICATION ORDERS OF THREE MILLION IN THE U.K. ALONE.
ACROSS THE WORLD, THIS ONE TITLE IS GOING TO ACCOUNT FOR FORTY PERCENT OF TOTAL BOOK SALES THIS YEAR.
SO YEAH, ANNIE, I'D SAY WE'RE LOOKING GOOD.
113
SECURITY
269
SECURITY
THAT'S WONDERFUL. MEANWHILE, THE BOOK ITSELF IS A BARELY LITERATE STEW OF STOCK TROPES AND CHEAP RIPOFFS, INCLUDING SOME CHARMLESS STEALS FROM ROWLING, GAIMAN, WYNNE JONES AND UNCLE TOM COBLEY.
SO MY REAL QUESTION IS HOW ARE YOU MANAGING TO LIVE WITH YOURSELF?
FOR THE LOVE OF CHRIST, ANNIE, WHAT DO YOU EXPECT ME TO SAY?
NOTHING, I SUPPOSE. I JUST EXPECT YOU TO BE ASHAMED. YOU KNOW WILSON TAYLOR DIDN'T WRITE THIS PIG-SWILL.
NO. WHAT I KNOW IS THAT WE NEED THIS PIG-SWILL.
AMAZON IS KICKING THE SHIT OUT OF US WITH ENFORCE-ABLE DISCOUNTS, WE'RE HEMORRHAGING SALES TO BOOTLEG DOWNLOADS, AND HALF THE POPULATION WOULD RATHER WATCH MOVIES ON THEIR PHONES THAN READ A BOOK.
THE LIGHT AT THE END OF THE TUNNEL IS A SURGICAL LASER.
SO DON'T PISS ON MY PARTY, ANNIE, PLEASE.
NOT UNTIL I'VE AT LEAST HAD A SLICE OF CAKE AND SOME ICE CREAM.
931

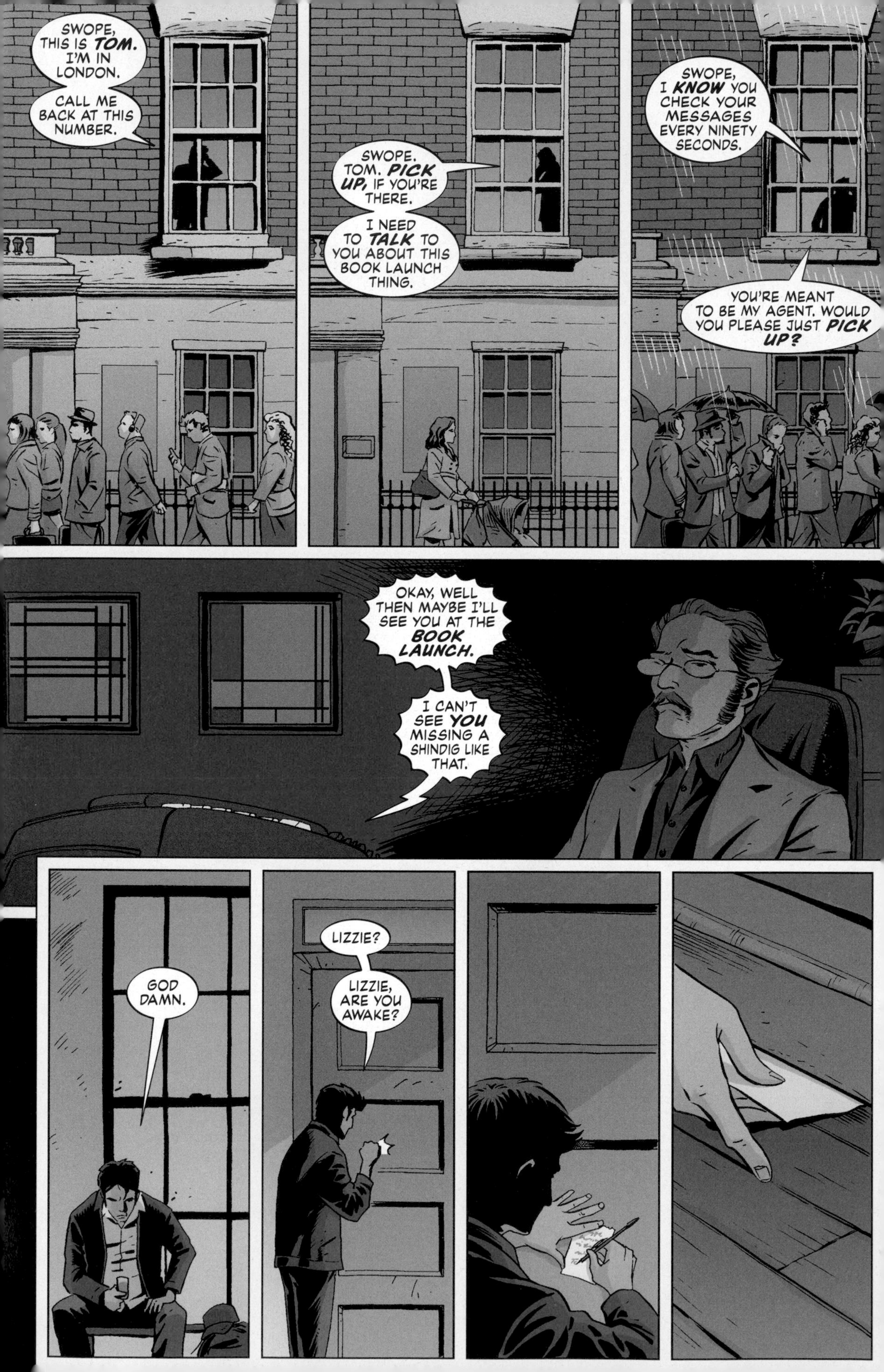
SWOPE, THIS IS TOM. I'M IN LONDON.
CALL ME BACK AT THIS NUMBER.
SWOPE. TOM. PICK UP, IF YOU'RE THERE.
I NEED TO TALK TO YOU ABOUT THIS BOOK LAUNCH THING.
SWOPE, I KNOW YOU CHECK YOUR MESSAGES EVERY NINETY SECONDS.
YOU'RE MEANT TO BE MY AGENT. WOULD YOU PLEASE JUST PICK UP?
OKAY, WELL THEN MAYBE I'LL SEE YOU AT THE BOOK LAUNCH.
I CAN'T SEE YOU MISSING A SHINDIG LIKE THAT.
GOD DAMN.
LIZZIE?
LIZZIE, ARE YOU AWAKE?

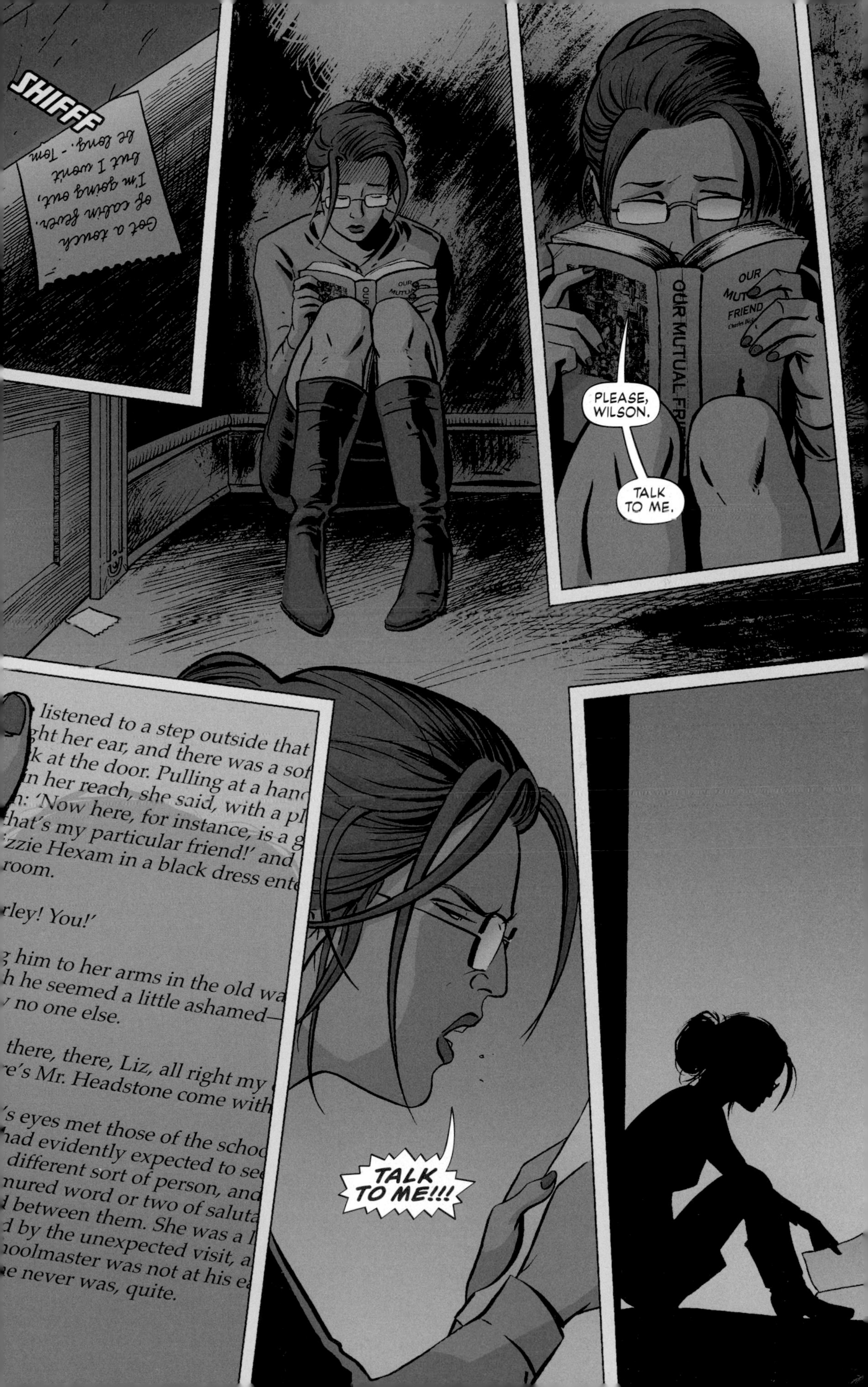
SHIFFF
Got a touch of cabin fever. I'm going out, but I won't be long. - Tom
OUR MUTUAL FRIEND
PLEASE, WILSON.
TALK TO ME.
listened to a step outside that
ght her ear, and there was a sof
k at the door. Pulling at a hand
n her reach, she said, with a pl
n: 'Now here, for instance, is a g
hat's my particular friend!' and
izzie Hexam in a black dress ente
room.
rley! You!'
g him to her arms in the old wa
h he seemed a little ashamed—
no one else.
there, there, Liz, all right my
re's Mr. Headstone come with
's eyes met those of the schoo
had evidently expected to se
different sort of person, and
nured word or two of saluta
d between them. She was a l
d by the unexpected visit, a
hoolmaster was not at his ea
e never was, quite.
TALK TO ME!!!

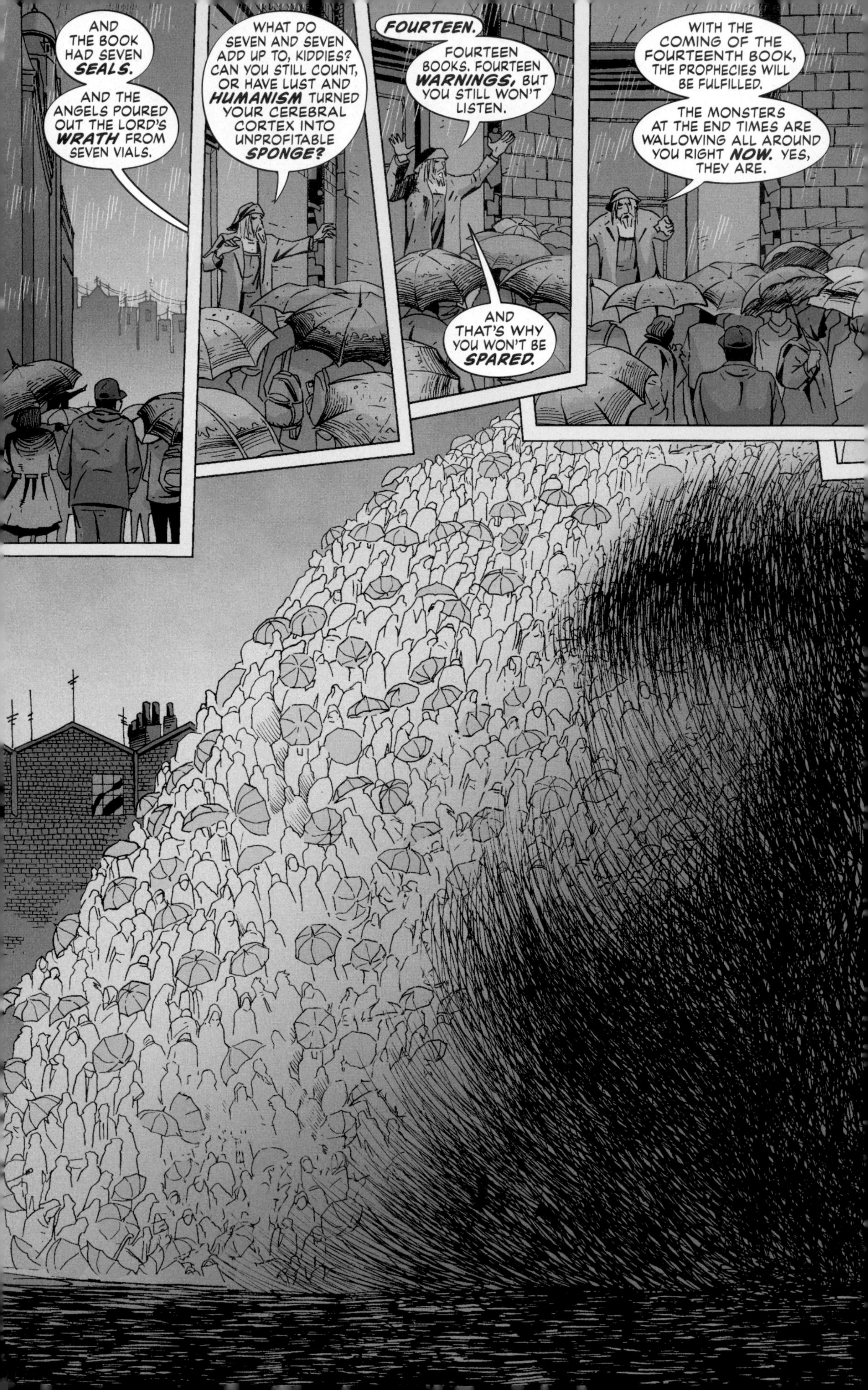

AND THE BOOK HAD SEVEN SEALS.
AND THE ANGELS POURED OUT THE LORD'S WRATH FROM SEVEN VIALS.
WHAT DO SEVEN AND SEVEN ADD UP TO, KIDDIES? CAN YOU STILL COUNT, OR HAVE LUST AND HUMANISM TURNED YOUR CEREBRAL CORTEX INTO UNPROFITABLE SPONGE?
FOURTEEN.
FOURTEEN BOOKS. FOURTEEN WARNINGS, BUT YOU STILL WON'T LISTEN.
AND THAT'S WHY YOU WON'T BE SPARED.
WITH THE COMING OF THE FOURTEENTH BOOK, THE PROPHECIES WILL BE FULFILLED.
THE MONSTERS AT THE END TIMES ARE WALLOWING ALL AROUND YOU RIGHT NOW. YES, THEY ARE.

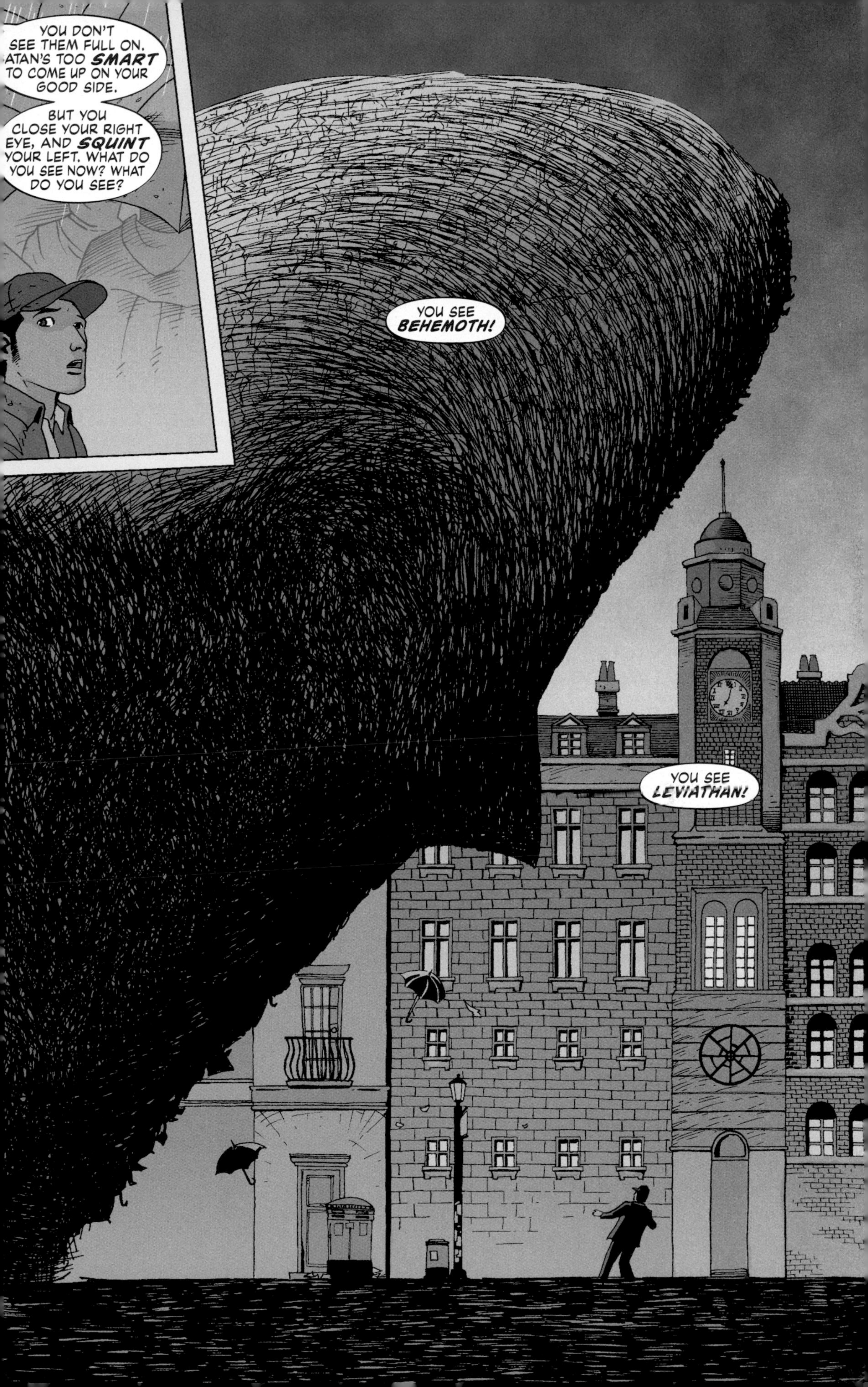

YOU DON'T SEE THEM FULL ON. SATAN'S TOO SMART TO COME UP ON YOUR GOOD SIDE.
BUT YOU CLOSE YOUR RIGHT EYE, AND SQUINT YOUR LEFT. WHAT DO YOU SEE NOW? WHAT DO YOU SEE?
YOU SEE BEHEMOTH!
YOU SEE LEVIATHAN!

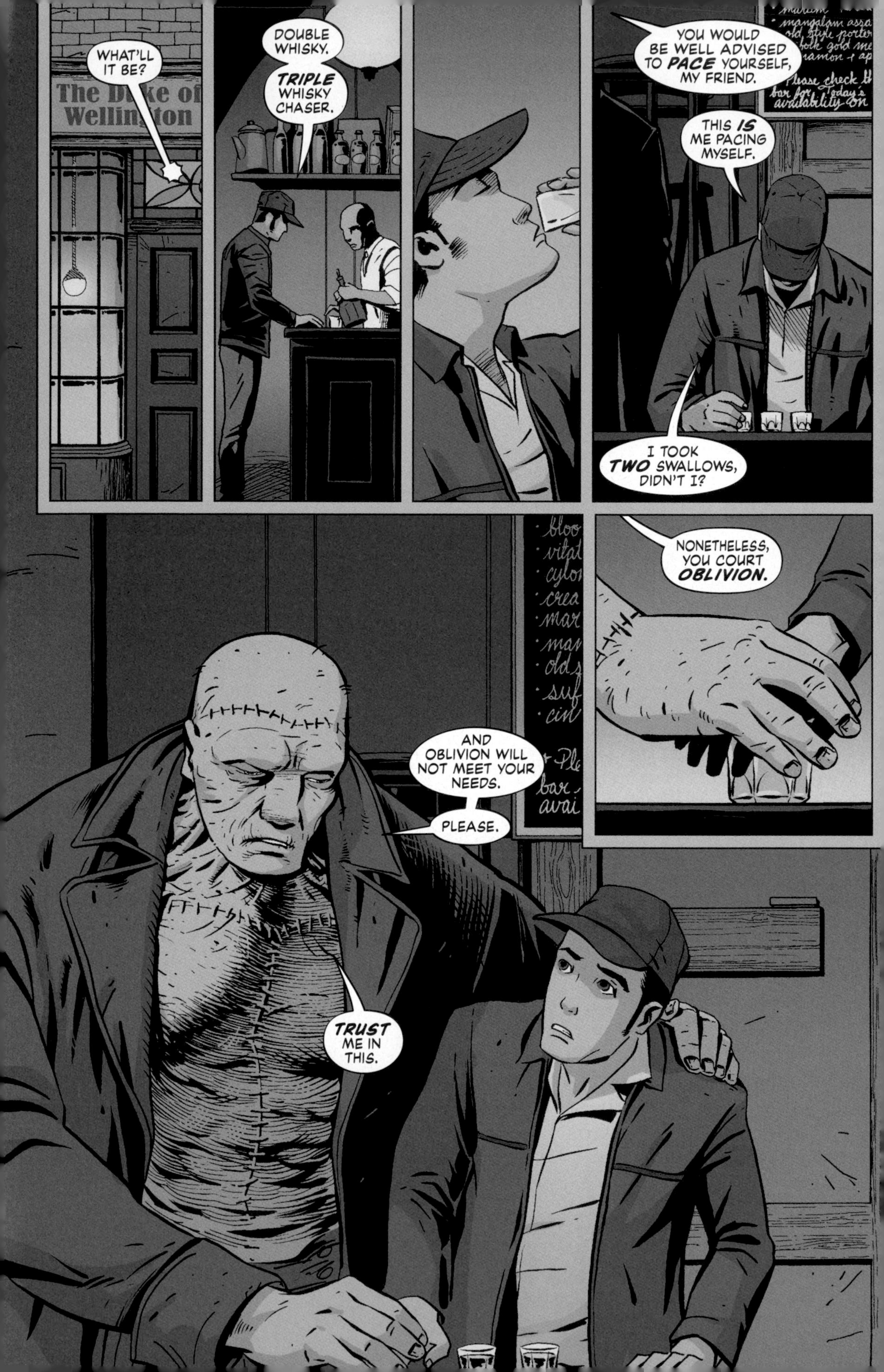
WHAT'LL IT BE?
DOUBLE WHISKY.
TRIPLE WHISKY CHASER.
YOU WOULD BE WELL ADVISED TO PACE YOURSELF, MY FRIEND.
THIS IS ME PACING MYSELF.
I TOOK TWO SWALLOWS, DIDN'T I?
NONETHELESS, YOU COURT OBLIVION.
AND OBLIVION WILL NOT MEET YOUR NEEDS.
PLEASE.
TRUST ME IN THIS.

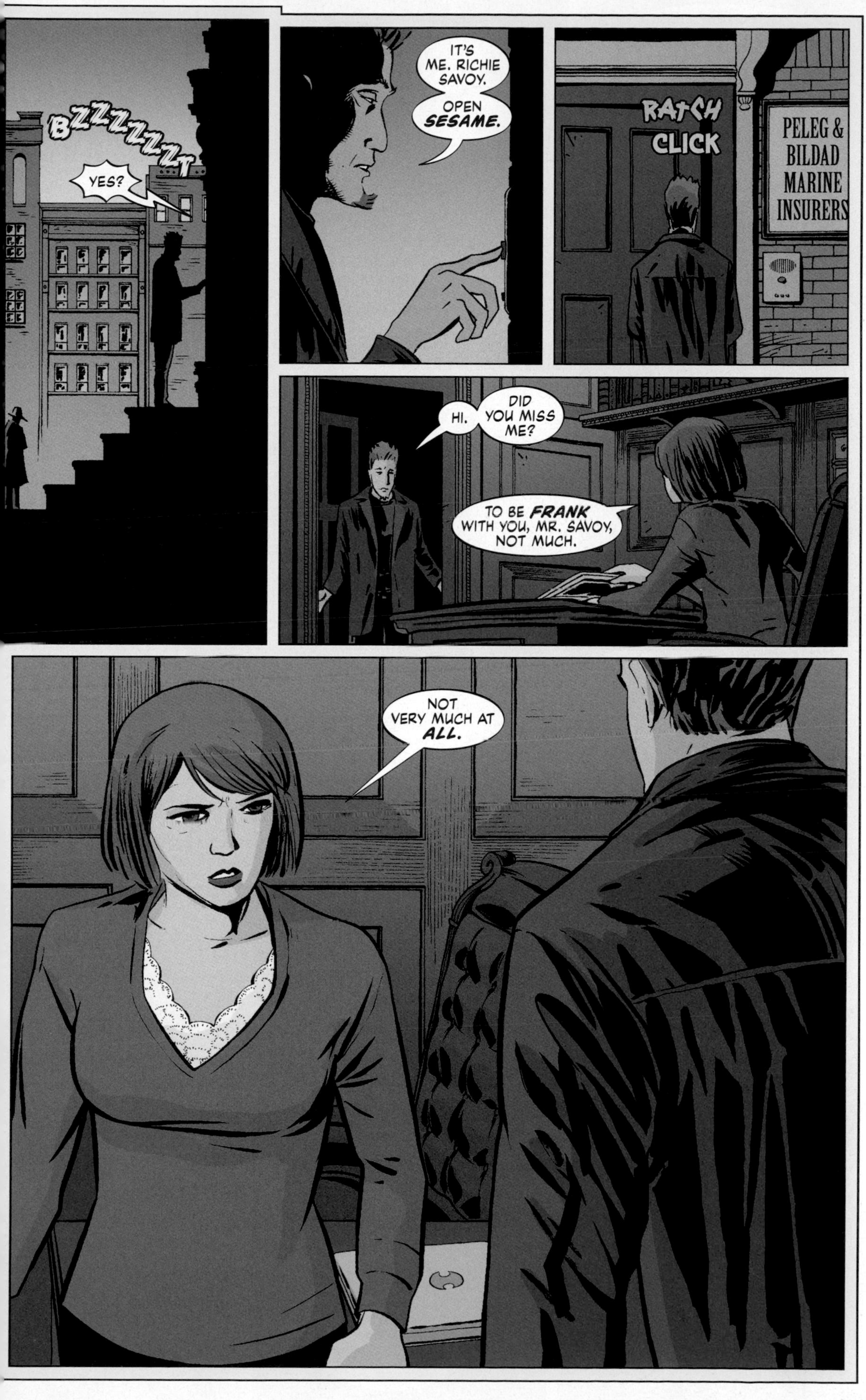
BZZZZZZZZT
YES?
IT'S ME. RICHIE SAVOY.
OPEN SESAME.
RATCH
CLICK
PELEG & BILDAD MARINE INSURERS
HI.
DID YOU MISS ME?
TO BE FRANK WITH YOU, MR. SAVOY, NOT MUCH.
NOT VERY MUCH AT ALL.

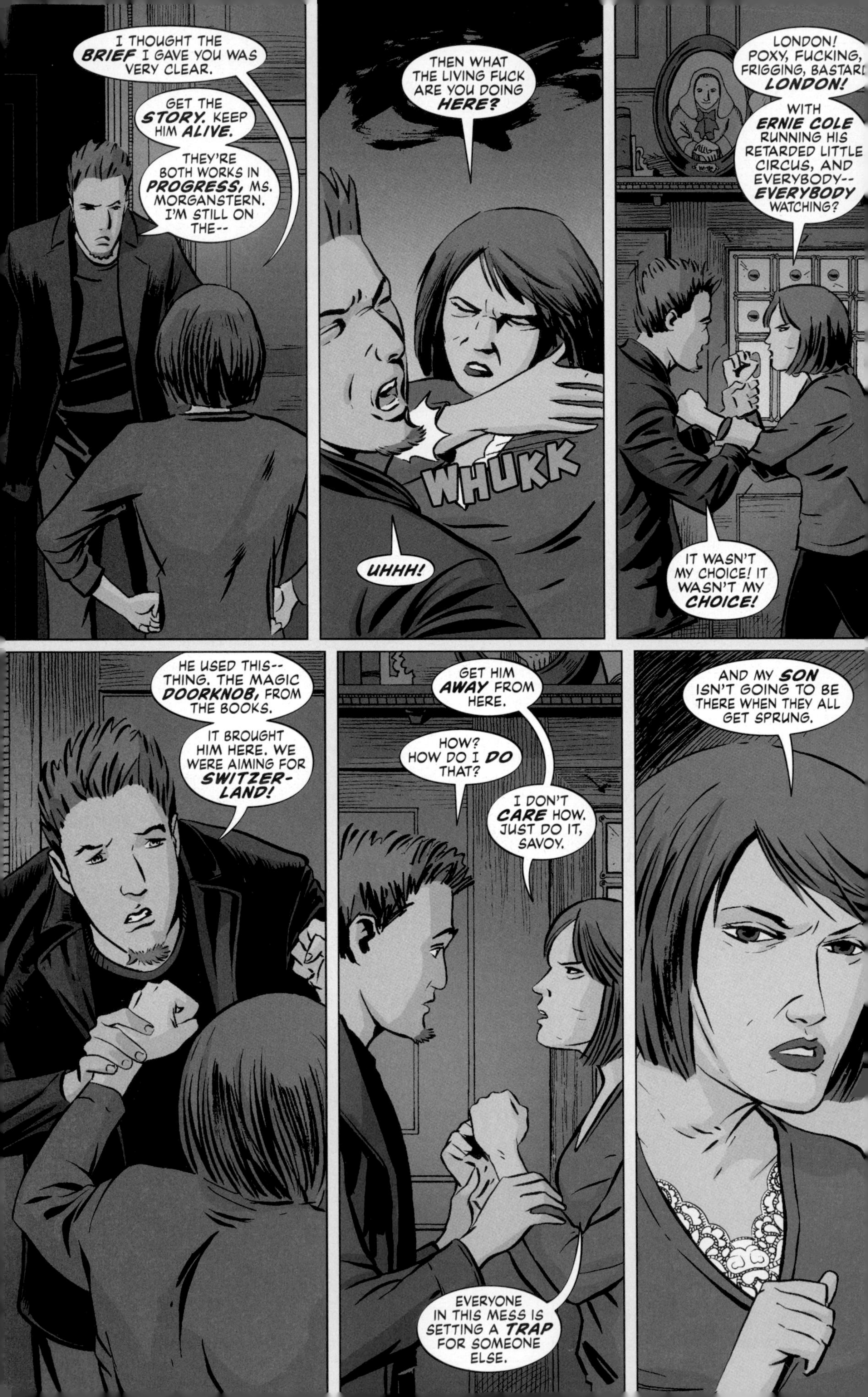
I THOUGHT THE BRIEF I GAVE YOU WAS VERY CLEAR.
GET THE STORY. KEEP HIM ALIVE.
THEY'RE BOTH WORKS IN PROGRESS, MS. MORGANSTERN. I'M STILL ON THE--
THEN WHAT THE LIVING FUCK ARE YOU DOING HERE?
WHUKK
UHHH!
LONDON! POXY, FUCKING, FRIGGING, BASTARD LONDON!
WITH ERNIE COLE RUNNING HIS RETARDED LITTLE CIRCUS, AND EVERYBODY-- EVERYBODY WATCHING?
IT WASN'T MY CHOICE! IT WASN'T MY CHOICE!
HE USED THIS-- THING. THE MAGIC DOORKNOB, FROM THE BOOKS.
IT BROUGHT HIM HERE. WE WERE AIMING FOR SWITZER-LAND!
GET HIM AWAY FROM HERE.
HOW? HOW DO I DO THAT?
I DON'T CARE HOW. JUST DO IT, SAVOY.
EVERYONE IN THIS MESS IS SETTING A TRAP FOR SOMEONE ELSE.
AND MY SON ISN'T GOING TO BE THERE WHEN THEY ALL GET SPRUNG.

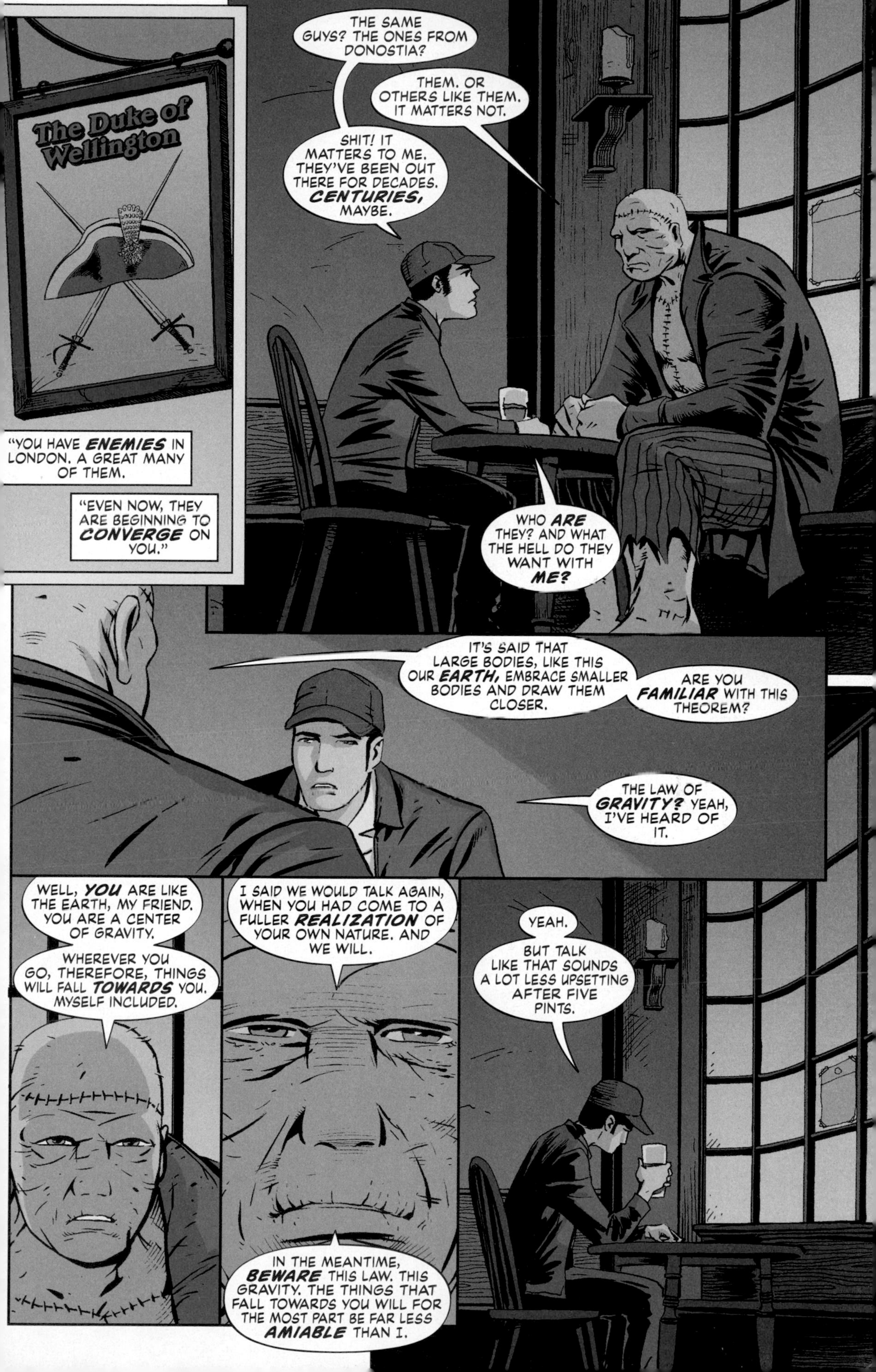
The Duke of Wellington
"YOU HAVE ENEMIES IN LONDON. A GREAT MANY OF THEM.
"EVEN NOW, THEY ARE BEGINNING TO CONVERGE ON YOU."
THE SAME GUYS? THE ONES FROM DONOSTIA?
THEM. OR OTHERS LIKE THEM. IT MATTERS NOT.
SHIT! IT MATTERS TO ME. THEY'VE BEEN OUT THERE FOR DECADES. CENTURIES, MAYBE.
WHO ARE THEY? AND WHAT THE HELL DO THEY WANT WITH ME?
IT'S SAID THAT LARGE BODIES, LIKE THIS OUR EARTH, EMBRACE SMALLER BODIES AND DRAW THEM CLOSER.
ARE YOU FAMILIAR WITH THIS THEOREM?
THE LAW OF GRAVITY? YEAH, I'VE HEARD OF IT.
WELL, YOU ARE LIKE THE EARTH, MY FRIEND. YOU ARE A CENTER OF GRAVITY.
WHEREVER YOU GO, THEREFORE, THINGS WILL FALL TOWARDS YOU. MYSELF INCLUDED.
I SAID WE WOULD TALK AGAIN, WHEN YOU HAD COME TO A FULLER REALIZATION OF YOUR OWN NATURE. AND WE WILL.
IN THE MEANTIME, BEWARE THIS LAW. THIS GRAVITY. THE THINGS THAT FALL TOWARDS YOU WILL FOR THE MOST PART BE FAR LESS AMIABLE THAN I.
YEAH.
BUT TALK LIKE THAT SOUNDS A LOT LESS UPSETTING AFTER FIVE PINTS.

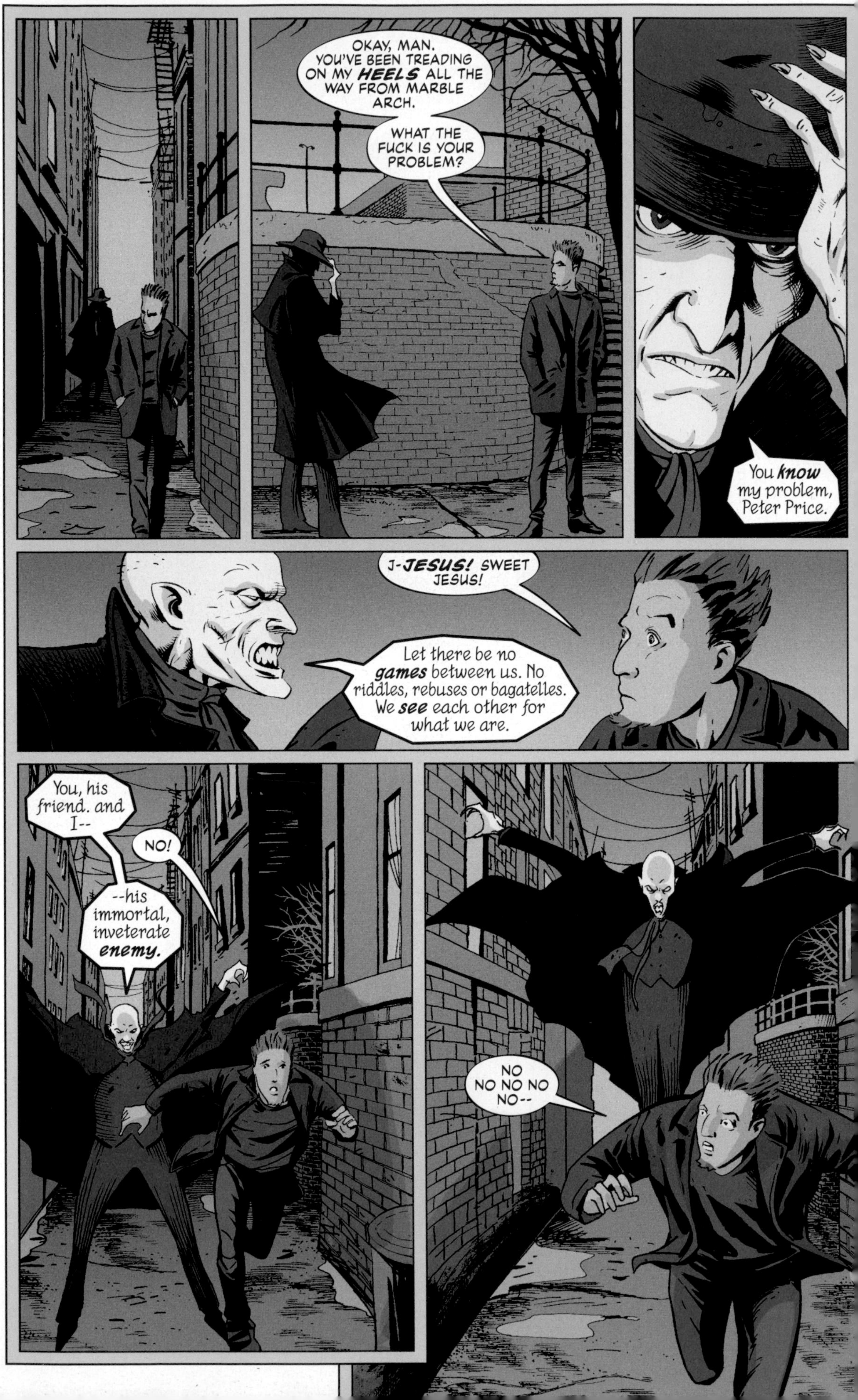
OKAY, MAN. YOU'VE BEEN TREADING ON MY HEELS ALL THE WAY FROM MARBLE ARCH.
WHAT THE FUCK IS YOUR PROBLEM?
You know my problem, Peter Price.
J-JESUS! SWEET JESUS!
Let there be no games between us. No riddles, rebuses or bagatelles. We see each other for what we are.
You, his friend. and I--
NO!
--his immortal, inveterate enemy.
NO NO NO NO NO--

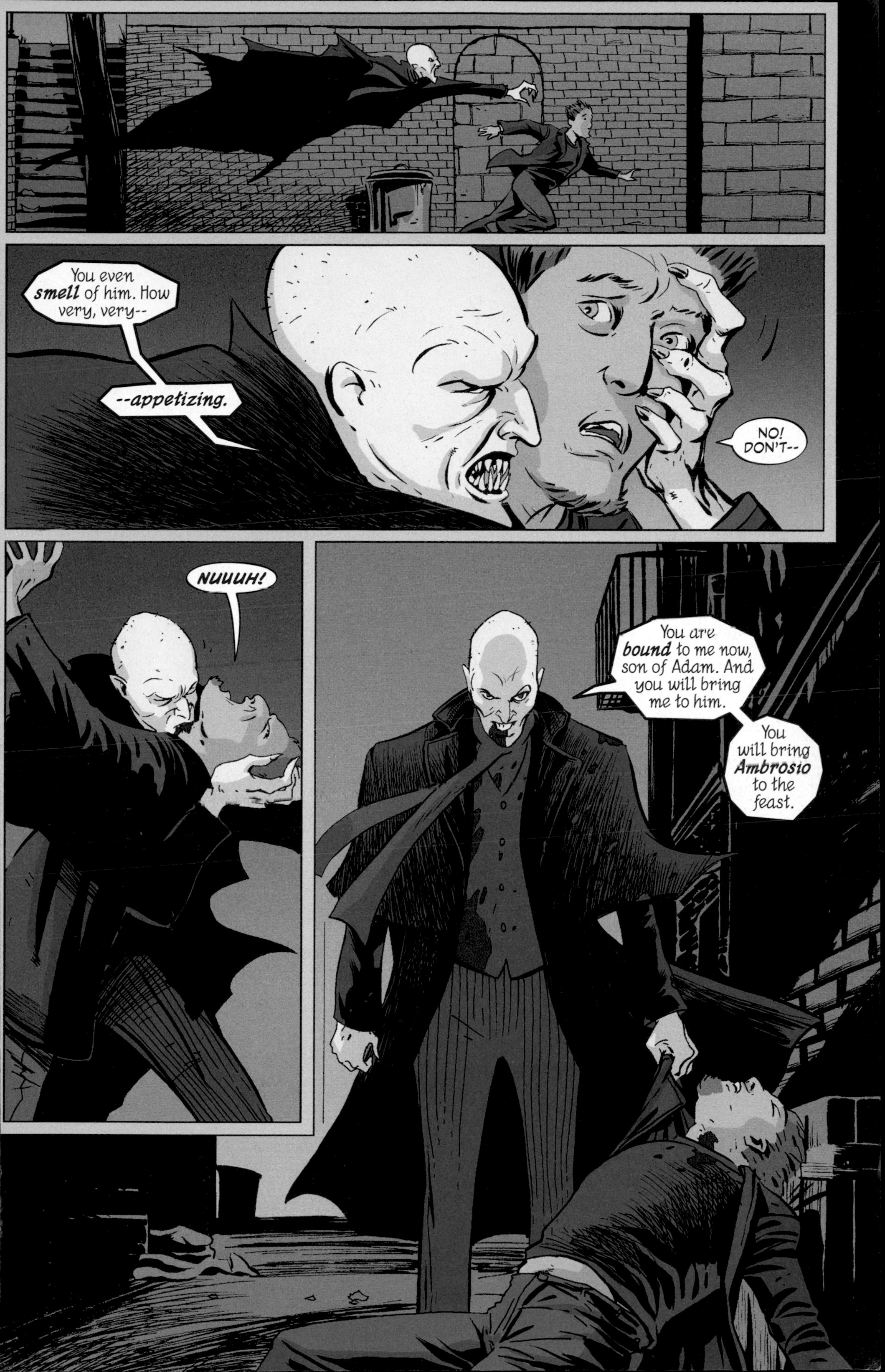
You even **smell** of him. How very, very--
--*appetizing.*
NO! DON'T--
NUUUH!
You are **bound** to me now, son of Adam. And you will bring me to him.
You will bring **Ambrosio** to the feast.

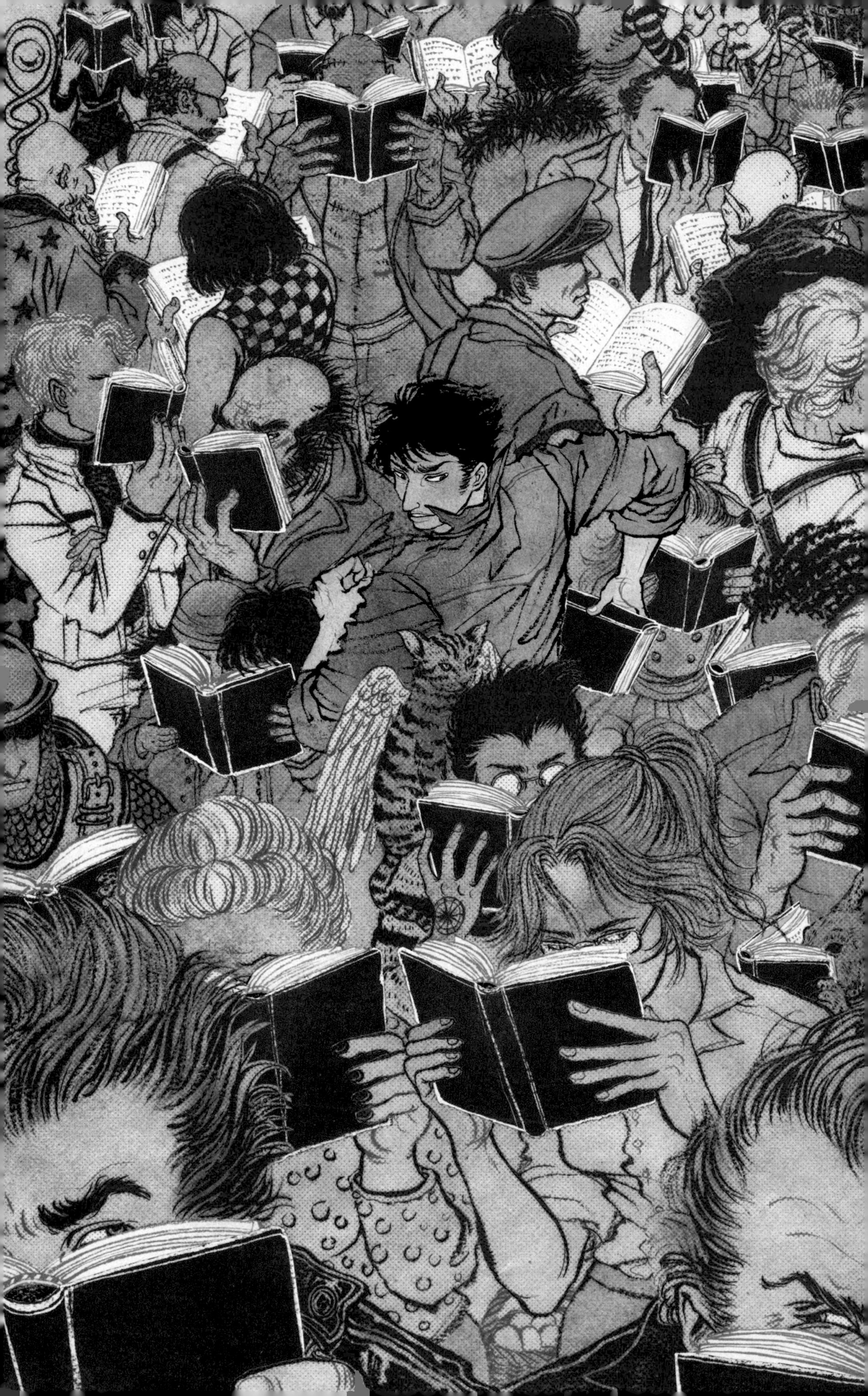

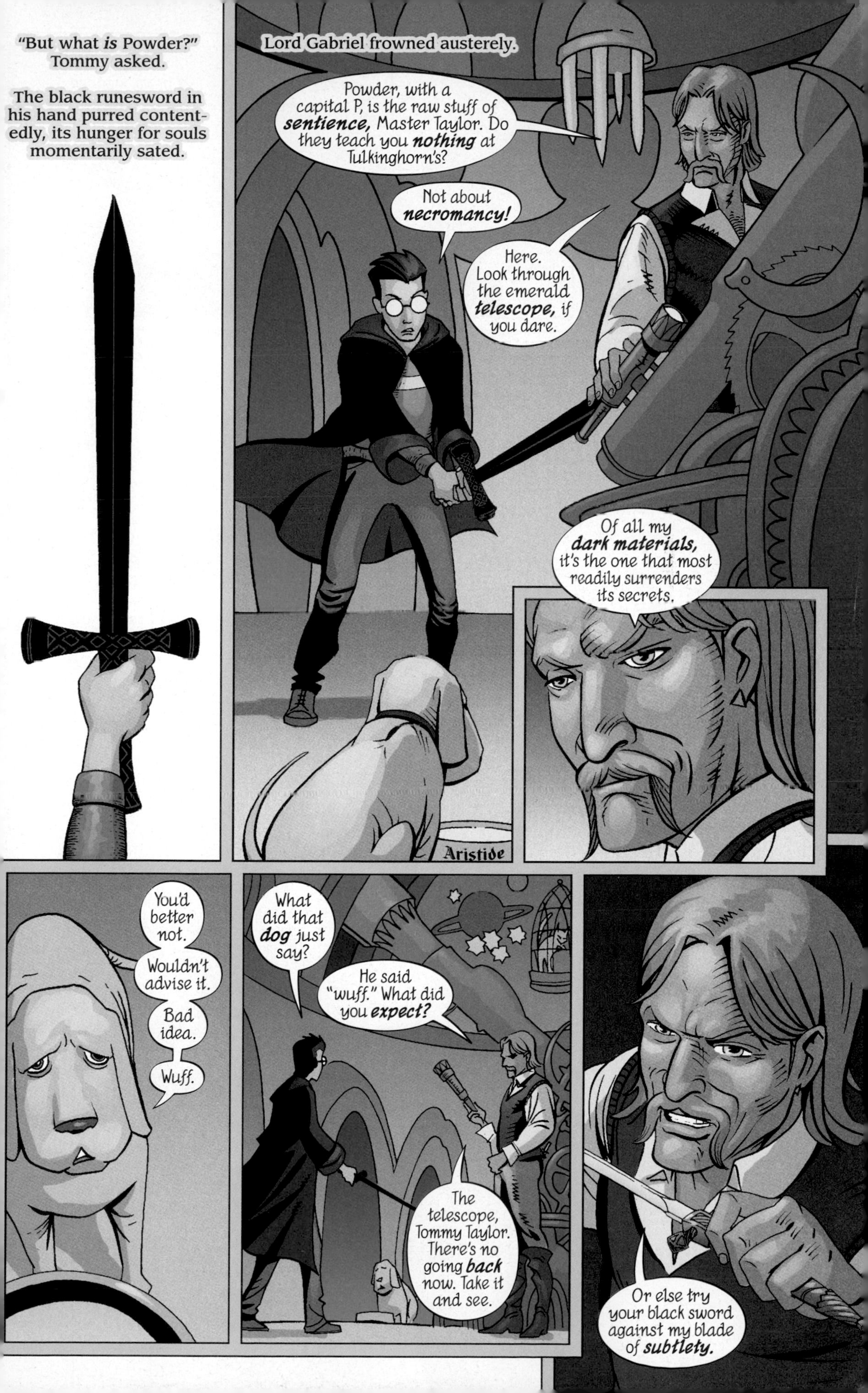
"But what *is* Powder?" Tommy asked.
The black runesword in his hand purred contentedly, its hunger for souls momentarily sated.
Lord Gabriel frowned austerely.
Powder, with a capital P, is the raw stuff of ***sentience,*** Master Taylor. Do they teach you ***nothing*** at Tulkinghorn's?
Not about ***necromancy!***
Here. Look through the emerald ***telescope,*** if you dare.
Of all my ***dark materials,*** it's the one that most readily surrenders its secrets.
Aristide
You'd better not.
Wouldn't advise it.
Bad idea.
Wuff.
What did that ***dog*** just say?
He said "wuff." What did you ***expect?***
The telescope, Tommy Taylor. There's no going ***back*** now. Take it and see.
Or else try your black sword against my blade of ***subtlety.***

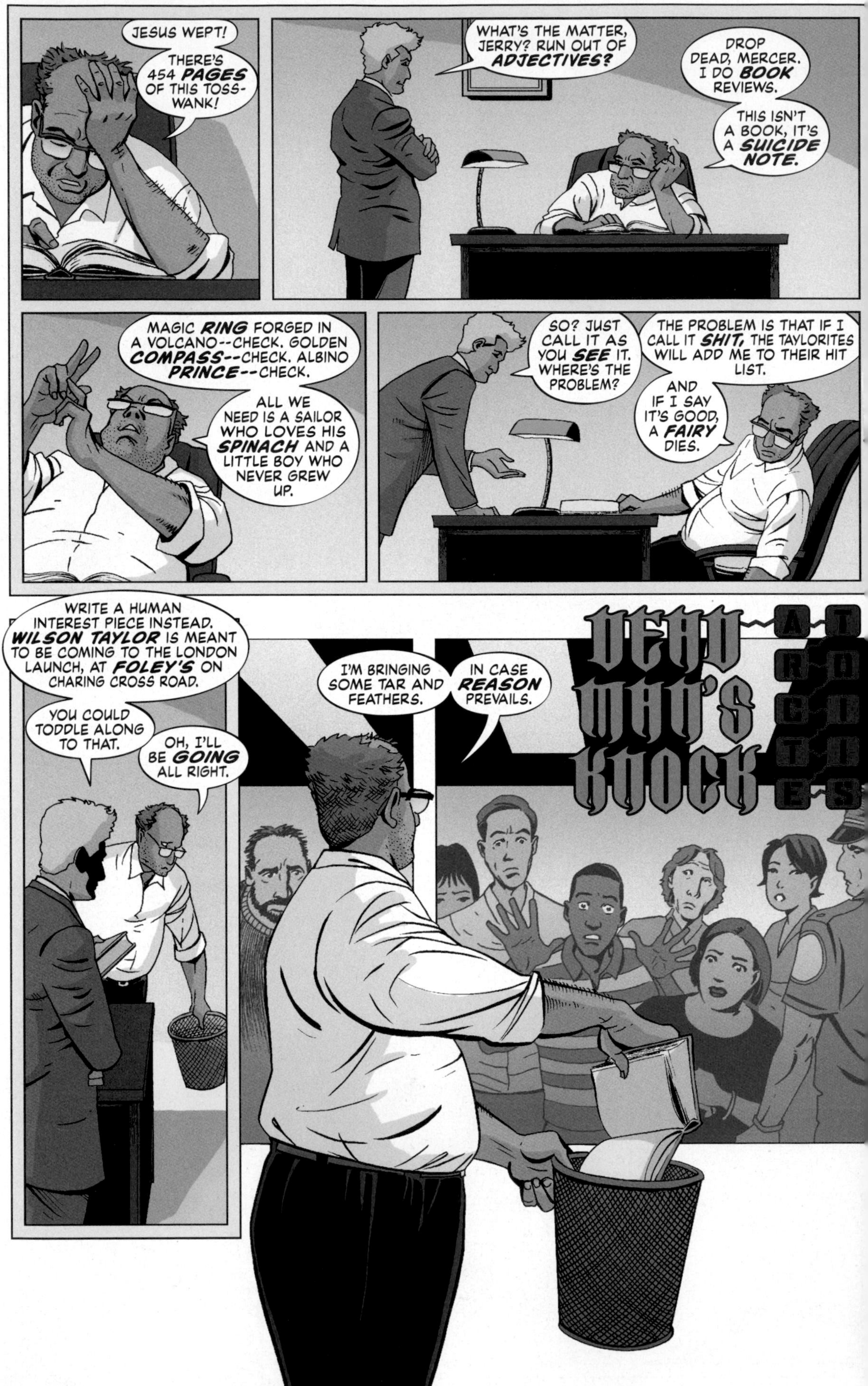
JESUS WEPT!
THERE'S 454 PAGES OF THIS TOSS-WANK!
WHAT'S THE MATTER, JERRY? RUN OUT OF ADJECTIVES?
DROP DEAD, MERCER. I DO BOOK REVIEWS.
THIS ISN'T A BOOK, IT'S A SUICIDE NOTE.
MAGIC RING FORGED IN A VOLCANO--CHECK. GOLDEN COMPASS--CHECK. ALBINO PRINCE--CHECK.
ALL WE NEED IS A SAILOR WHO LOVES HIS SPINACH AND A LITTLE BOY WHO NEVER GREW UP.
SO? JUST CALL IT AS YOU SEE IT. WHERE'S THE PROBLEM?
THE PROBLEM IS THAT IF I CALL IT SHIT, THE TAYLORITES WILL ADD ME TO THEIR HIT LIST.
AND IF I SAY IT'S GOOD, A FAIRY DIES.
WRITE A HUMAN INTEREST PIECE INSTEAD. WILSON TAYLOR IS MEANT TO BE COMING TO THE LONDON LAUNCH, AT FOLEY'S ON CHARING CROSS ROAD.
YOU COULD TODDLE ALONG TO THAT.
OH, I'LL BE GOING ALL RIGHT.
I'M BRINGING SOME TAR AND FEATHERS.
IN CASE REASON PREVAILS.
DEAD MAN'S KNOCK
A RECITE TOMORROWS

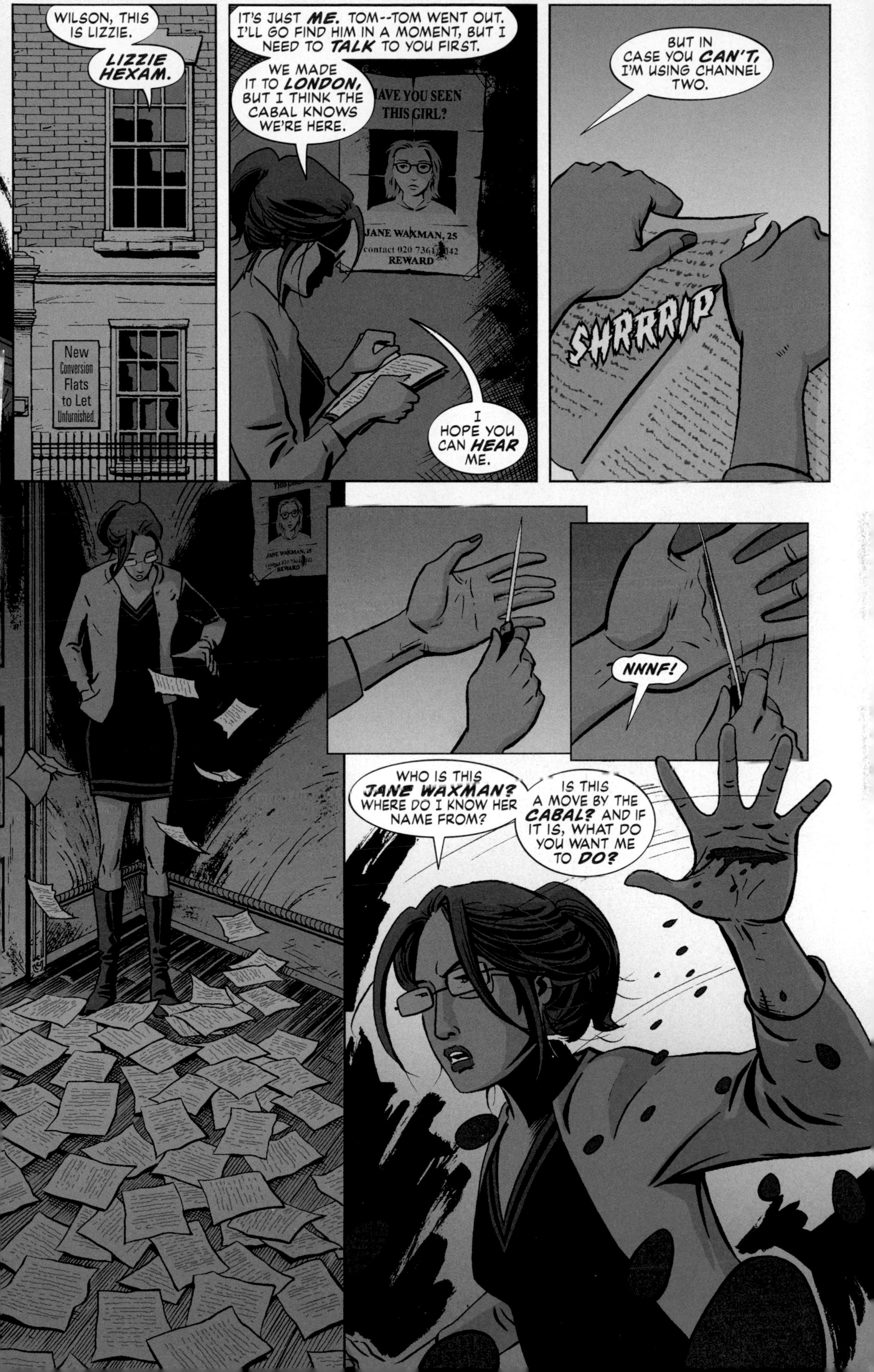
WILSON, THIS IS LIZZIE.
LIZZIE HEXAM.
New Conversion Flats to Let Unfurnished.
IT'S JUST ME. TOM--TOM WENT OUT. I'LL GO FIND HIM IN A MOMENT, BUT I NEED TO TALK TO YOU FIRST.
WE MADE IT TO LONDON, BUT I THINK THE CABAL KNOWS WE'RE HERE.
HAVE YOU SEEN THIS GIRL?
JANE WAXMAN, 25
REWARD
I HOPE YOU CAN HEAR ME.
BUT IN CASE YOU CAN'T, I'M USING CHANNEL TWO.
SHRRRIP
NNNF!
WHO IS THIS JANE WAXMAN? WHERE DO I KNOW HER NAME FROM?
IS THIS A MOVE BY THE CABAL? AND IF IT IS, WHAT DO YOU WANT ME TO DO?

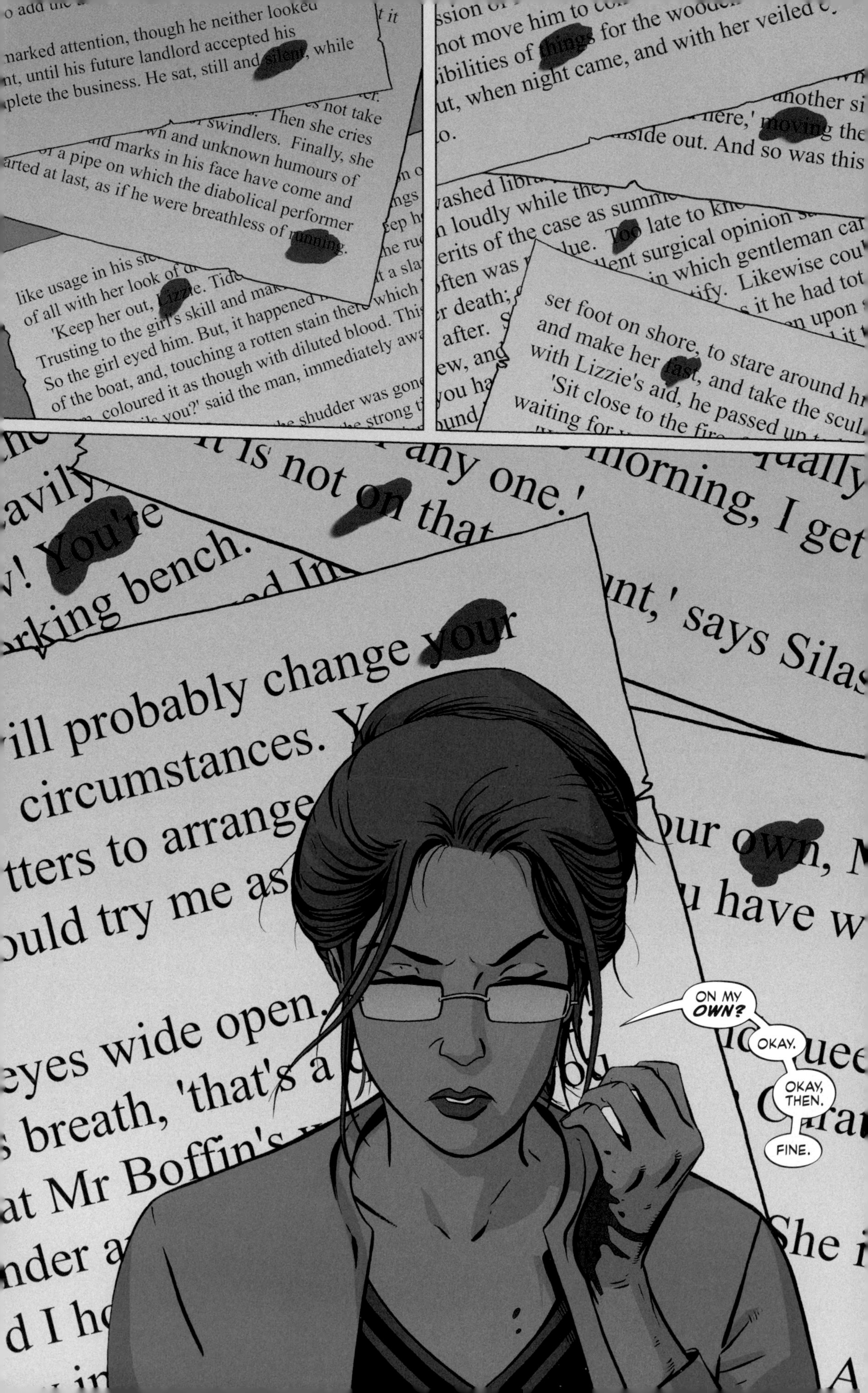
ON MY OWN?
OKAY.
OKAY, THEN.
FINE.

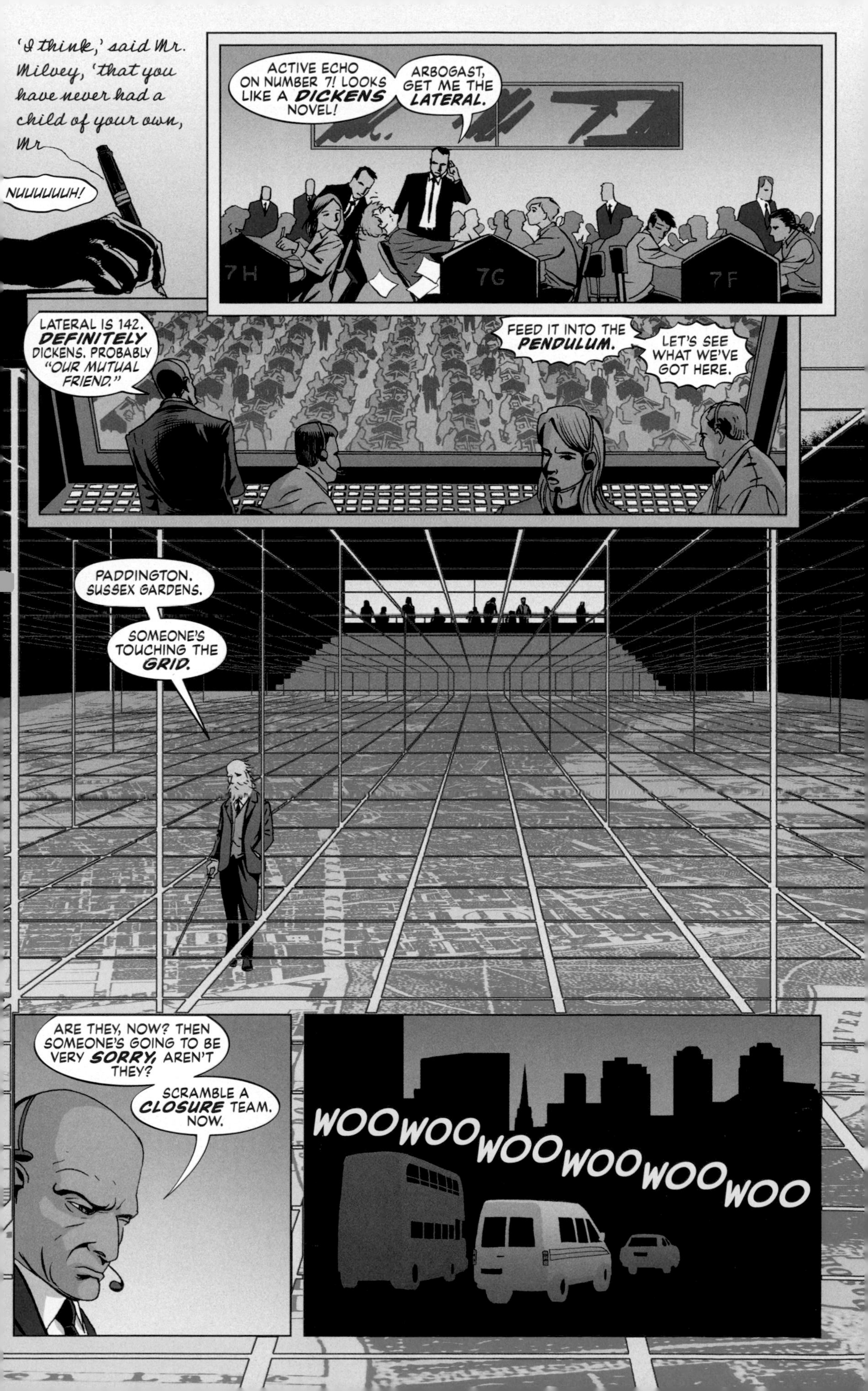
'I think,' said Mr. Milvey, 'that you have never had a child of your own, Mr
NUUUUUUH!
ACTIVE ECHO ON NUMBER 7! LOOKS LIKE A DICKENS NOVEL!
ARBOGAST, GET ME THE LATERAL.
7H
7G
7F
LATERAL IS 142. DEFINITELY DICKENS. PROBABLY "OUR MUTUAL FRIEND."
FEED IT INTO THE PENDULUM.
LET'S SEE WHAT WE'VE GOT HERE.
PADDINGTON. SUSSEX GARDENS.
SOMEONE'S TOUCHING THE GRID.
ARE THEY, NOW? THEN SOMEONE'S GOING TO BE VERY SORRY, AREN'T THEY?
SCRAMBLE A CLOSURE TEAM. NOW.
WOO WOO WOO WOO WOO WOO

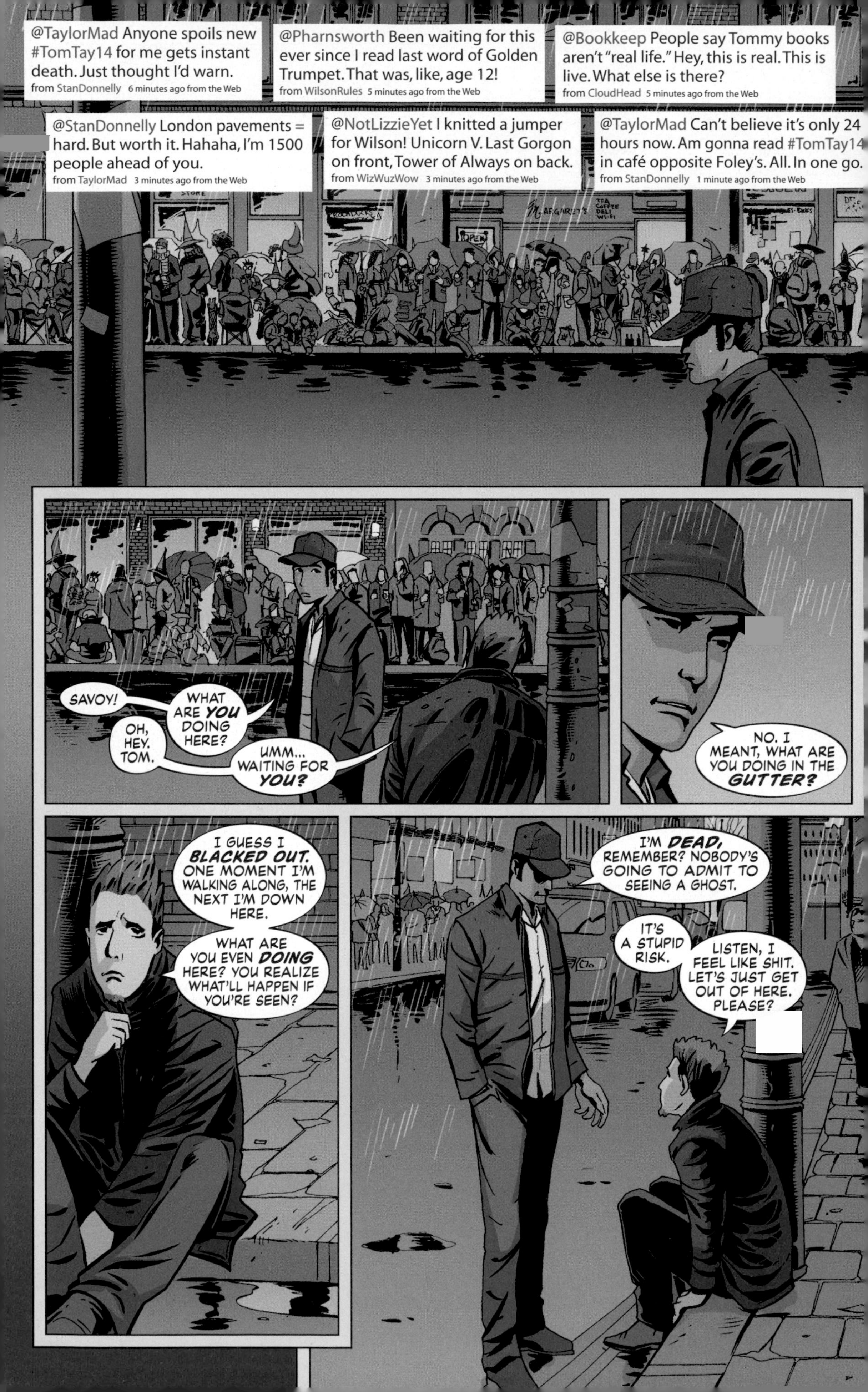

@TaylorMad Anyone spoils new #TomTay14 for me gets instant death. Just thought I'd warn.
from StanDonnelly 6 minutes ago from the Web
@Pharnsworth Been waiting for this ever since I read last word of Golden Trumpet. That was, like, age 12!
from WilsonRules 5 minutes ago from the Web
@Bookkeep People say Tommy books aren't "real life." Hey, this is real. This is live. What else is there?
from CloudHead 5 minutes ago from the Web
@StanDonnelly London pavements = hard. But worth it. Hahaha, I'm 1500 people ahead of you.
from TaylorMad 3 minutes ago from the Web
@NotLizzieYet I knitted a jumper for Wilson! Unicorn V. Last Gorgon on front, Tower of Always on back.
from WizWuzWow 3 minutes ago from the Web
@TaylorMad Can't believe it's only 24 hours now. Am gonna read #TomTay14 in café opposite Foley's. All. In one go.
from StanDonnelly 1 minute ago from the Web
OPEN
SAVOY!
OH, HEY. TOM.
WHAT ARE *YOU* DOING HERE?
UMM... WAITING FOR *YOU?*
NO. I MEANT, WHAT ARE YOU DOING IN THE *GUTTER?*
I GUESS I *BLACKED OUT.* ONE MOMENT I'M WALKING ALONG, THE NEXT I'M DOWN HERE.
WHAT ARE YOU EVEN *DOING* HERE? YOU REALIZE WHAT'LL HAPPEN IF YOU'RE SEEN?
I'M *DEAD,* REMEMBER? NOBODY'S GOING TO ADMIT TO SEEING A GHOST.
IT'S A STUPID RISK.
LISTEN, I FEEL LIKE SHIT. LET'S JUST GET OUT OF HERE. PLEASE?

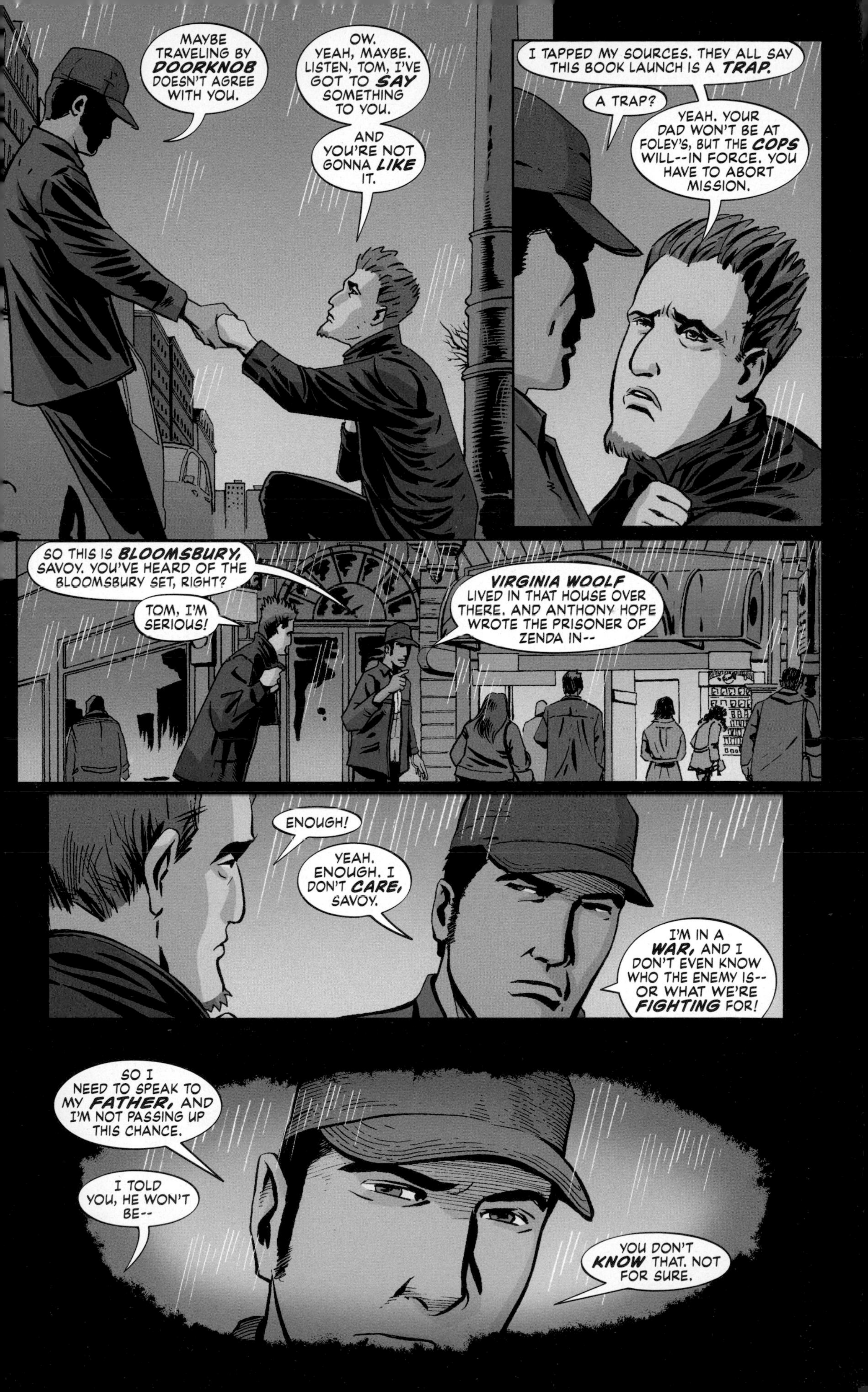
MAYBE TRAVELING BY DOORKNOB DOESN'T AGREE WITH YOU.
OW. YEAH, MAYBE. LISTEN, TOM, I'VE GOT TO SAY SOMETHING TO YOU.
AND YOU'RE NOT GONNA LIKE IT.
I TAPPED MY SOURCES. THEY ALL SAY THIS BOOK LAUNCH IS A TRAP.
A TRAP?
YEAH. YOUR DAD WON'T BE AT FOLEY'S, BUT THE COPS WILL--IN FORCE. YOU HAVE TO ABORT MISSION.
SO THIS IS BLOOMSBURY, SAVOY. YOU'VE HEARD OF THE BLOOMSBURY SET, RIGHT?
TOM, I'M SERIOUS!
VIRGINIA WOOLF LIVED IN THAT HOUSE OVER THERE. AND ANTHONY HOPE WROTE THE PRISONER OF ZENDA IN--
ENOUGH!
YEAH. ENOUGH. I DON'T CARE, SAVOY.
I'M IN A WAR, AND I DON'T EVEN KNOW WHO THE ENEMY IS-- OR WHAT WE'RE FIGHTING FOR!
SO I NEED TO SPEAK TO MY FATHER, AND I'M NOT PASSING UP THIS CHANCE.
I TOLD YOU, HE WON'T BE--
YOU DON'T KNOW THAT. NOT FOR SURE.

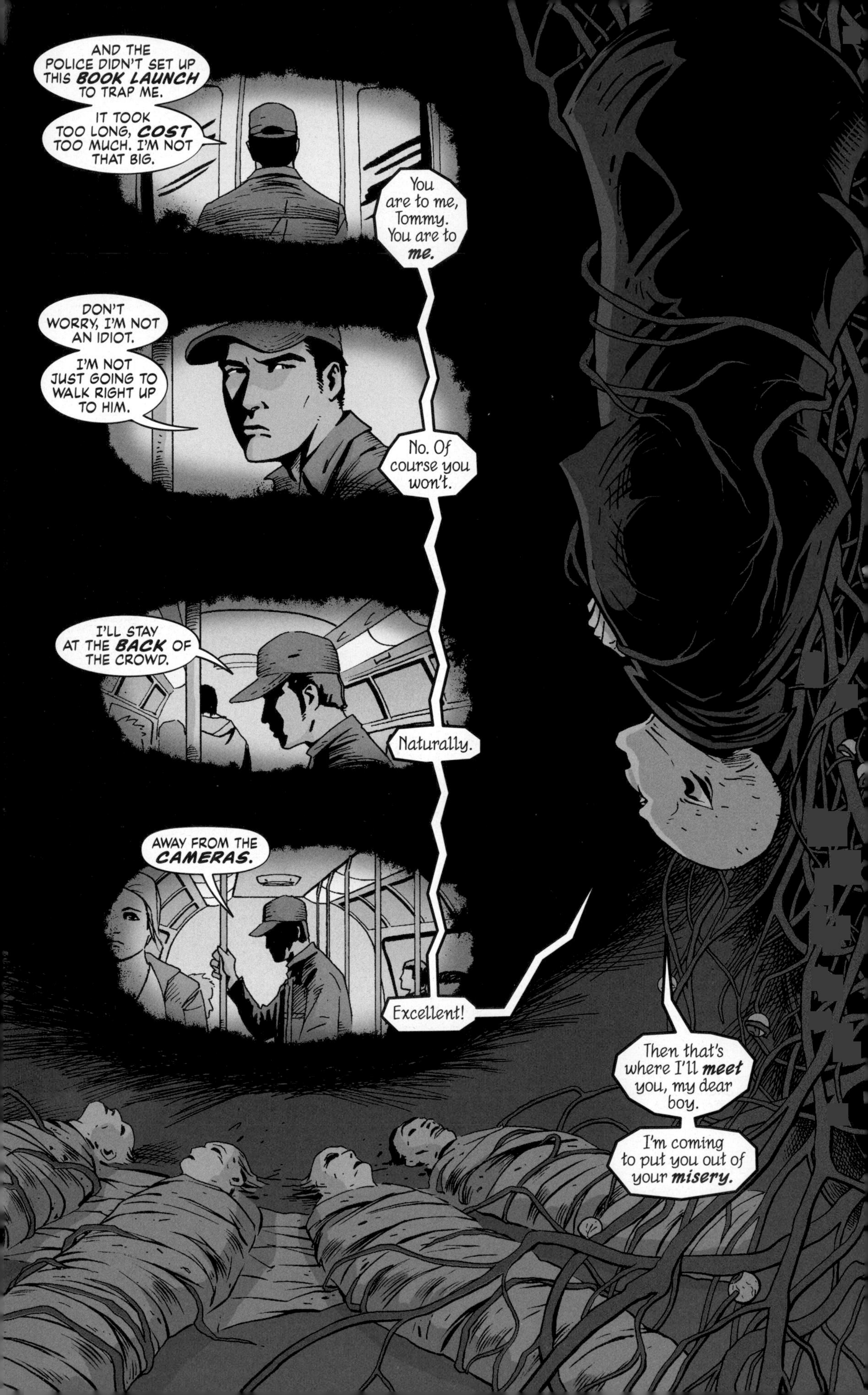
AND THE POLICE DIDN'T SET UP THIS BOOK LAUNCH TO TRAP ME.
IT TOOK TOO LONG, COST TOO MUCH. I'M NOT THAT BIG.
You are to me, Tommy. You are to me.
DON'T WORRY, I'M NOT AN IDIOT.
I'M NOT JUST GOING TO WALK RIGHT UP TO HIM.
No. Of course you won't.
I'LL STAY AT THE BACK OF THE CROWD.
Naturally.
AWAY FROM THE CAMERAS.
Excellent!
Then that's where I'll meet you, my dear boy.
I'm coming to put you out of your misery.

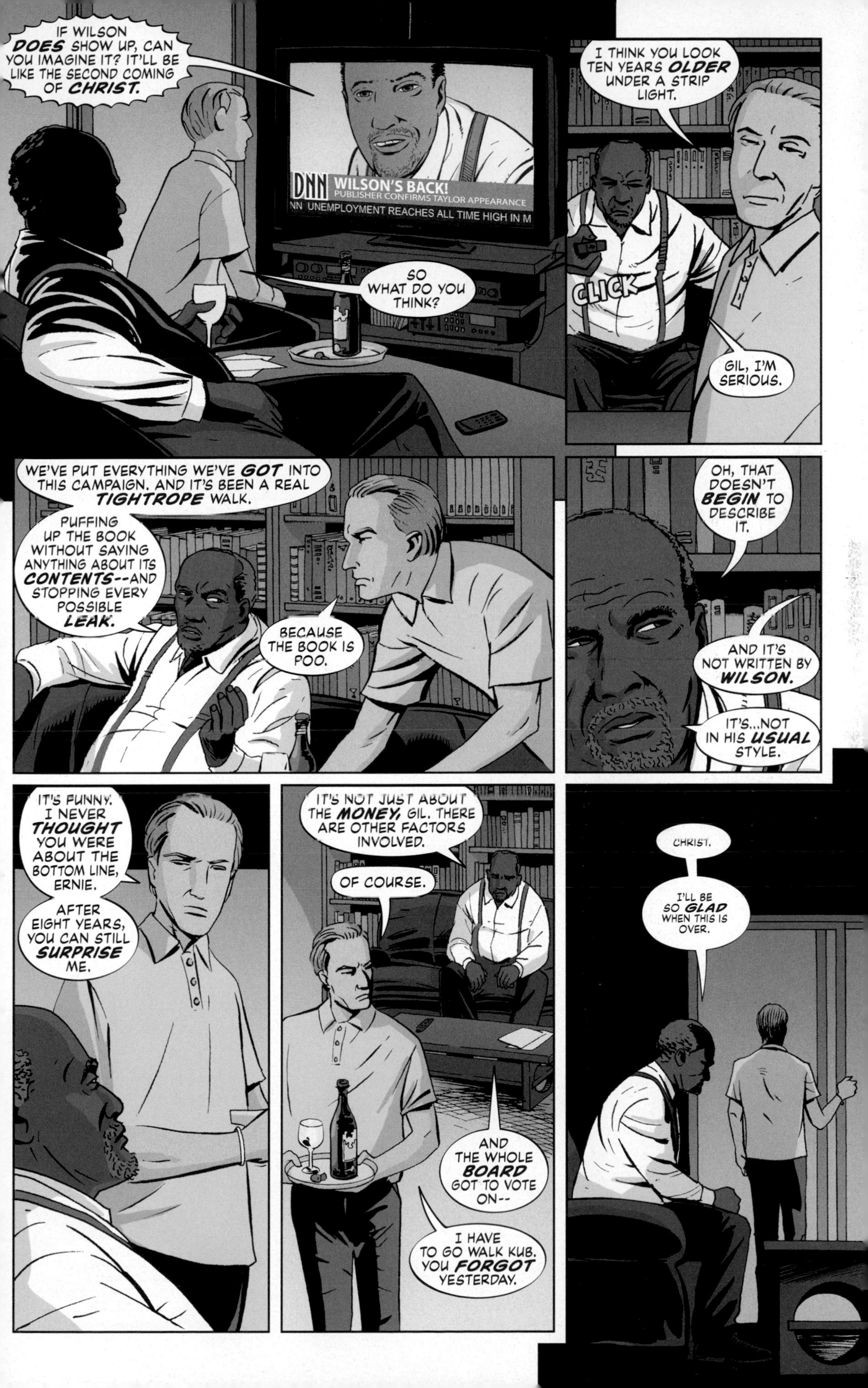
IF WILSON DOES SHOW UP, CAN YOU IMAGINE IT? IT'LL BE LIKE THE SECOND COMING OF CHRIST.
DNN WILSON'S BACK!
PUBLISHER CONFIRMS TAYLOR APPEARANCE
NN UNEMPLOYMENT REACHES ALL TIME HIGH IN M
SO WHAT DO YOU THINK?
I THINK YOU LOOK TEN YEARS OLDER UNDER A STRIP LIGHT.
CLICK
GIL, I'M SERIOUS.
WE'VE PUT EVERYTHING WE'VE GOT INTO THIS CAMPAIGN. AND IT'S BEEN A REAL TIGHTROPE WALK.
PUFFING UP THE BOOK WITHOUT SAYING ANYTHING ABOUT ITS CONTENTS--AND STOPPING EVERY POSSIBLE LEAK.
BECAUSE THE BOOK IS POO.
OH, THAT DOESN'T BEGIN TO DESCRIBE IT.
AND IT'S NOT WRITTEN BY WILSON.
IT'S...NOT IN HIS USUAL STYLE.
IT'S FUNNY. I NEVER THOUGHT YOU WERE ABOUT THE BOTTOM LINE, ERNIE.
AFTER EIGHT YEARS, YOU CAN STILL SURPRISE ME.
IT'S NOT JUST ABOUT THE MONEY, GIL. THERE ARE OTHER FACTORS INVOLVED.
OF COURSE.
AND THE WHOLE BOARD GOT TO VOTE ON--
I HAVE TO GO WALK KUB. YOU FORGOT YESTERDAY.
CHRIST.
I'LL BE SO GLAD WHEN THIS IS OVER.

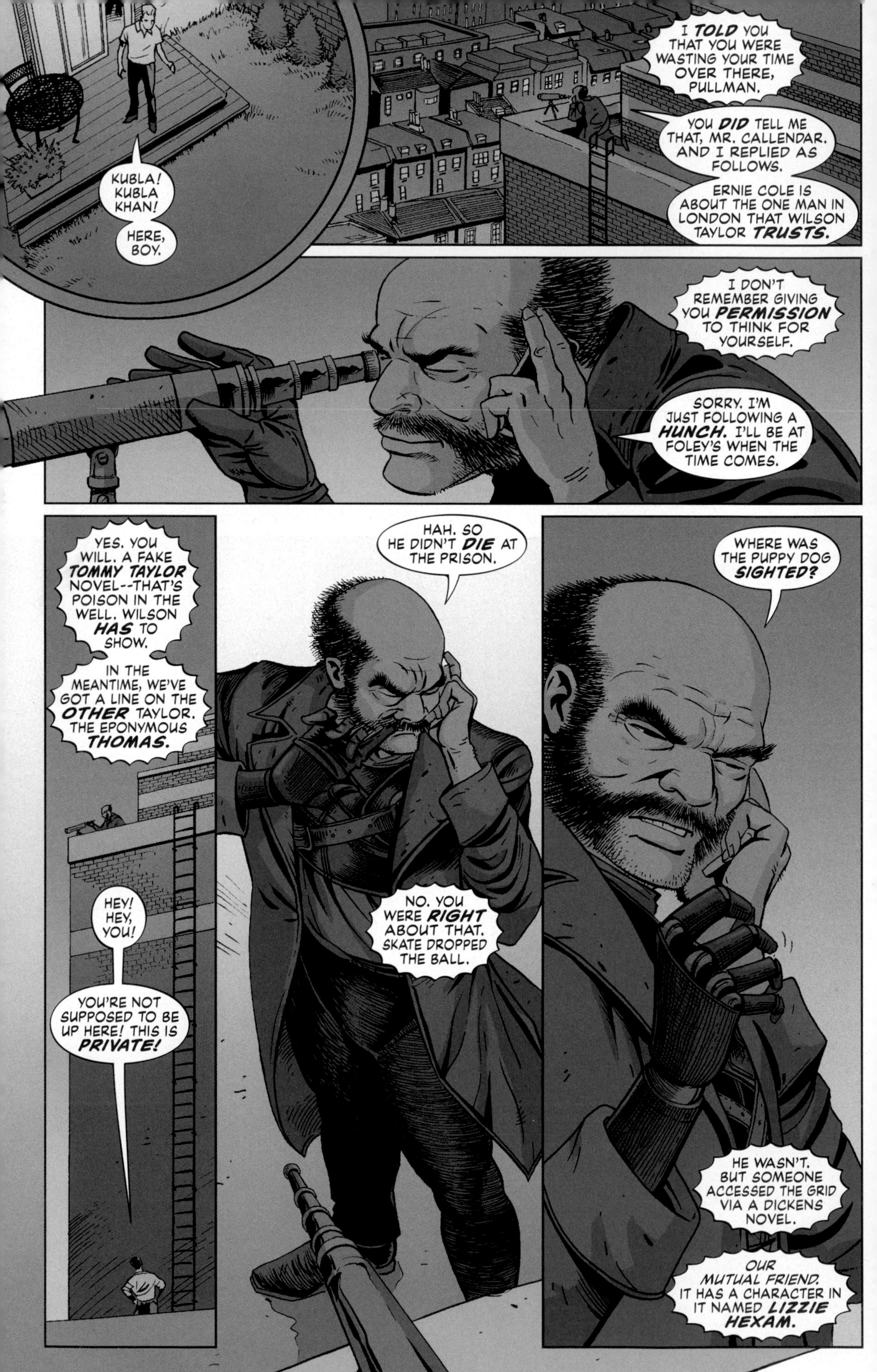

KUBLA! KUBLA KHAN!
HERE, BOY.
I TOLD YOU THAT YOU WERE WASTING YOUR TIME OVER THERE, PULLMAN.
YOU DID TELL ME THAT, MR. CALLENDAR. AND I REPLIED AS FOLLOWS.
ERNIE COLE IS ABOUT THE ONE MAN IN LONDON THAT WILSON TAYLOR TRUSTS.
I DON'T REMEMBER GIVING YOU PERMISSION TO THINK FOR YOURSELF.
SORRY. I'M JUST FOLLOWING A HUNCH. I'LL BE AT FOLEY'S WHEN THE TIME COMES.
YES. YOU WILL. A FAKE TOMMY TAYLOR NOVEL--THAT'S POISON IN THE WELL. WILSON HAS TO SHOW.
IN THE MEANTIME, WE'VE GOT A LINE ON THE OTHER TAYLOR. THE EPONYMOUS THOMAS.
HAH. SO HE DIDN'T DIE AT THE PRISON.
NO. YOU WERE RIGHT ABOUT THAT. SKATE DROPPED THE BALL.
HEY! HEY, YOU!
YOU'RE NOT SUPPOSED TO BE UP HERE! THIS IS PRIVATE!
WHERE WAS THE PUPPY DOG SIGHTED?
HE WASN'T. BUT SOMEONE ACCESSED THE GRID VIA A DICKENS NOVEL.
OUR MUTUAL FRIEND. IT HAS A CHARACTER IN IT NAMED LIZZIE HEXAM.

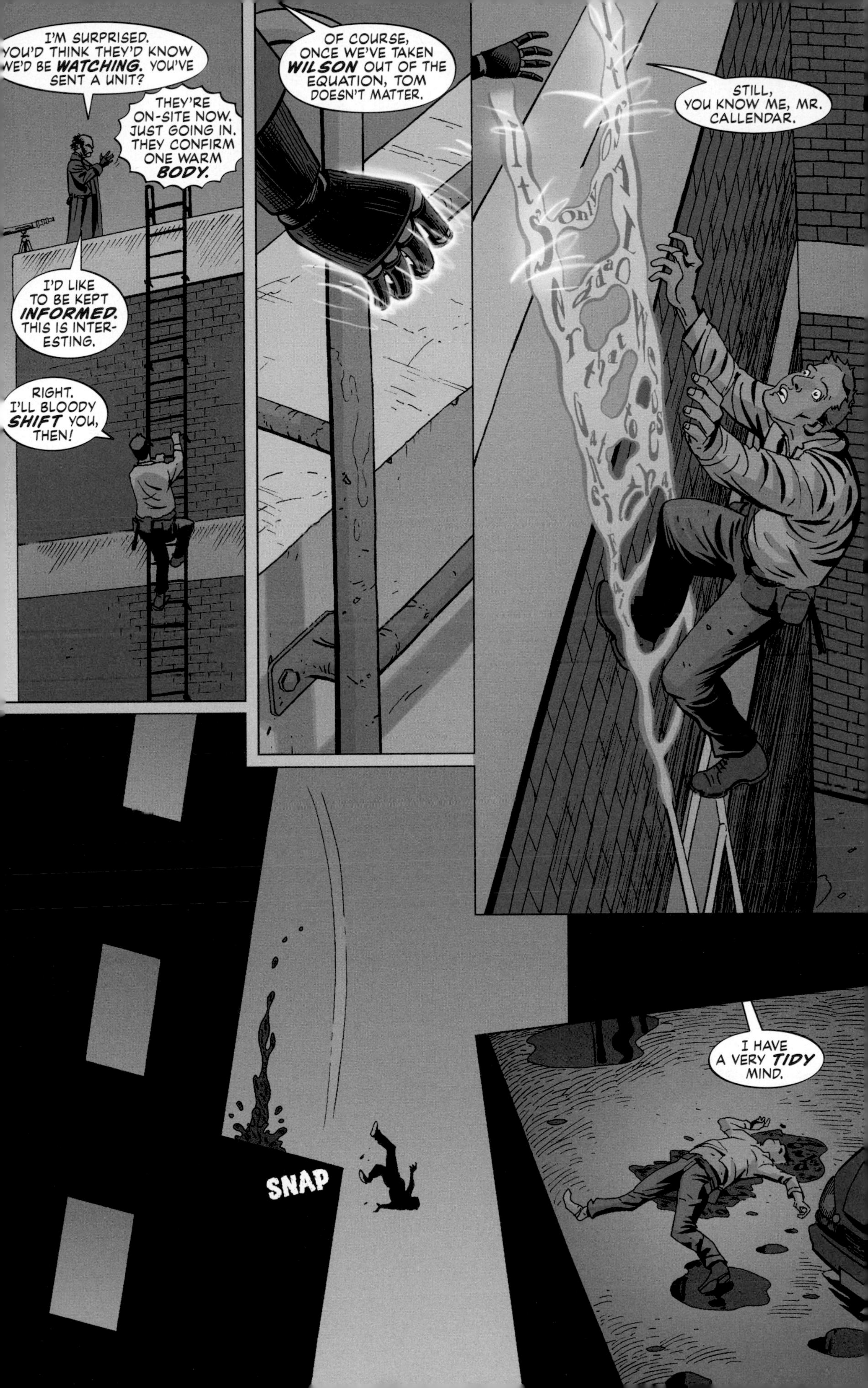
I'M SURPRISED. YOU'D THINK THEY'D KNOW WE'D BE ***WATCHING.*** YOU'VE SENT A UNIT?
THEY'RE ON-SITE NOW. JUST GOING IN. THEY CONFIRM ONE WARM ***BODY.***
I'D LIKE TO BE KEPT ***INFORMED.*** THIS IS INTER-ESTING.
RIGHT. I'LL BLOODY ***SHIFT*** YOU, THEN!
OF COURSE, ONCE WE'VE TAKEN ***WILSON*** OUT OF THE EQUATION, TOM DOESN'T MATTER.
STILL, YOU KNOW ME, MR. CALLENDAR.
SNAP
I HAVE A VERY ***TIDY*** MIND.

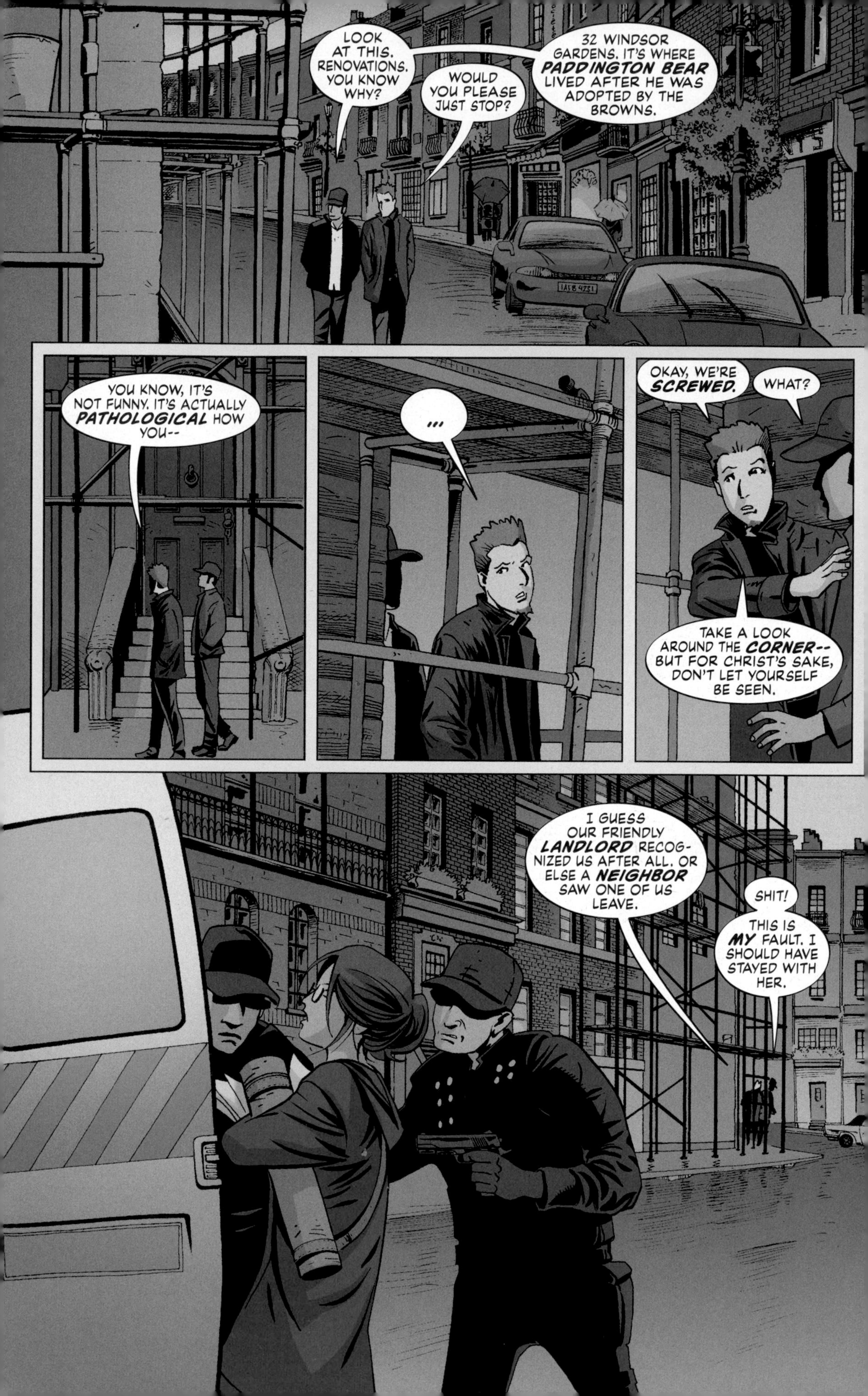
LOOK AT THIS. RENOVATIONS. YOU KNOW WHY?
32 WINDSOR GARDENS. IT'S WHERE **PADDINGTON BEAR** LIVED AFTER HE WAS ADOPTED BY THE BROWNS.
WOULD YOU PLEASE JUST STOP?
YOU KNOW, IT'S NOT FUNNY. IT'S ACTUALLY **PATHOLOGICAL** HOW YOU--
...
OKAY, WE'RE **SCREWED.**
WHAT?
TAKE A LOOK AROUND THE **CORNER**-- BUT FOR CHRIST'S SAKE, DON'T LET YOURSELF BE SEEN.
I GUESS OUR FRIENDLY **LANDLORD** RECOGNIZED US AFTER ALL. OR ELSE A **NEIGHBOR** SAW ONE OF US LEAVE.
SHIT!
THIS IS **MY** FAULT. I SHOULD HAVE STAYED WITH HER.

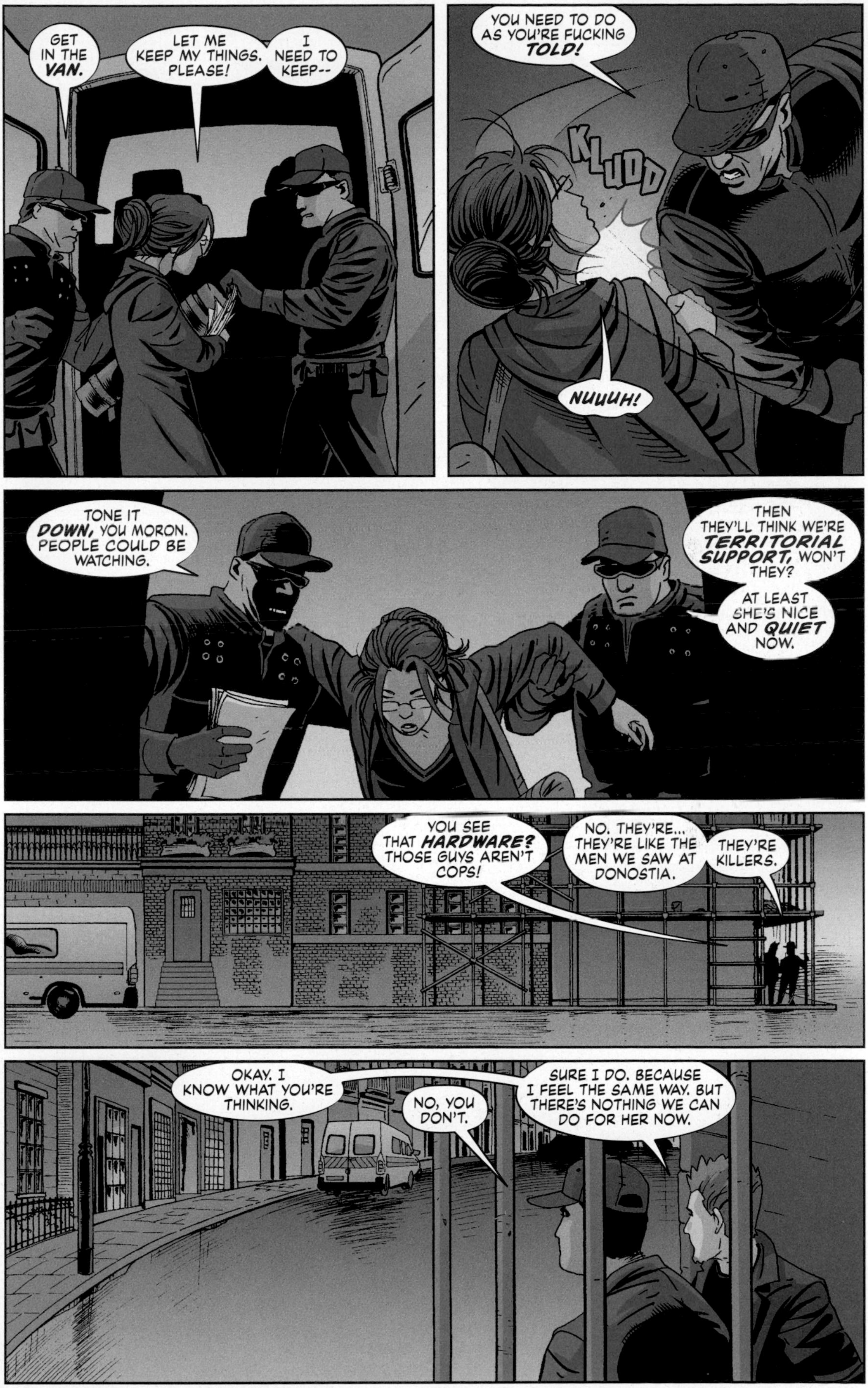
GET IN THE VAN.
LET ME KEEP MY THINGS. PLEASE!
I NEED TO KEEP--
YOU NEED TO DO AS YOU'RE FUCKING TOLD!
KLUDD
NUUUH!
TONE IT DOWN, YOU MORON. PEOPLE COULD BE WATCHING.
THEN THEY'LL THINK WE'RE TERRITORIAL SUPPORT, WON'T THEY?
AT LEAST SHE'S NICE AND QUIET NOW.
YOU SEE THAT HARDWARE? THOSE GUYS AREN'T COPS!
NO. THEY'RE... THEY'RE LIKE THE MEN WE SAW AT DONOSTIA.
THEY'RE KILLERS.
OKAY. I KNOW WHAT YOU'RE THINKING.
NO, YOU DON'T.
SURE I DO. BECAUSE I FEEL THE SAME WAY. BUT THERE'S NOTHING WE CAN DO FOR HER NOW.

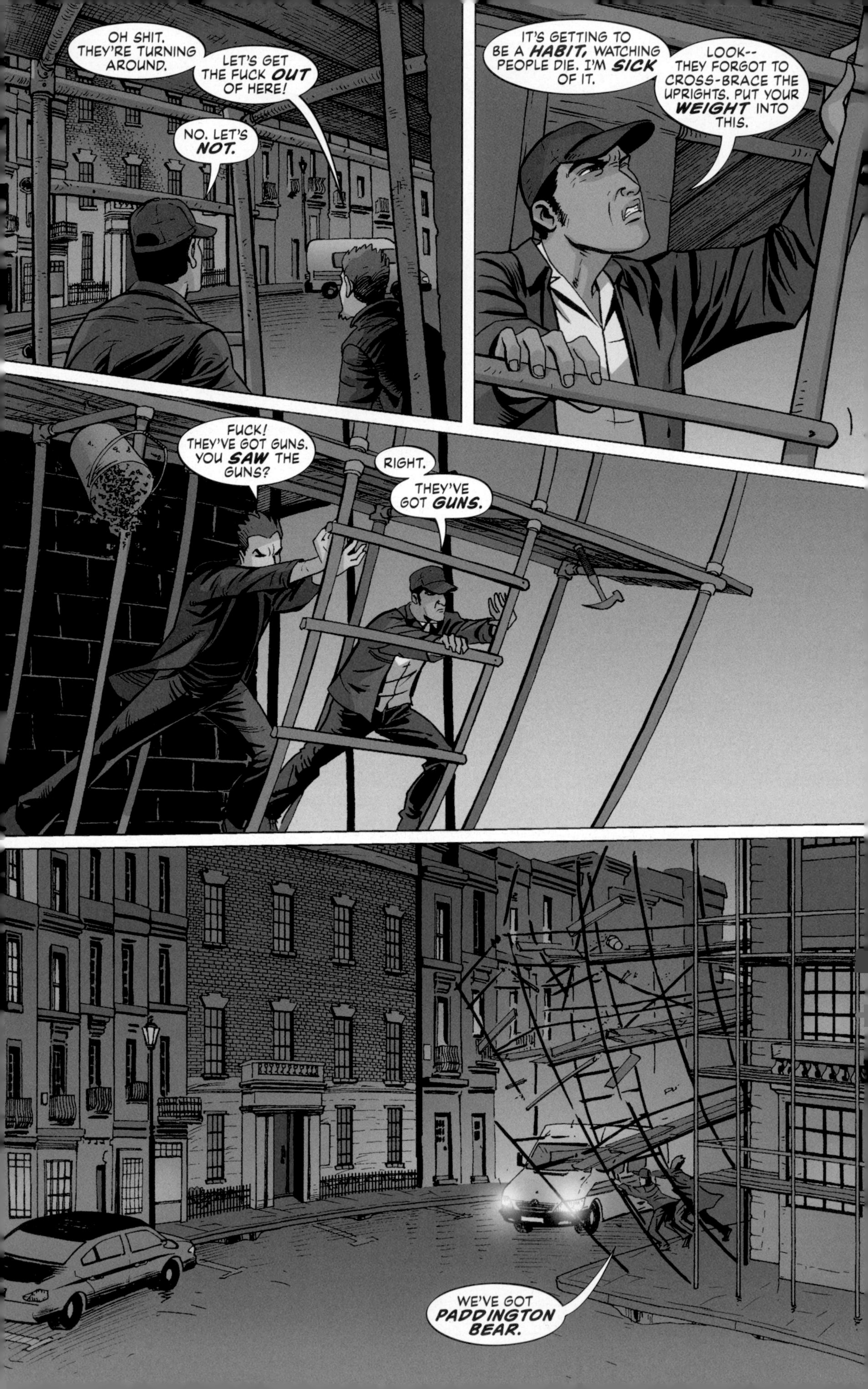
OH SHIT. THEY'RE TURNING AROUND.
LET'S GET THE FUCK OUT OF HERE!
NO. LET'S NOT.
IT'S GETTING TO BE A HABIT, WATCHING PEOPLE DIE. I'M SICK OF IT.
LOOK-- THEY FORGOT TO CROSS-BRACE THE UPRIGHTS. PUT YOUR WEIGHT INTO THIS.
FUCK! THEY'VE GOT GUNS. YOU SAW THE GUNS?
RIGHT.
THEY'VE GOT GUNS.
WE'VE GOT PADDINGTON BEAR.

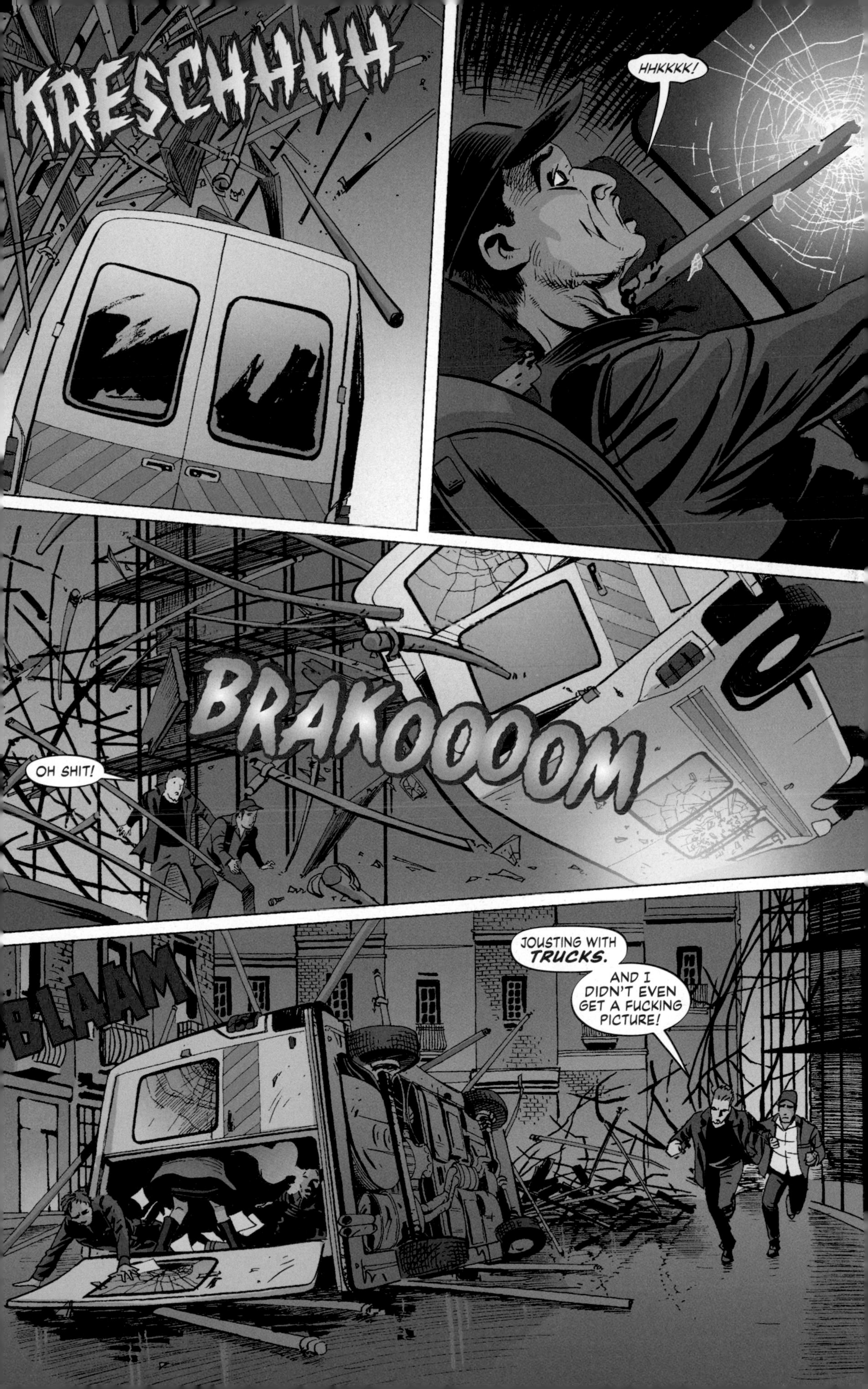
KRESCHHHH
HHKKKK!
BRAKOOOOM
OH SHIT!
BLAAM
JOUSTING WITH TRUCKS.
AND I DIDN'T EVEN GET A FUCKING PICTURE!

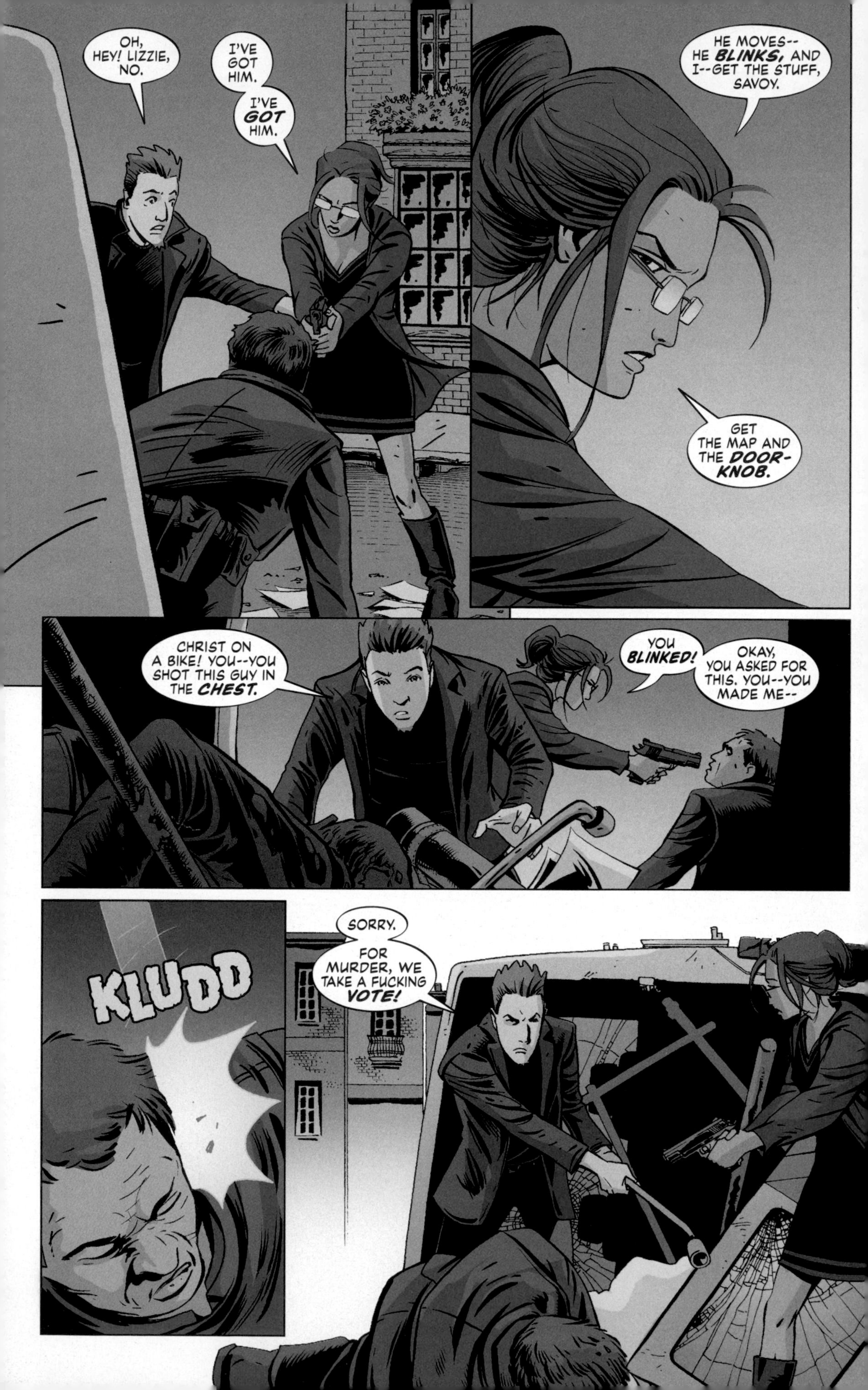

OH, HEY! LIZZIE, NO.
I'VE GOT HIM.
I'VE *GOT* HIM.
HE MOVES-- HE *BLINKS,* AND I--GET THE STUFF, SAVOY.
GET THE MAP AND THE *DOOR-KNOB.*
CHRIST ON A BIKE! YOU--YOU SHOT THIS GUY IN THE *CHEST.*
YOU *BLINKED!*
OKAY, YOU ASKED FOR THIS. YOU--YOU MADE ME--
KLUDD
SORRY.
FOR MURDER, WE TAKE A FUCKING *VOTE!*

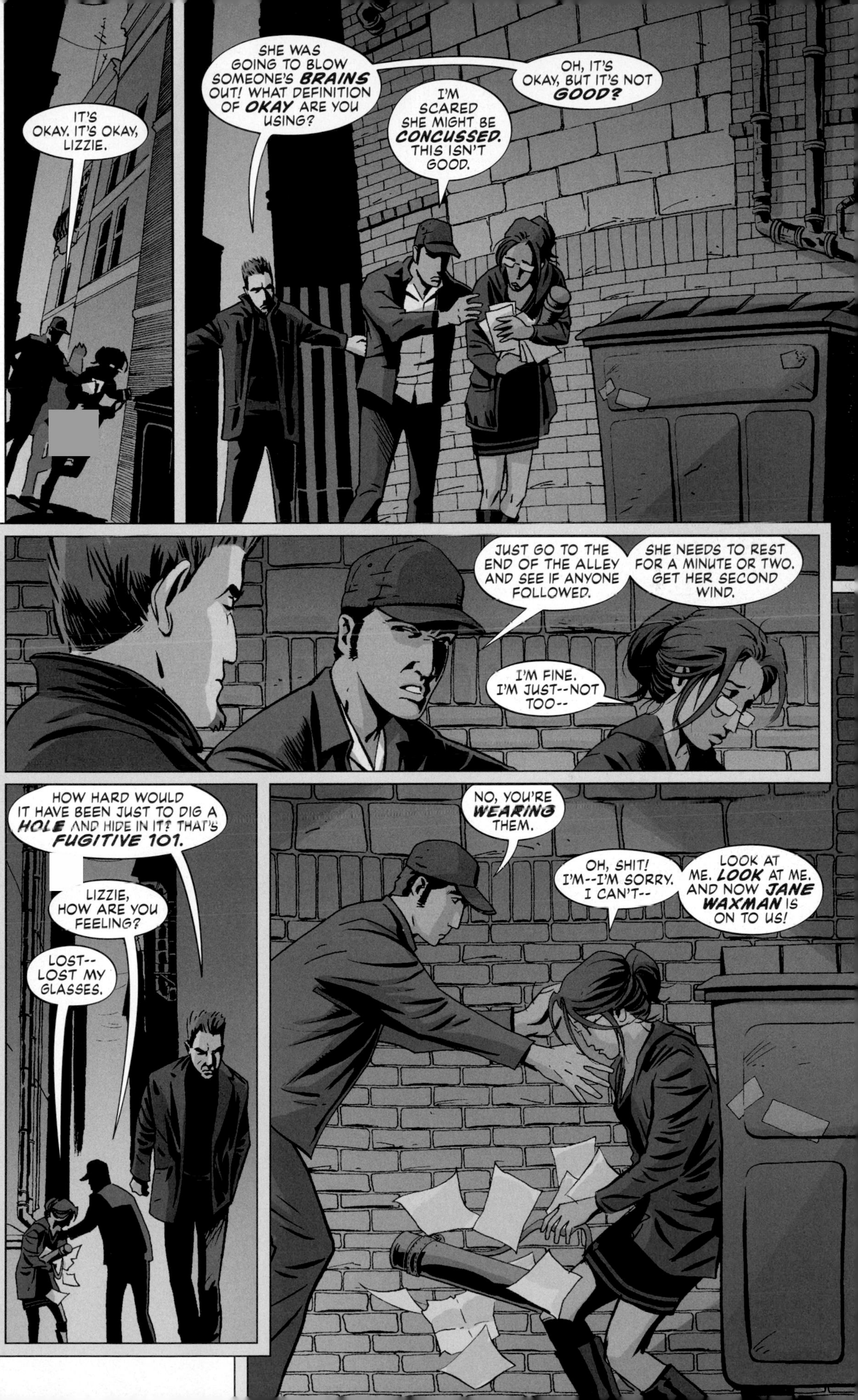
IT'S OKAY. IT'S OKAY, LIZZIE.
SHE WAS GOING TO BLOW SOMEONE'S BRAINS OUT! WHAT DEFINITION OF OKAY ARE YOU USING?
I'M SCARED SHE MIGHT BE CONCUSSED. THIS ISN'T GOOD.
OH, IT'S OKAY, BUT IT'S NOT GOOD?
JUST GO TO THE END OF THE ALLEY AND SEE IF ANYONE FOLLOWED.
SHE NEEDS TO REST FOR A MINUTE OR TWO. GET HER SECOND WIND.
I'M FINE. I'M JUST--NOT TOO--
HOW HARD WOULD IT HAVE BEEN JUST TO DIG A HOLE AND HIDE IN IT? THAT'S FUGITIVE 101.
LIZZIE, HOW ARE YOU FEELING?
LOST-- LOST MY GLASSES.
NO, YOU'RE WEARING THEM.
OH, SHIT! I'M--I'M SORRY. I CAN'T--
LOOK AT ME. LOOK AT ME. AND NOW JANE WAXMAN IS ON TO US!

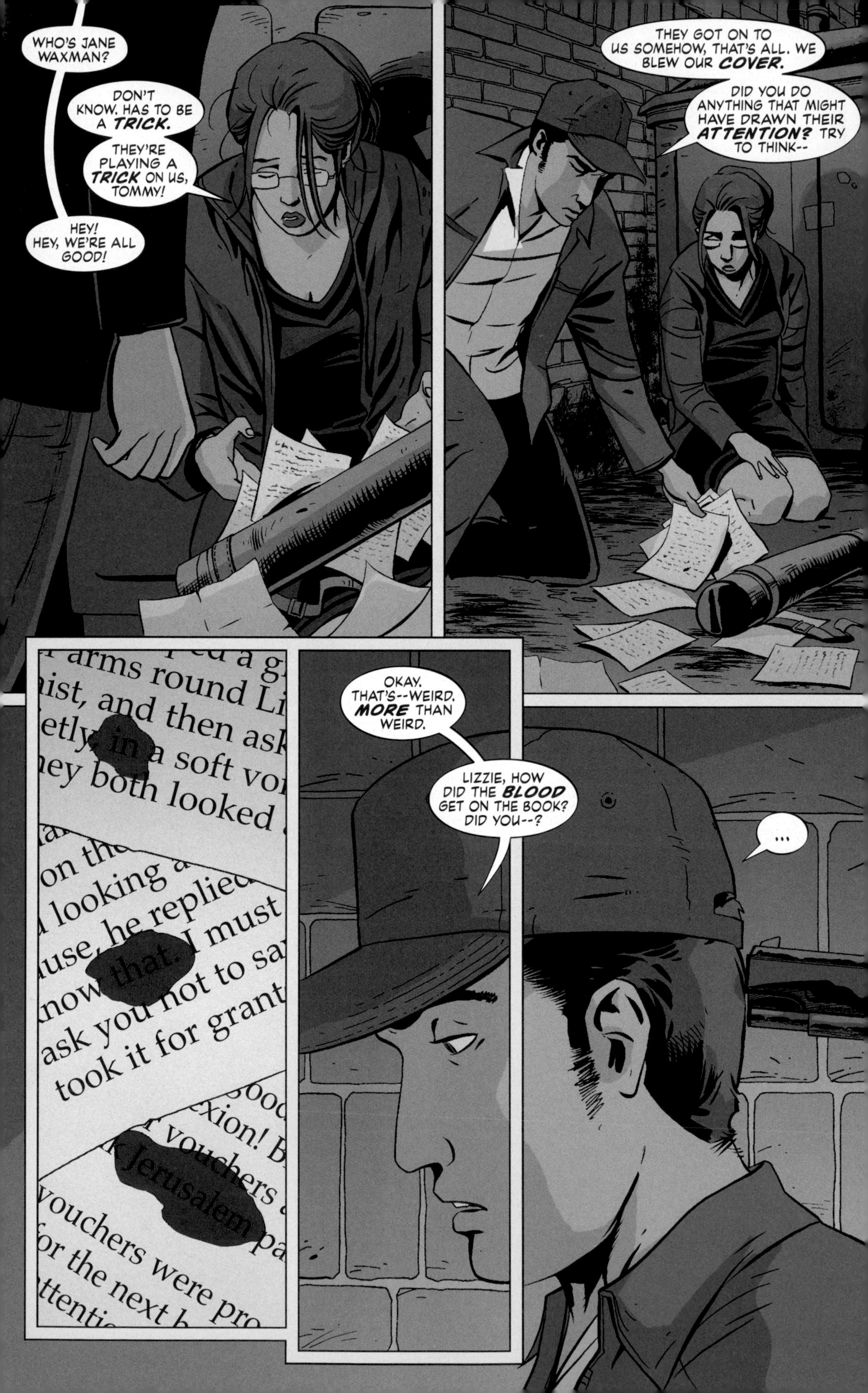
WHO'S JANE WAXMAN?
DON'T KNOW. HAS TO BE A TRICK.
THEY'RE PLAYING A TRICK ON US, TOMMY!
HEY! HEY, WE'RE ALL GOOD!
THEY GOT ON TO US SOMEHOW, THAT'S ALL. WE BLEW OUR COVER.
DID YOU DO ANYTHING THAT MIGHT HAVE DRAWN THEIR ATTENTION? TRY TO THINK--
OKAY. THAT'S--WEIRD. MORE THAN WEIRD.
LIZZIE, HOW DID THE BLOOD GET ON THE BOOK? DID YOU--?
...

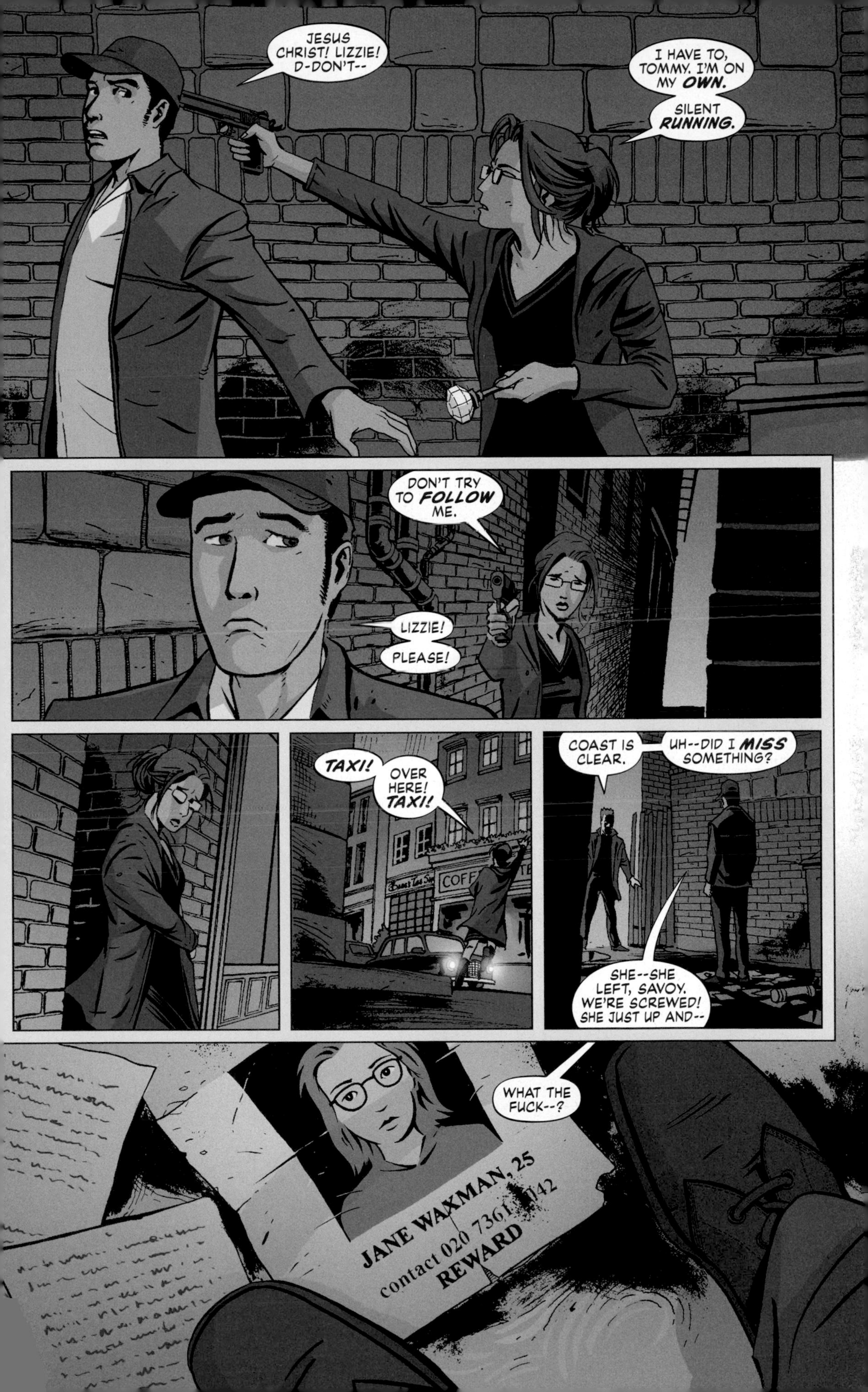
JESUS CHRIST! LIZZIE! D-DON'T--
I HAVE TO, TOMMY. I'M ON MY OWN.
SILENT RUNNING.
DON'T TRY TO FOLLOW ME.
LIZZIE!
PLEASE!
TAXI!
OVER HERE! TAXI!
COAST IS CLEAR.
UH--DID I MISS SOMETHING?
SHE--SHE LEFT, SAVOY. WE'RE SCREWED! SHE JUST UP AND--
WHAT THE FUCK--?
JANE WAXMAN, 25
contact 020 7361 142
REWARD

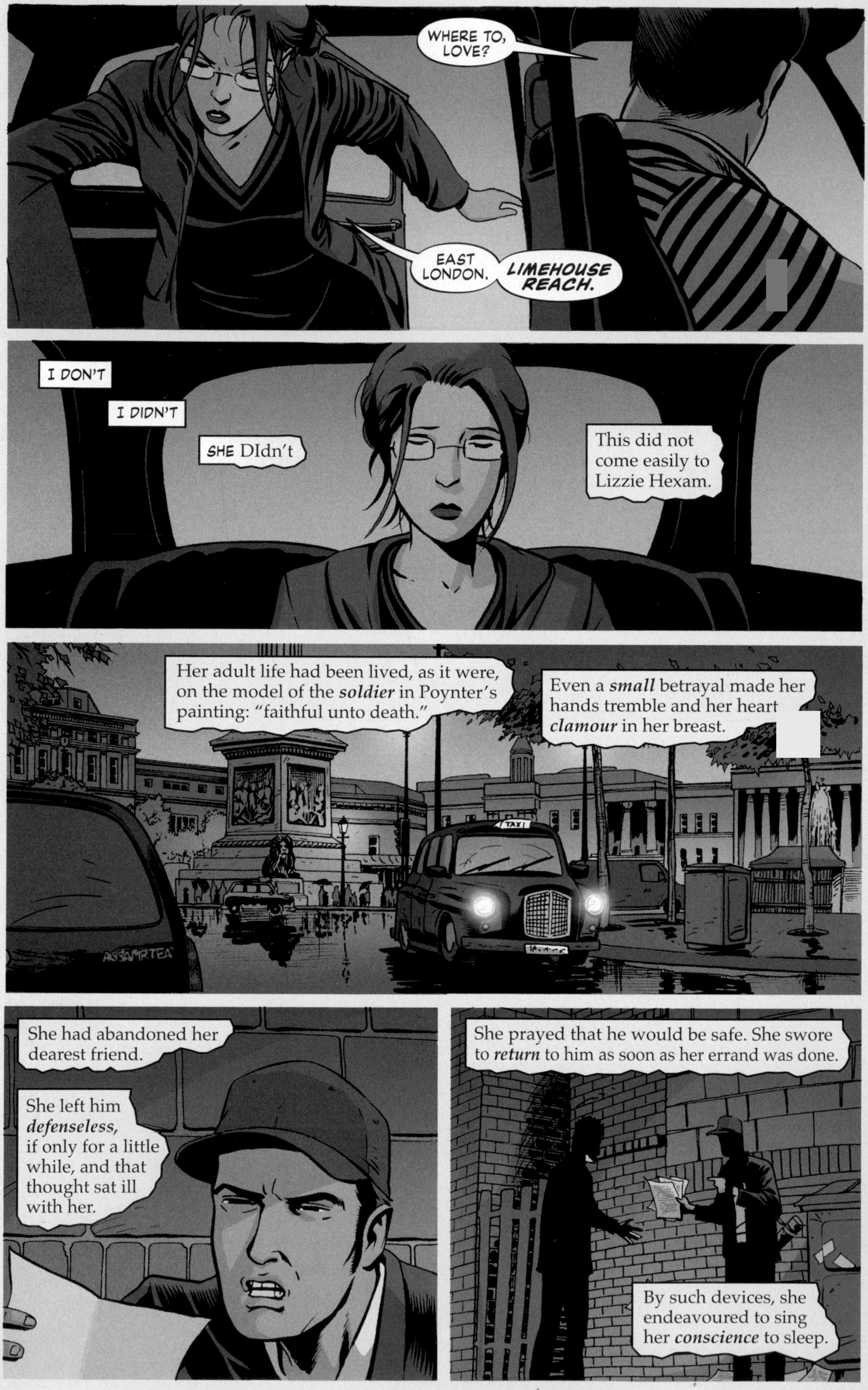
WHERE TO, LOVE?
EAST LONDON.
LIMEHOUSE REACH.
I DON'T
I DIDN'T
SHE DIdn't
This did not come easily to Lizzie Hexam.
Her adult life had been lived, as it were, on the model of the *soldier* in Poynter's painting: "faithful unto death."
Even a *small* betrayal made her hands tremble and her heart *clamour* in her breast.
TAXI
She had abandoned her dearest friend.
She left him *defenseless,* if only for a little while, and that thought sat ill with her.
She prayed that he would be safe. She swore to *return* to him as soon as her errand was done.
By such devices, she endeavoured to sing her *conscience* to sleep.

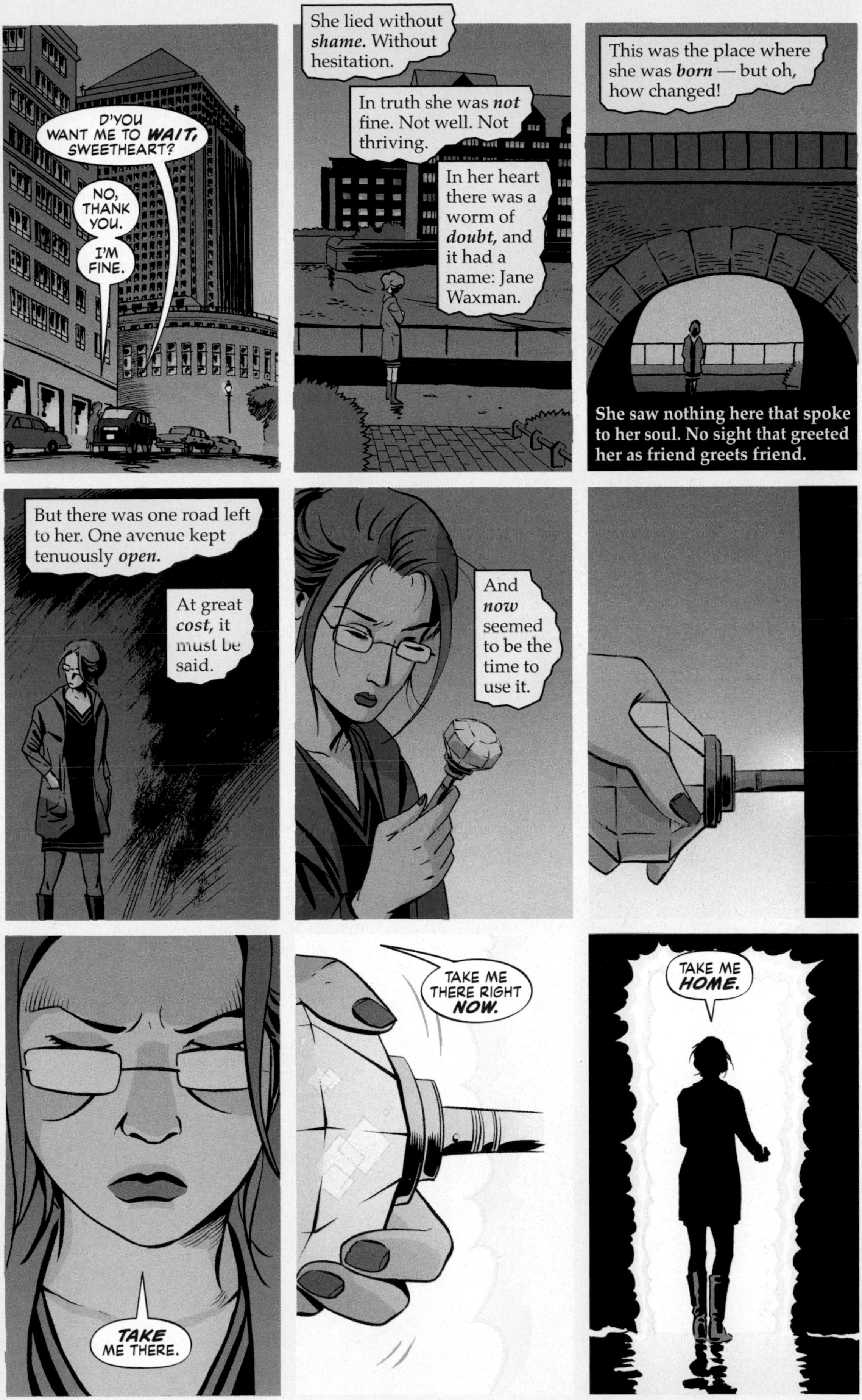
D'YOU WANT ME TO WAIT, SWEETHEART?
NO, THANK YOU.
I'M FINE.
She lied without shame. Without hesitation.
In truth she was not fine. Not well. Not thriving.
In her heart there was a worm of doubt, and it had a name: Jane Waxman.
This was the place where she was born — but oh, how changed!
She saw nothing here that spoke to her soul. No sight that greeted her as friend greets friend.
But there was one road left to her. One avenue kept tenuously open.
At great cost, it must be said.
And now seemed to be the time to use it.
TAKE ME THERE.
TAKE ME THERE RIGHT NOW.
TAKE ME HOME.

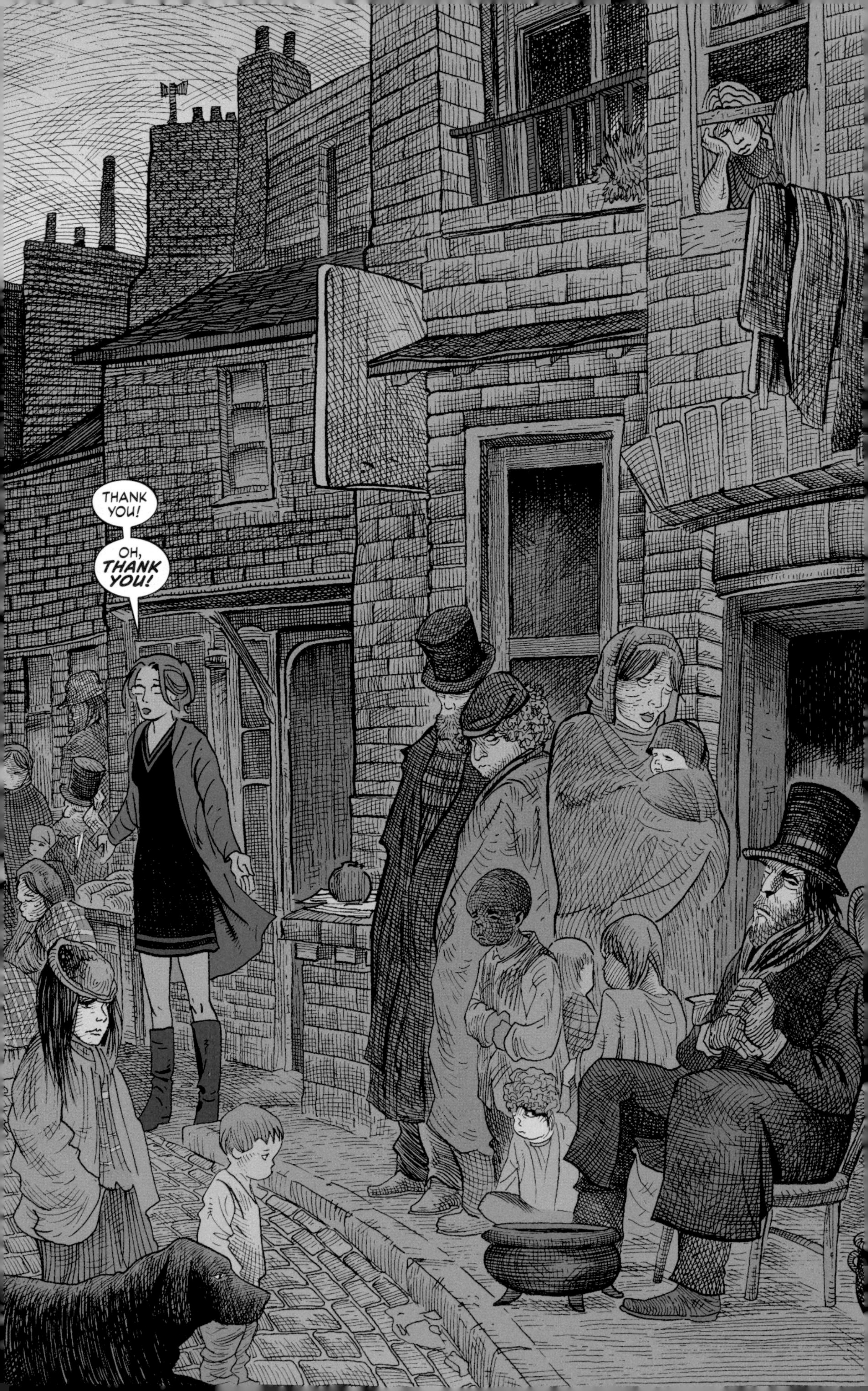
THANK YOU!
OH, *THANK YOU!*

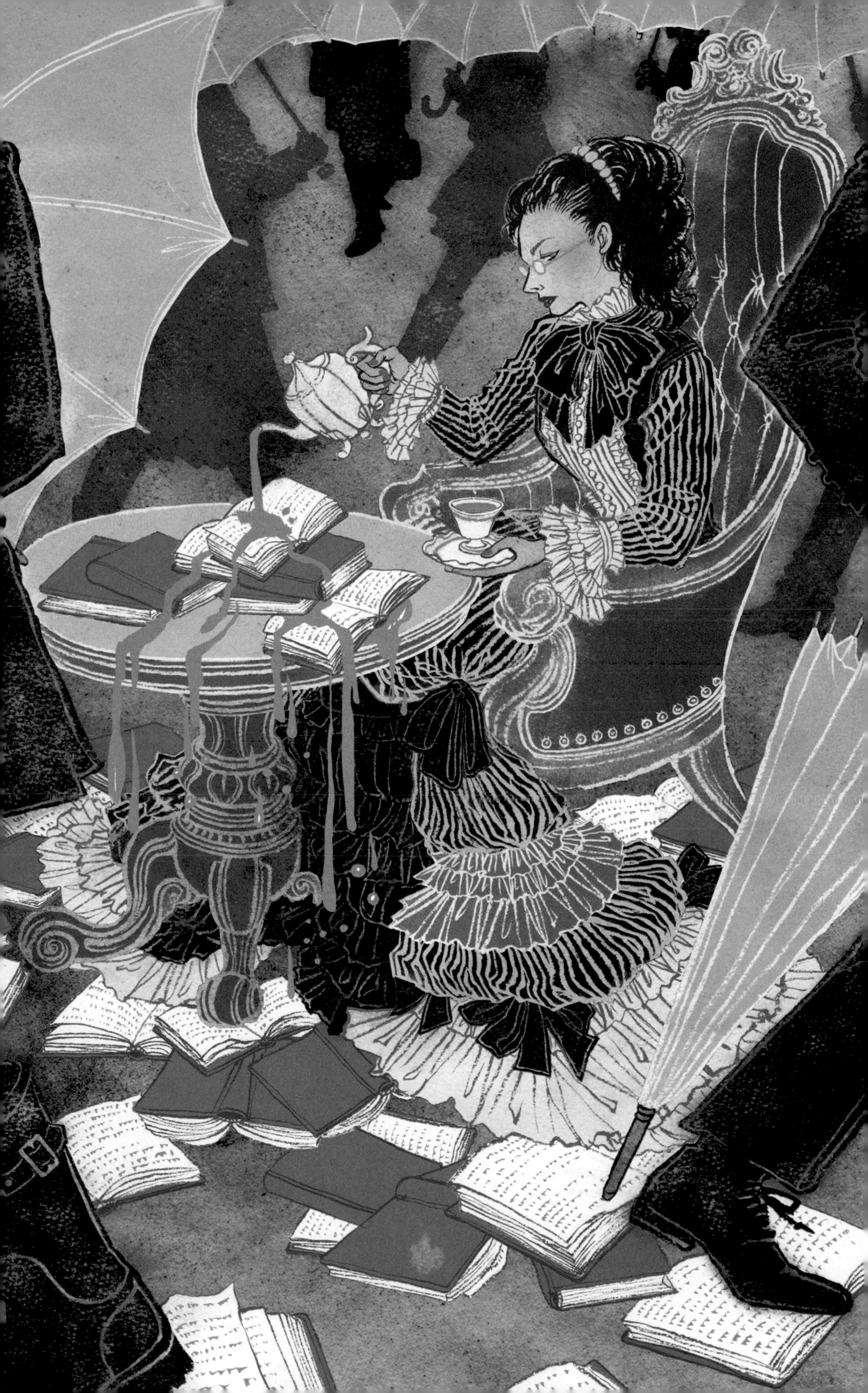

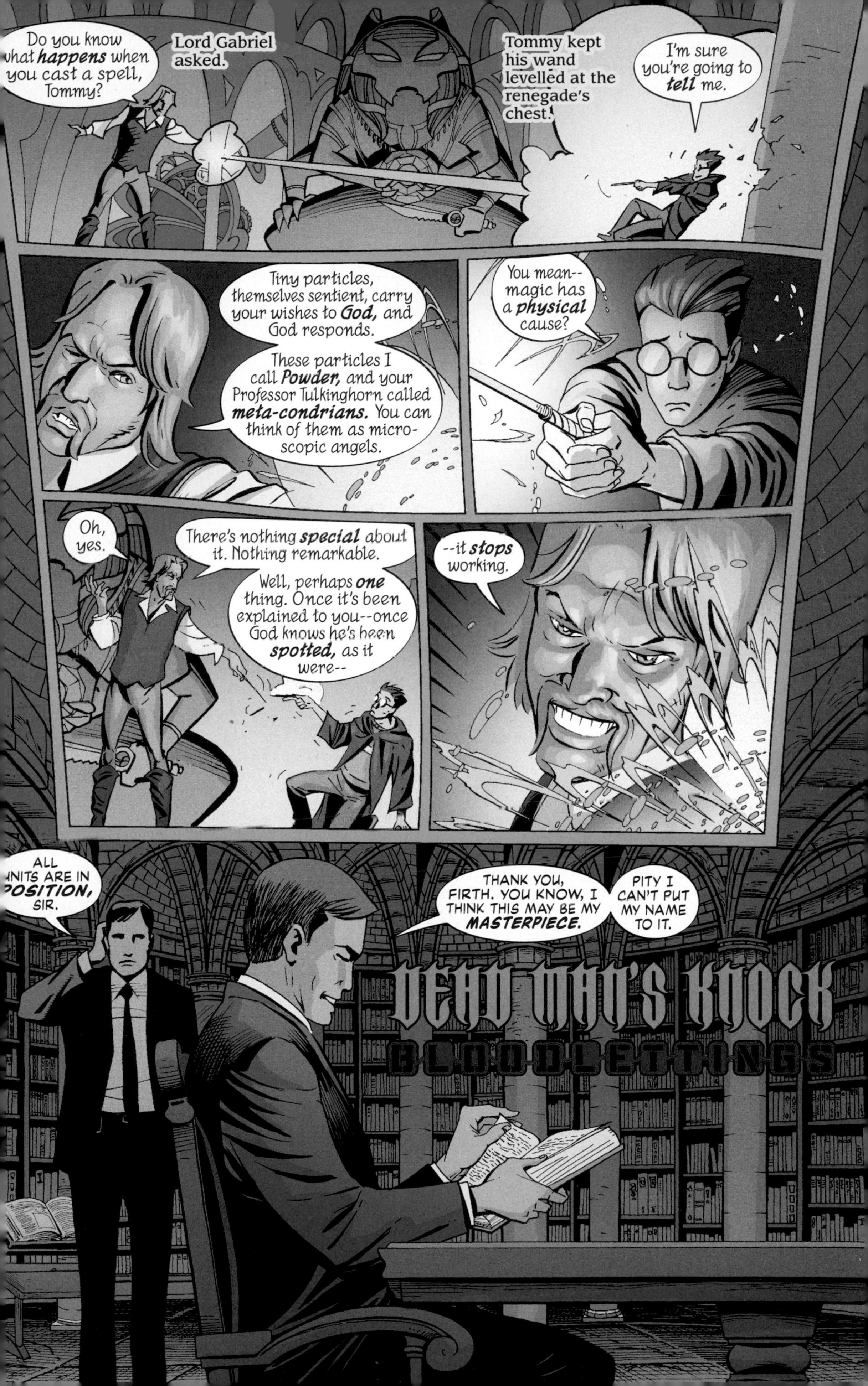
Do you know what happens when you cast a spell, Tommy?
Lord Gabriel asked.
Tommy kept his wand levelled at the renegade's chest.
I'm sure you're going to tell me.
Tiny particles, themselves sentient, carry your wishes to God, and God responds.
These particles I call Powder, and your Professor Tulkinghorn called meta-condrians. You can think of them as microscopic angels.
You mean--magic has a physical cause?
Oh, yes.
There's nothing special about it. Nothing remarkable.
Well, perhaps one thing. Once it's been explained to you--once God knows he's been spotted, as it were--
--it stops working.
ALL UNITS ARE IN POSITION, SIR.
THANK YOU, FIRTH. YOU KNOW, I THINK THIS MAY BE MY MASTERPIECE.
PITY I CAN'T PUT MY NAME TO IT.
DEAD MAN'S KNOCK
BLOODLETTINGS

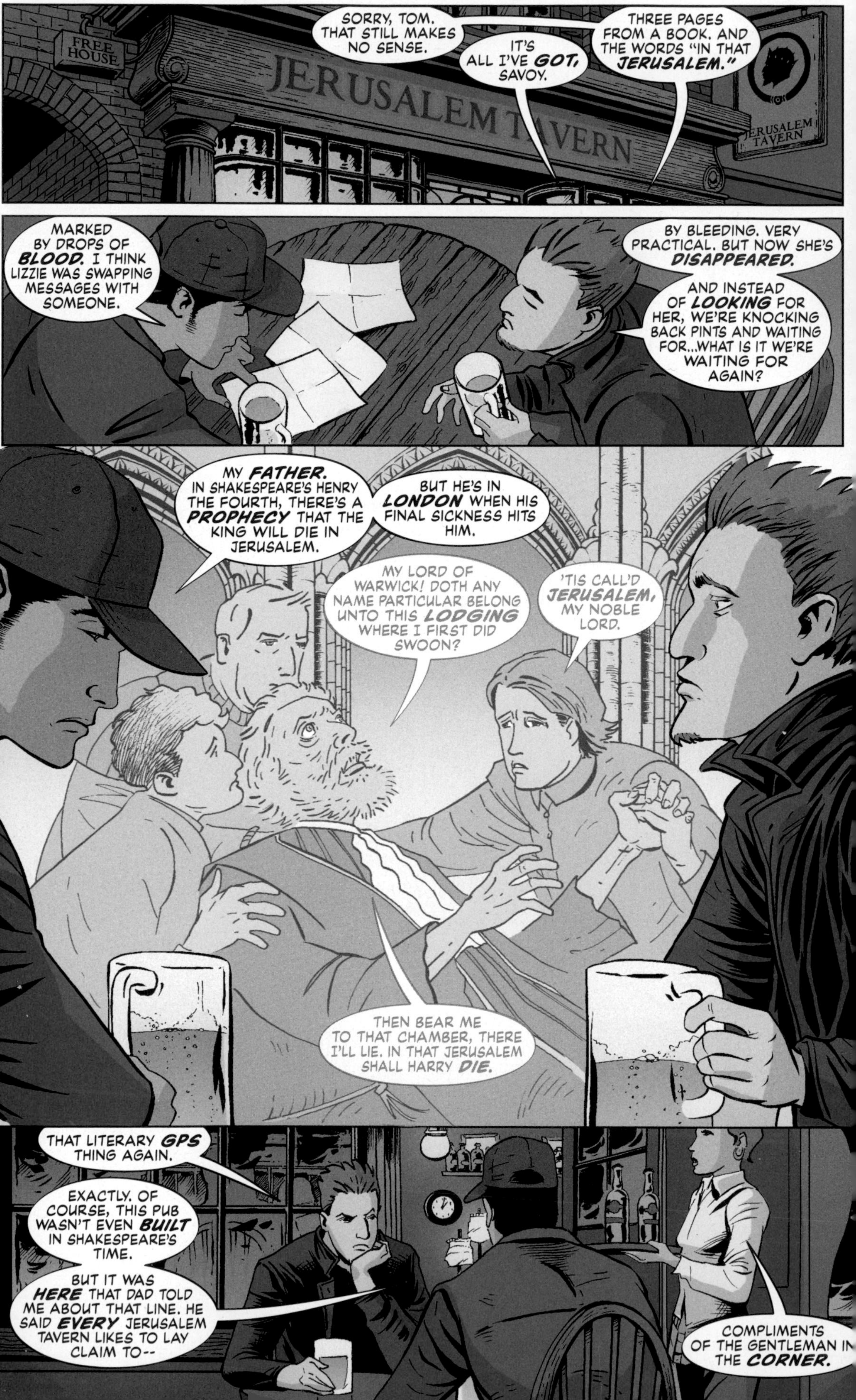
FREE HOUSE
JERUSALEM TAVERN
SORRY, TOM. THAT STILL MAKES NO SENSE.
THREE PAGES FROM A BOOK. AND THE WORDS "IN THAT JERUSALEM."
IT'S ALL I'VE GOT, SAVOY.
JERUSALEM TAVERN
MARKED BY DROPS OF BLOOD. I THINK LIZZIE WAS SWAPPING MESSAGES WITH SOMEONE.
BY BLEEDING. VERY PRACTICAL. BUT NOW SHE'S DISAPPEARED.
AND INSTEAD OF LOOKING FOR HER, WE'RE KNOCKING BACK PINTS AND WAITING FOR...WHAT IS IT WE'RE WAITING FOR AGAIN?
MY FATHER. IN SHAKESPEARE'S HENRY THE FOURTH, THERE'S A PROPHECY THAT THE KING WILL DIE IN JERUSALEM.
BUT HE'S IN LONDON WHEN HIS FINAL SICKNESS HITS HIM.
MY LORD OF WARWICK! DOTH ANY NAME PARTICULAR BELONG UNTO THIS LODGING WHERE I FIRST DID SWOON?
'TIS CALL'D JERUSALEM, MY NOBLE LORD.
THEN BEAR ME TO THAT CHAMBER, THERE I'LL LIE. IN THAT JERUSALEM SHALL HARRY DIE.
THAT LITERARY GPS THING AGAIN.
EXACTLY. OF COURSE, THIS PUB WASN'T EVEN BUILT IN SHAKESPEARE'S TIME.
BUT IT WAS HERE THAT DAD TOLD ME ABOUT THAT LINE. HE SAID EVERY JERUSALEM TAVERN LIKES TO LAY CLAIM TO--
COMPLIMENTS OF THE GENTLEMAN IN THE CORNER.

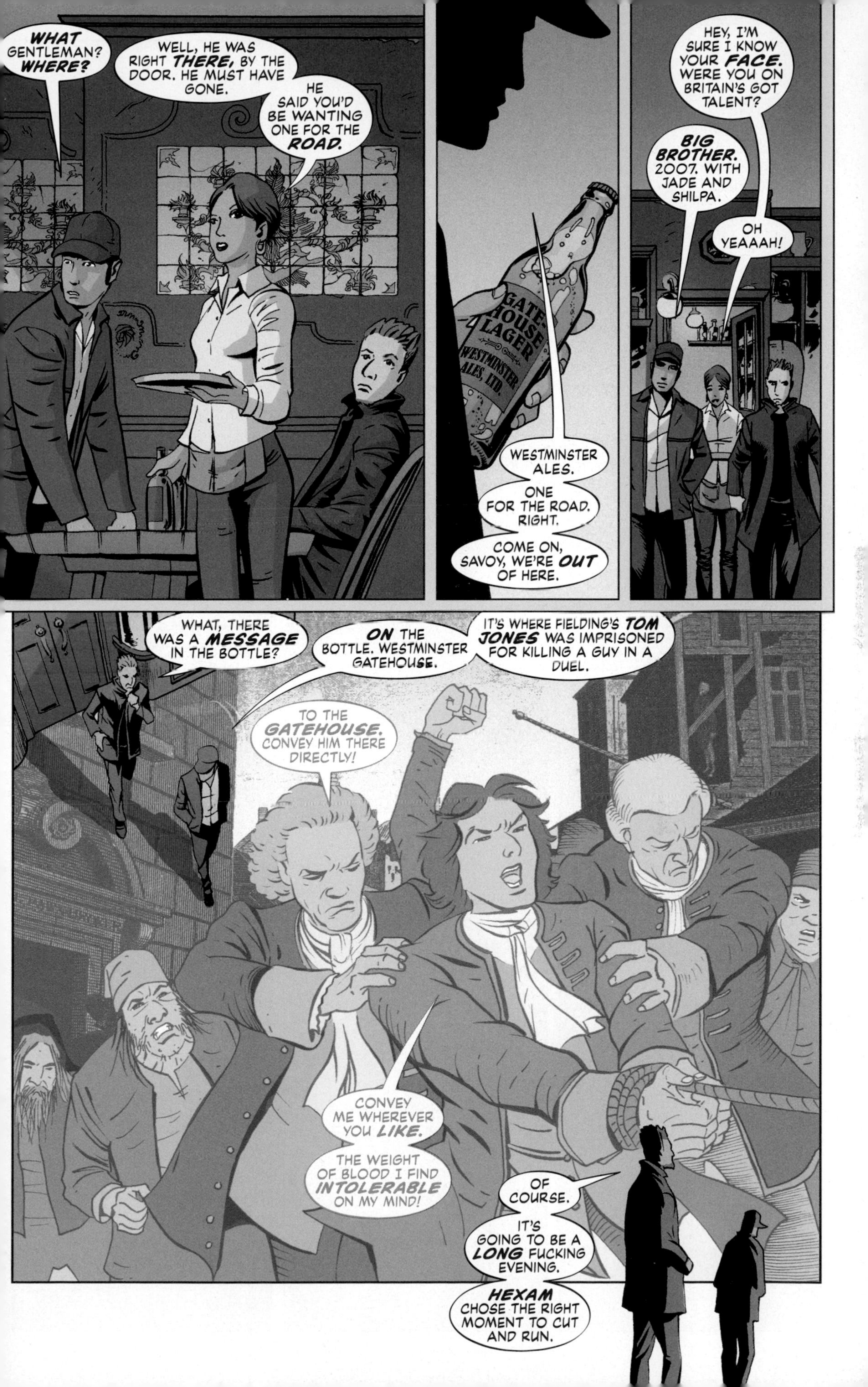

WHAT GENTLEMAN? WHERE?
WELL, HE WAS RIGHT THERE, BY THE DOOR. HE MUST HAVE GONE.
HE SAID YOU'D BE WANTING ONE FOR THE ROAD.
GATE-HOUSE LAGER WESTMINSTER ALES, LTD.
WESTMINSTER ALES.
ONE FOR THE ROAD. RIGHT.
COME ON, SAVOY, WE'RE OUT OF HERE.
HEY, I'M SURE I KNOW YOUR FACE. WERE YOU ON BRITAIN'S GOT TALENT?
BIG BROTHER. 2007. WITH JADE AND SHILPA.
OH YEAAAH!
WHAT, THERE WAS A MESSAGE IN THE BOTTLE?
ON THE BOTTLE. WESTMINSTER GATEHOUSE.
IT'S WHERE FIELDING'S TOM JONES WAS IMPRISONED FOR KILLING A GUY IN A DUEL.
TO THE GATEHOUSE. CONVEY HIM THERE DIRECTLY!
CONVEY ME WHEREVER YOU LIKE.
THE WEIGHT OF BLOOD I FIND INTOLERABLE ON MY MIND!
OF COURSE.
IT'S GOING TO BE A LONG FUCKING EVENING.
HEXAM CHOSE THE RIGHT MOMENT TO CUT AND RUN.

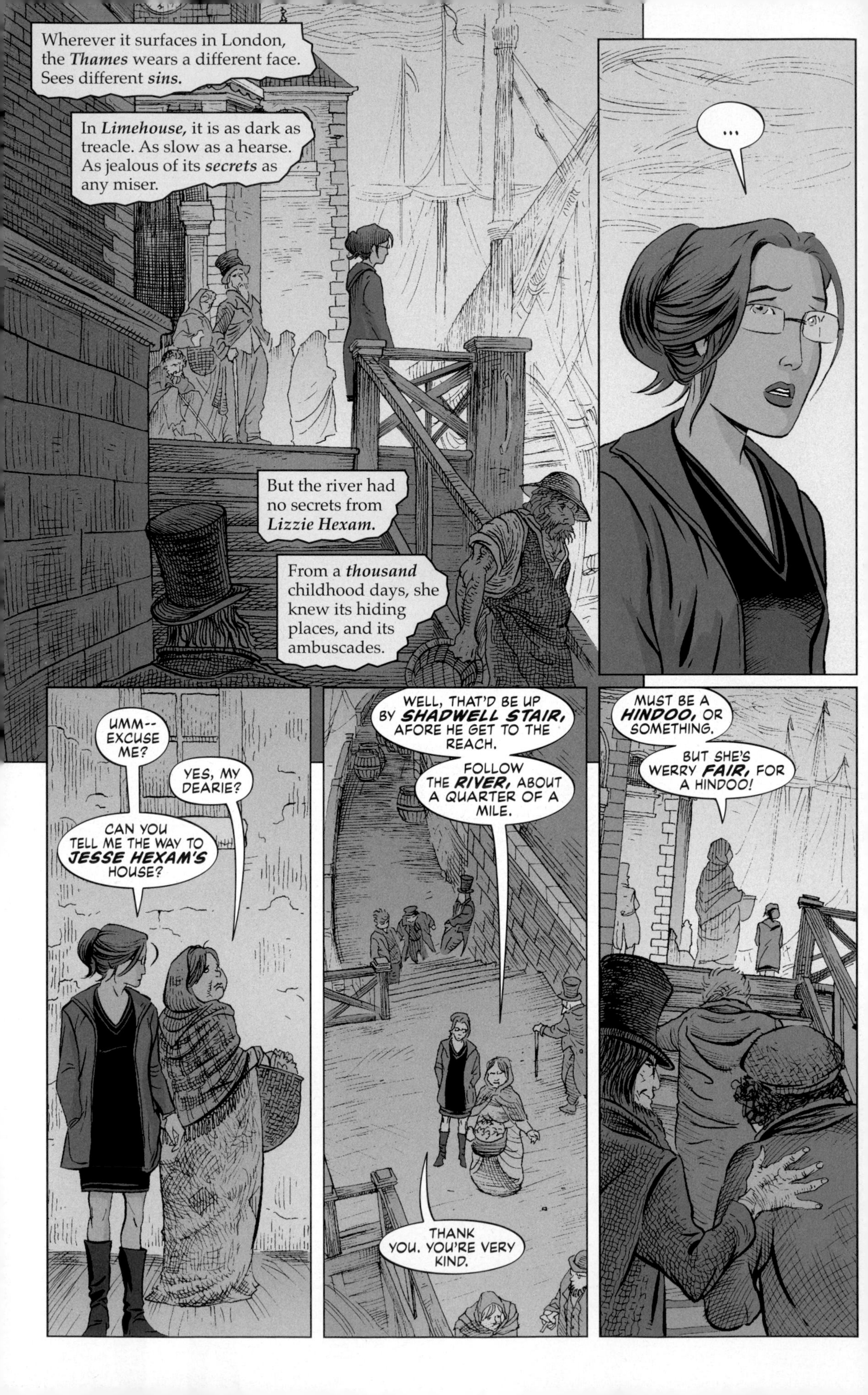
Wherever it surfaces in London, the *Thames* wears a different face. Sees different *sins.*
In *Limehouse,* it is as dark as treacle. As slow as a hearse. As jealous of its *secrets* as any miser.
But the river had no secrets from *Lizzie Hexam.*
From a *thousand* childhood days, she knew its hiding places, and its ambuscades.
...
UMM-- EXCUSE ME?
YES, MY DEARIE?
CAN YOU TELL ME THE WAY TO ***JESSE HEXAM'S*** HOUSE?
WELL, THAT'D BE UP BY ***SHADWELL STAIR,*** AFORE HE GET TO THE REACH.
FOLLOW THE ***RIVER,*** ABOUT A QUARTER OF A MILE.
THANK YOU. YOU'RE VERY KIND.
MUST BE A ***HINDOO,*** OR SOMETHING.
BUT SHE'S WERRY ***FAIR,*** FOR A HINDOO!

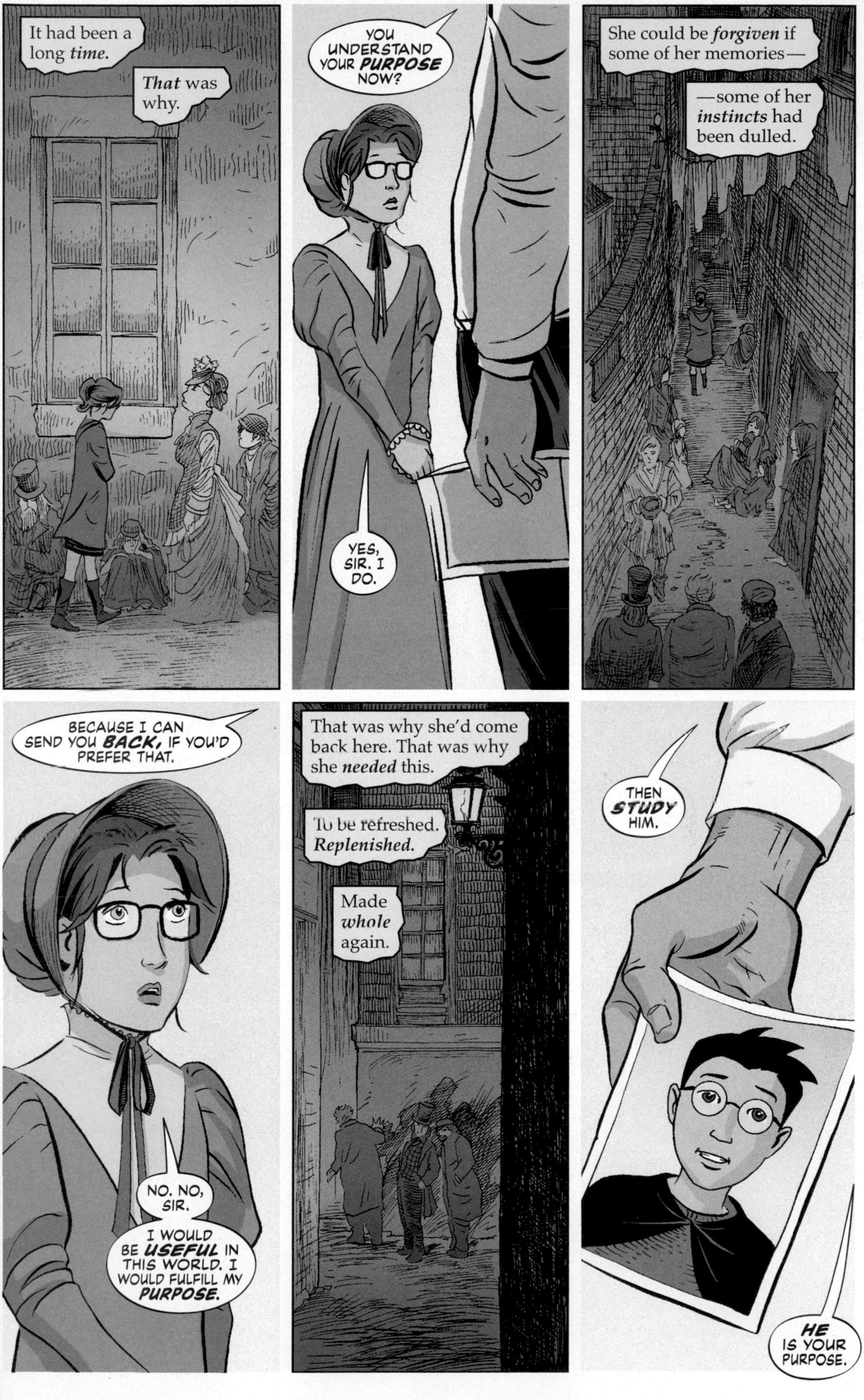
It had been a long *time.*
That was why.
YOU UNDERSTAND YOUR **PURPOSE** NOW?
YES, SIR. I DO.
She could be *forgiven* if some of her memories—
—some of her *instincts* had been dulled.
BECAUSE I CAN SEND YOU **BACK,** IF YOU'D PREFER THAT.
NO. NO, SIR.
I WOULD BE **USEFUL** IN THIS WORLD. I WOULD FULFILL MY **PURPOSE.**
That was why she'd come back here. That was why she *needed* this.
To be refreshed. *Replenished.*
Made *whole* again.
THEN **STUDY** HIM.
HE IS YOUR PURPOSE.

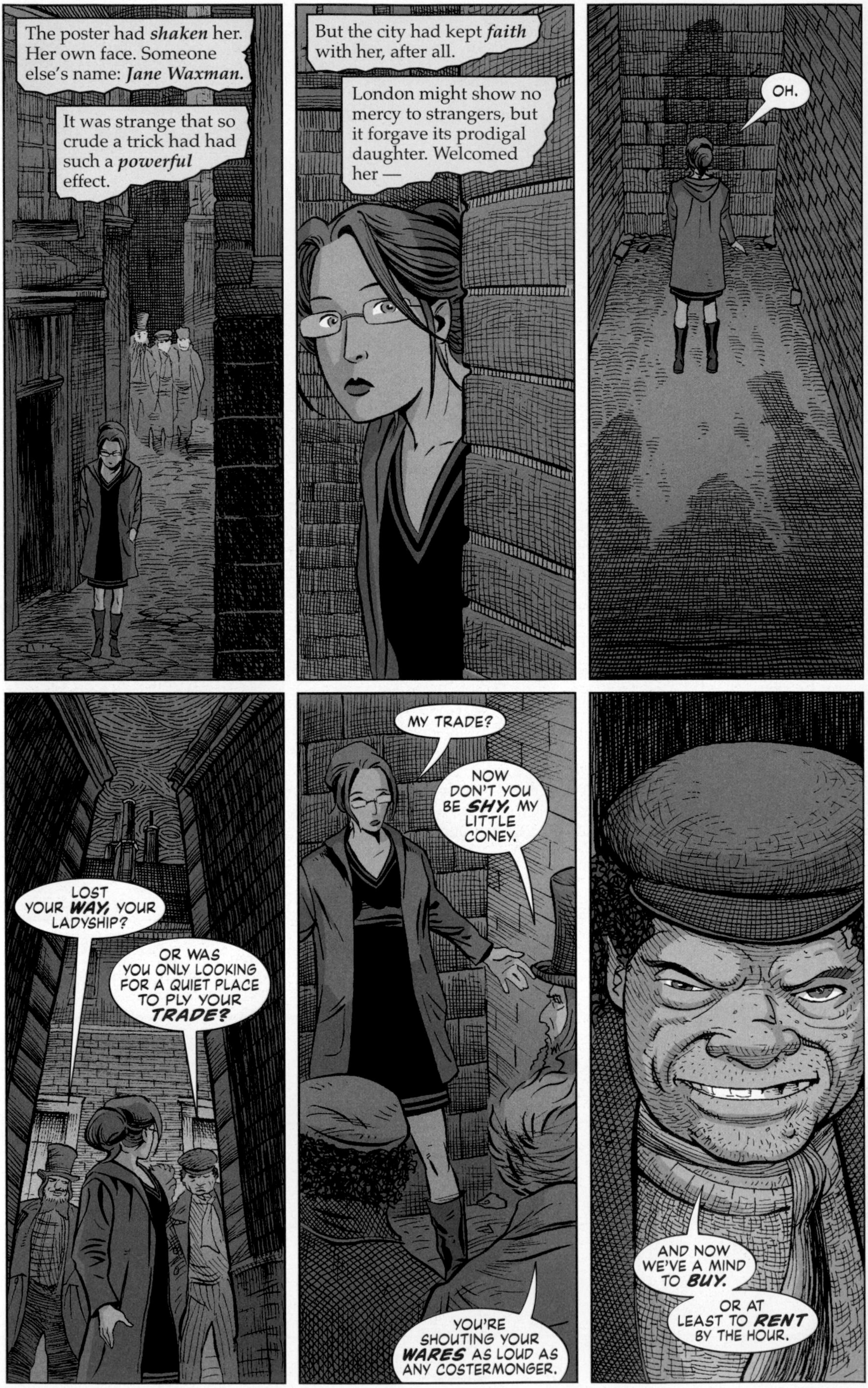

The poster had *shaken* her. Her own face. Someone else's name: *Jane Waxman.*
It was strange that so crude a trick had had such a *powerful* effect.
But the city had kept *faith* with her, after all.
London might show no mercy to strangers, but it forgave its prodigal daughter. Welcomed her —
OH.
LOST YOUR **WAY,** YOUR LADYSHIP?
OR WAS YOU ONLY LOOKING FOR A QUIET PLACE TO PLY YOUR **TRADE?**
MY TRADE?
NOW DON'T YOU BE **SHY,** MY LITTLE CONEY.
YOU'RE SHOUTING YOUR **WARES** AS LOUD AS ANY COSTERMONGER.
AND NOW WE'VE A MIND TO **BUY.**
OR AT LEAST TO **RENT** BY THE HOUR.

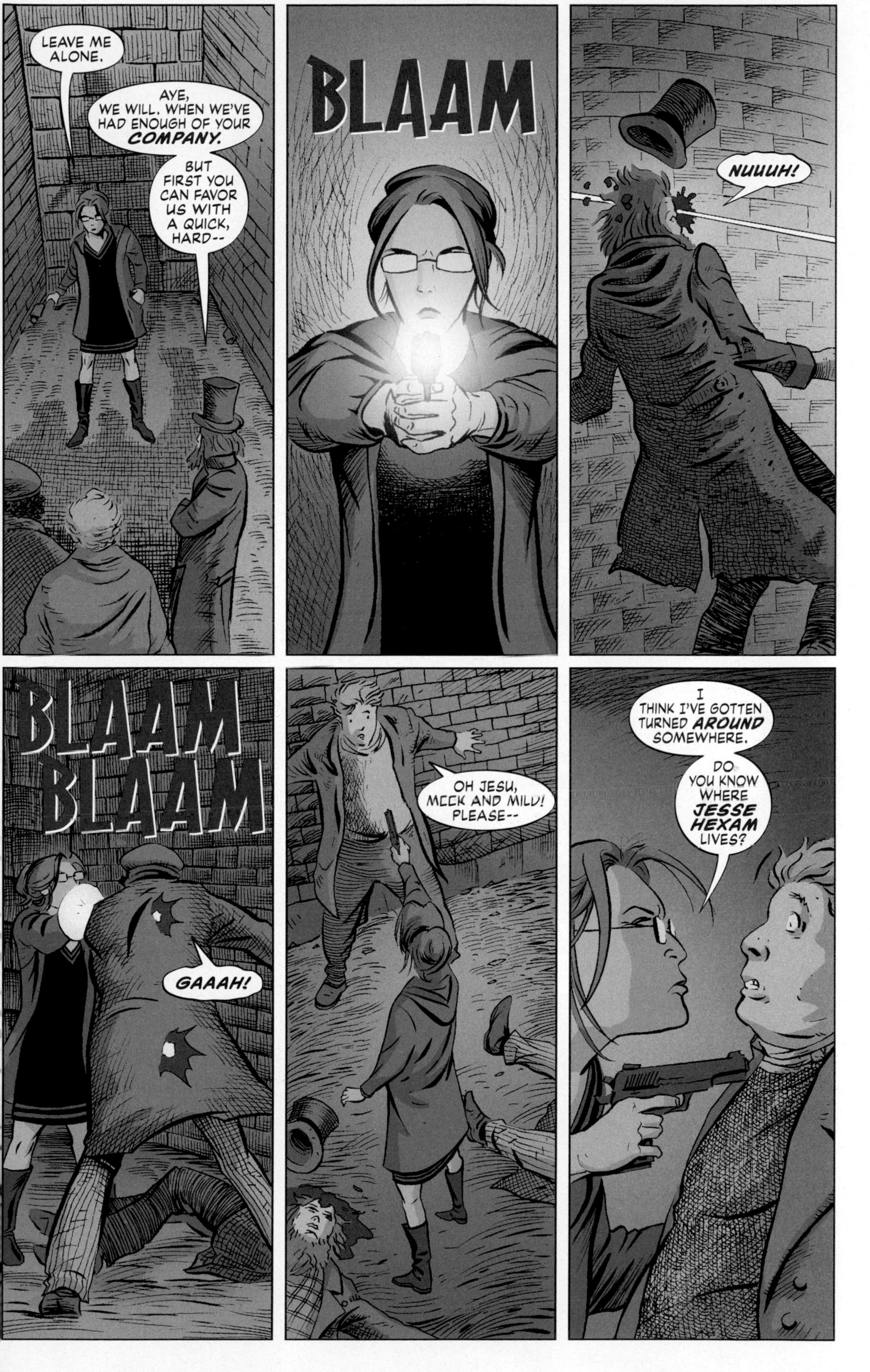
LEAVE ME ALONE.
AYE, WE WILL. WHEN WE'VE HAD ENOUGH OF YOUR *COMPANY.*
BUT FIRST YOU CAN FAVOR US WITH A QUICK, HARD--
BLAAM
NUUUH!
BLAAM BLAAM
GAAAH!
OH JESU, MEEK AND MILD! PLEASE--
I THINK I'VE GOTTEN TURNED *AROUND* SOMEWHERE.
DO YOU KNOW WHERE *JESSE HEXAM* LIVES?

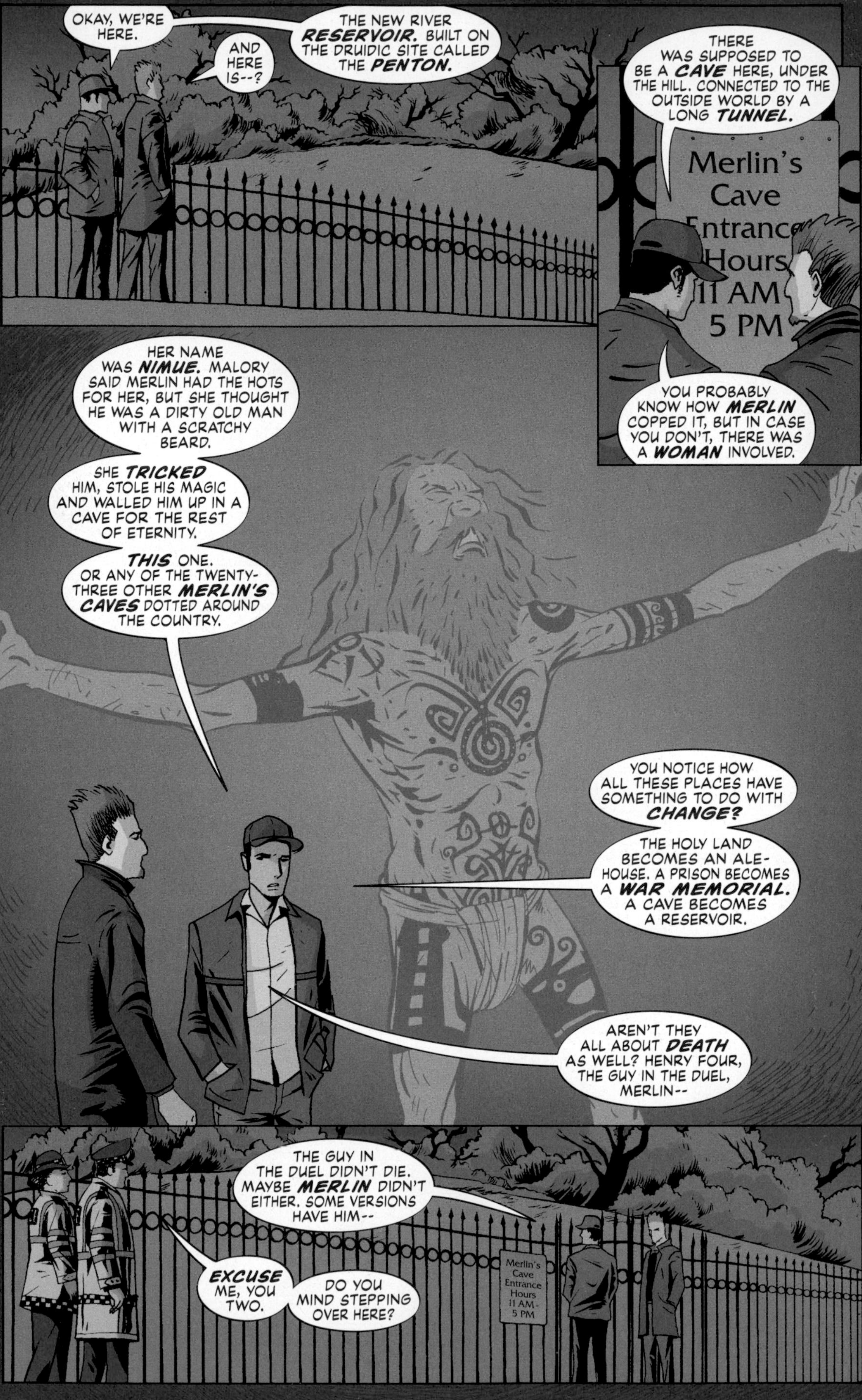
OKAY, WE'RE HERE.
THE NEW RIVER RESERVOIR. BUILT ON THE DRUIDIC SITE CALLED THE PENTON.
AND HERE IS--?
THERE WAS SUPPOSED TO BE A CAVE HERE, UNDER THE HILL. CONNECTED TO THE OUTSIDE WORLD BY A LONG TUNNEL.
Merlin's Cave Entrance Hours 11 AM 5 PM
YOU PROBABLY KNOW HOW MERLIN COPPED IT, BUT IN CASE YOU DON'T, THERE WAS A WOMAN INVOLVED.
HER NAME WAS NIMUE. MALORY SAID MERLIN HAD THE HOTS FOR HER, BUT SHE THOUGHT HE WAS A DIRTY OLD MAN WITH A SCRATCHY BEARD.
SHE TRICKED HIM, STOLE HIS MAGIC AND WALLED HIM UP IN A CAVE FOR THE REST OF ETERNITY.
THIS ONE. OR ANY OF THE TWENTY-THREE OTHER MERLIN'S CAVES DOTTED AROUND THE COUNTRY.
YOU NOTICE HOW ALL THESE PLACES HAVE SOMETHING TO DO WITH CHANGE?
THE HOLY LAND BECOMES AN ALE-HOUSE. A PRISON BECOMES A WAR MEMORIAL. A CAVE BECOMES A RESERVOIR.
AREN'T THEY ALL ABOUT DEATH AS WELL? HENRY FOUR, THE GUY IN THE DUEL, MERLIN--
THE GUY IN THE DUEL DIDN'T DIE. MAYBE MERLIN DIDN'T EITHER. SOME VERSIONS HAVE HIM--
EXCUSE ME, YOU TWO.
DO YOU MIND STEPPING OVER HERE?
Merlin's Cave Entrance Hours 11 AM-5 PM

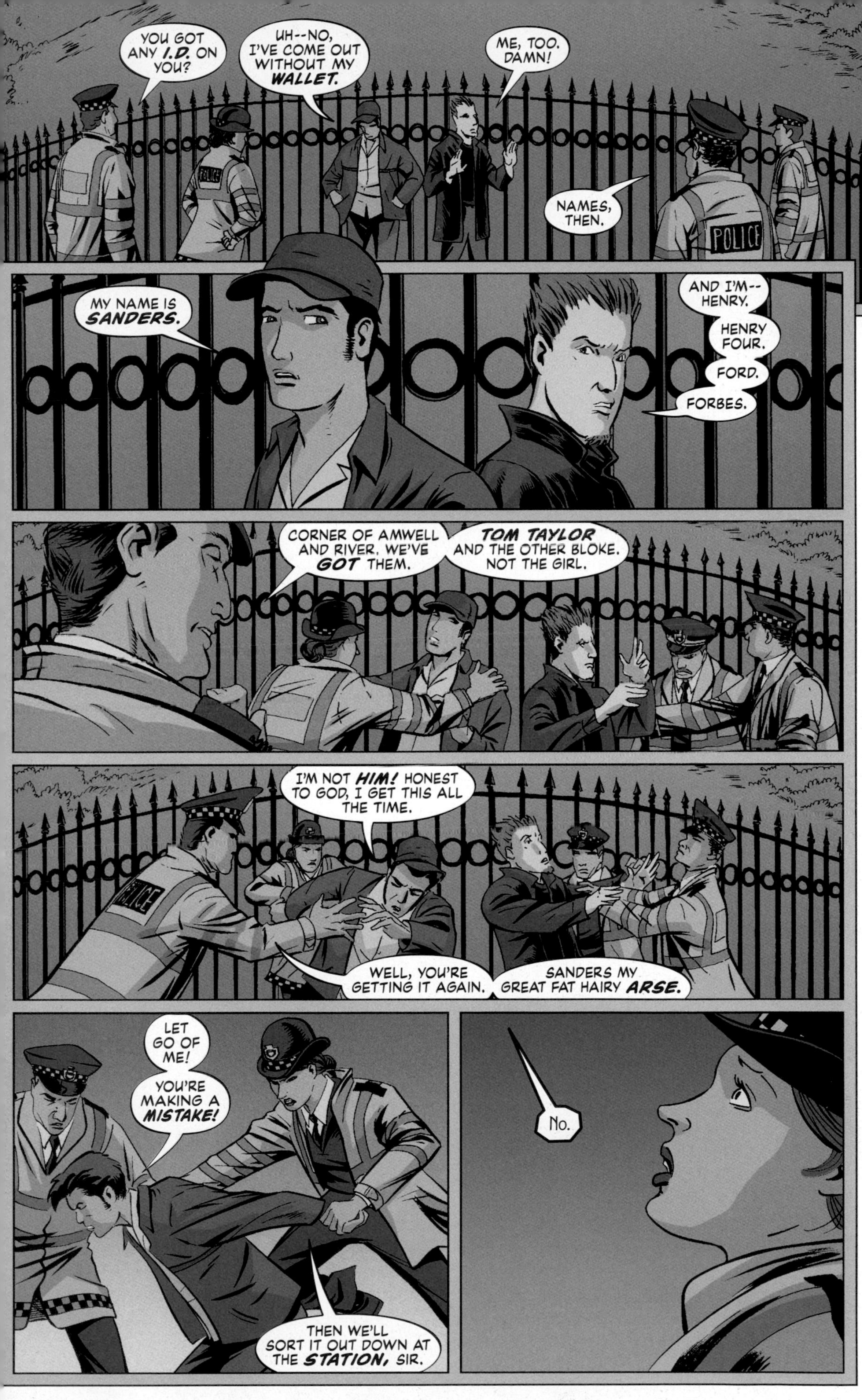

YOU GOT ANY I.D. ON YOU?
UH--NO, I'VE COME OUT WITHOUT MY WALLET.
ME, TOO. DAMN!
NAMES, THEN.
MY NAME IS SANDERS.
AND I'M-- HENRY.
HENRY FOUR.
FORD.
FORBES.
CORNER OF AMWELL AND RIVER. WE'VE GOT THEM.
TOM TAYLOR AND THE OTHER BLOKE. NOT THE GIRL.
I'M NOT HIM! HONEST TO GOD, I GET THIS ALL THE TIME.
WELL, YOU'RE GETTING IT AGAIN.
SANDERS MY GREAT FAT HAIRY ARSE.
LET GO OF ME!
YOU'RE MAKING A MISTAKE!
THEN WE'LL SORT IT OUT DOWN AT THE STATION, SIR.
No.

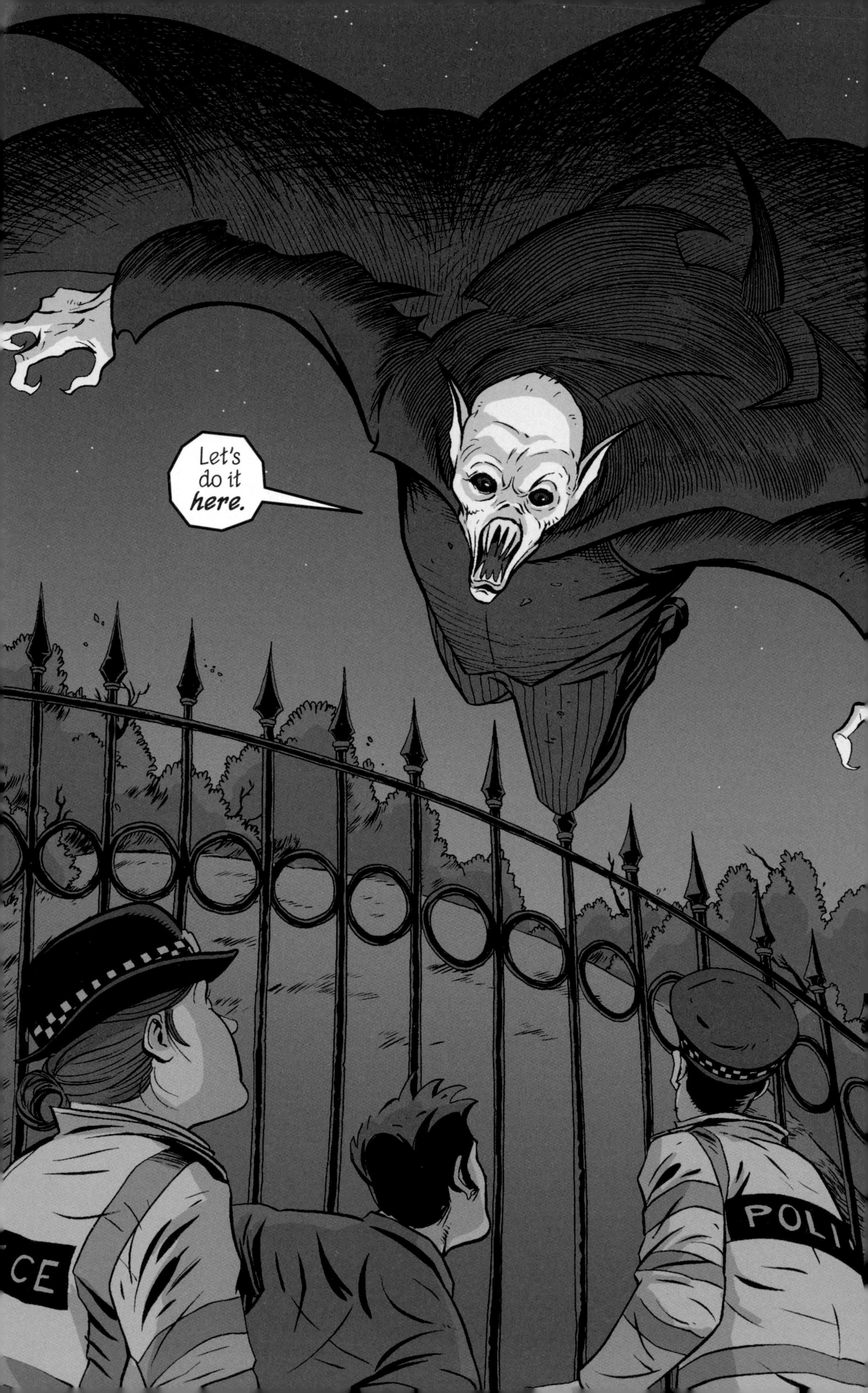
Let's do it *here.*
POLI
CE

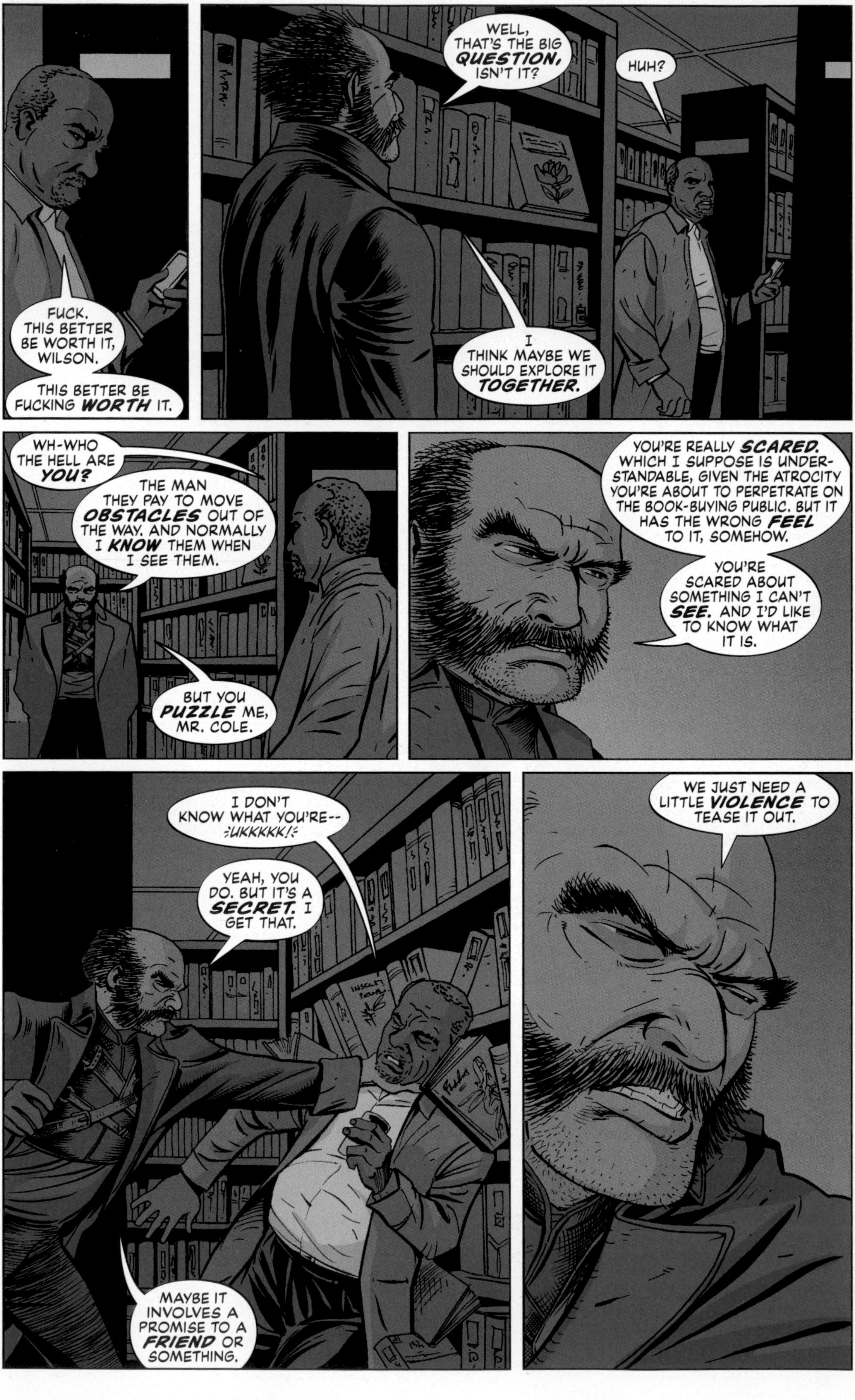
WELL, THAT'S THE BIG QUESTION, ISN'T IT?
HUH?
FUCK. THIS BETTER BE WORTH IT, WILSON.
THIS BETTER BE FUCKING WORTH IT.
I THINK MAYBE WE SHOULD EXPLORE IT TOGETHER.
WH-WHO THE HELL ARE YOU?
THE MAN THEY PAY TO MOVE OBSTACLES OUT OF THE WAY. AND NORMALLY I KNOW THEM WHEN I SEE THEM.
BUT YOU PUZZLE ME, MR. COLE.
YOU'RE REALLY SCARED. WHICH I SUPPOSE IS UNDER-STANDABLE, GIVEN THE ATROCITY YOU'RE ABOUT TO PERPETRATE ON THE BOOK-BUYING PUBLIC. BUT IT HAS THE WRONG FEEL TO IT, SOMEHOW.
YOU'RE SCARED ABOUT SOMETHING I CAN'T SEE. AND I'D LIKE TO KNOW WHAT IT IS.
I DON'T KNOW WHAT YOU'RE-- UKKKKK!
YEAH, YOU DO. BUT IT'S A SECRET. I GET THAT.
MAYBE IT INVOLVES A PROMISE TO A FRIEND OR SOMETHING.
WE JUST NEED A LITTLE VIOLENCE TO TEASE IT OUT.

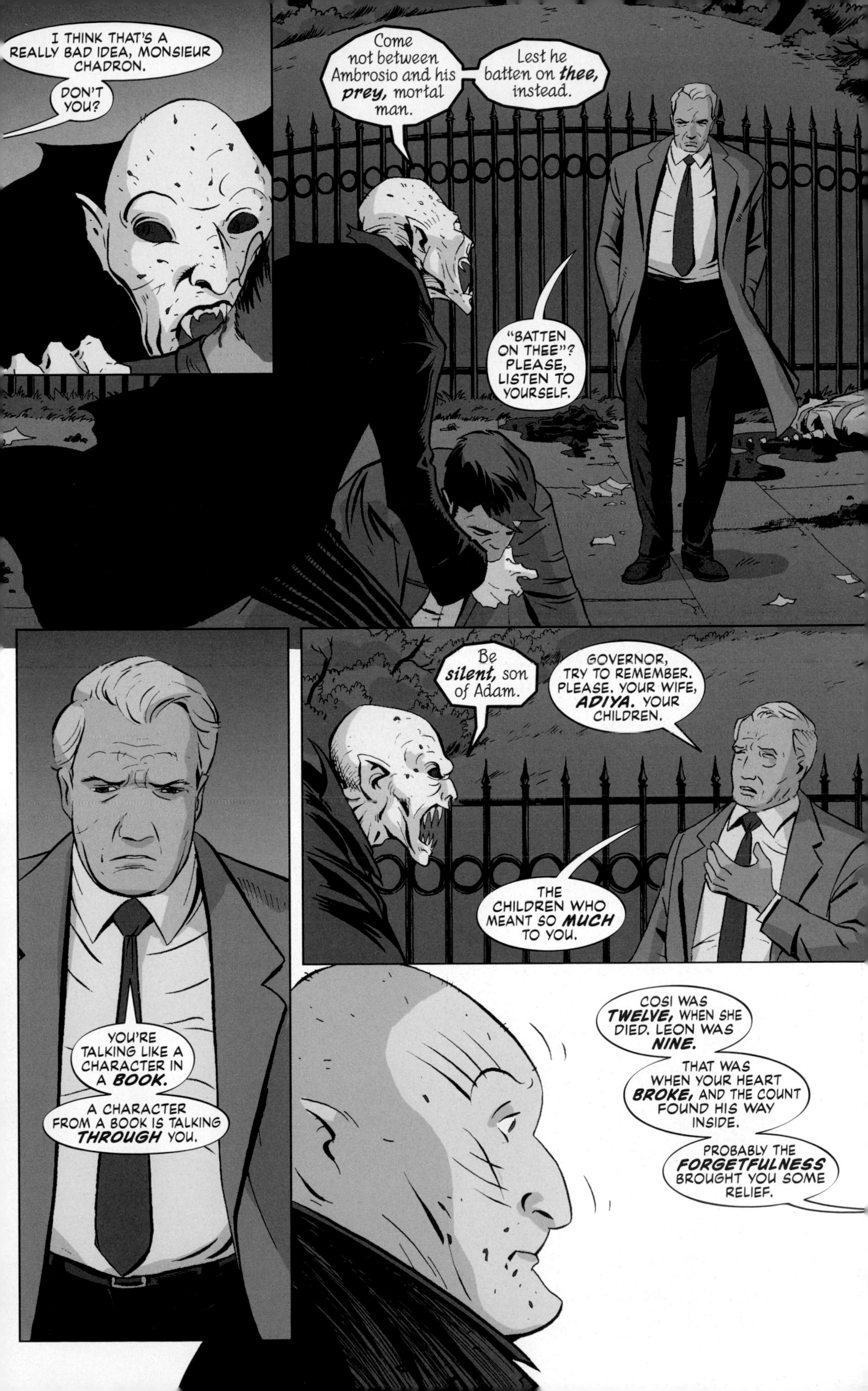

I THINK THAT'S A REALLY BAD IDEA, MONSIEUR CHADRON.
DON'T YOU?
Come not between Ambrosio and his *prey,* mortal man.
Lest he batten on *thee,* instead.
"BATTEN ON THEE"? PLEASE, LISTEN TO YOURSELF.
YOU'RE TALKING LIKE A CHARACTER IN A **BOOK.**
A CHARACTER FROM A BOOK IS TALKING **THROUGH** YOU.
Be *silent,* son of Adam.
GOVERNOR, TRY TO REMEMBER. PLEASE. YOUR WIFE, **ADIYA.** YOUR CHILDREN.
THE CHILDREN WHO MEANT SO **MUCH** TO YOU.
COSI WAS **TWELVE,** WHEN SHE DIED. LEON WAS **NINE.**
THAT WAS WHEN YOUR HEART **BROKE,** AND THE COUNT FOUND HIS WAY INSIDE.
PROBABLY THE **FORGETFULNESS** BROUGHT YOU SOME RELIEF.

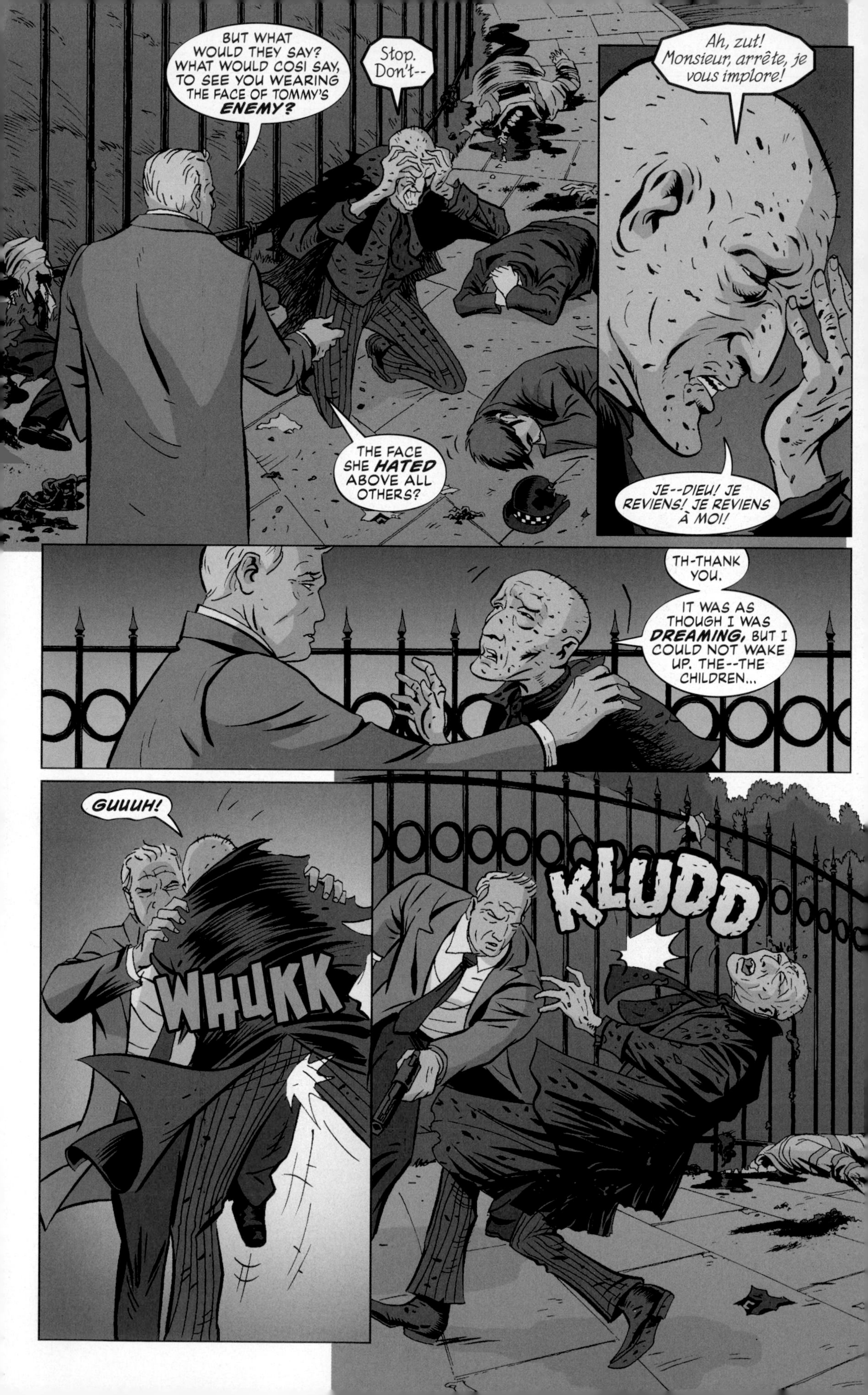
BUT WHAT WOULD THEY SAY? WHAT WOULD COSI SAY, TO SEE YOU WEARING THE FACE OF TOMMY'S ENEMY?
Stop. Don't--
THE FACE SHE HATED ABOVE ALL OTHERS?
Ah, zut! Monsieur, arrête, je vous implore!
JE--DIEU! JE REVIENS! JE REVIENS À MOI!
TH-THANK YOU.
IT WAS AS THOUGH I WAS DREAMING, BUT I COULD NOT WAKE UP. THE--THE CHILDREN...
GUUUH!
WHUKK
KLUDD

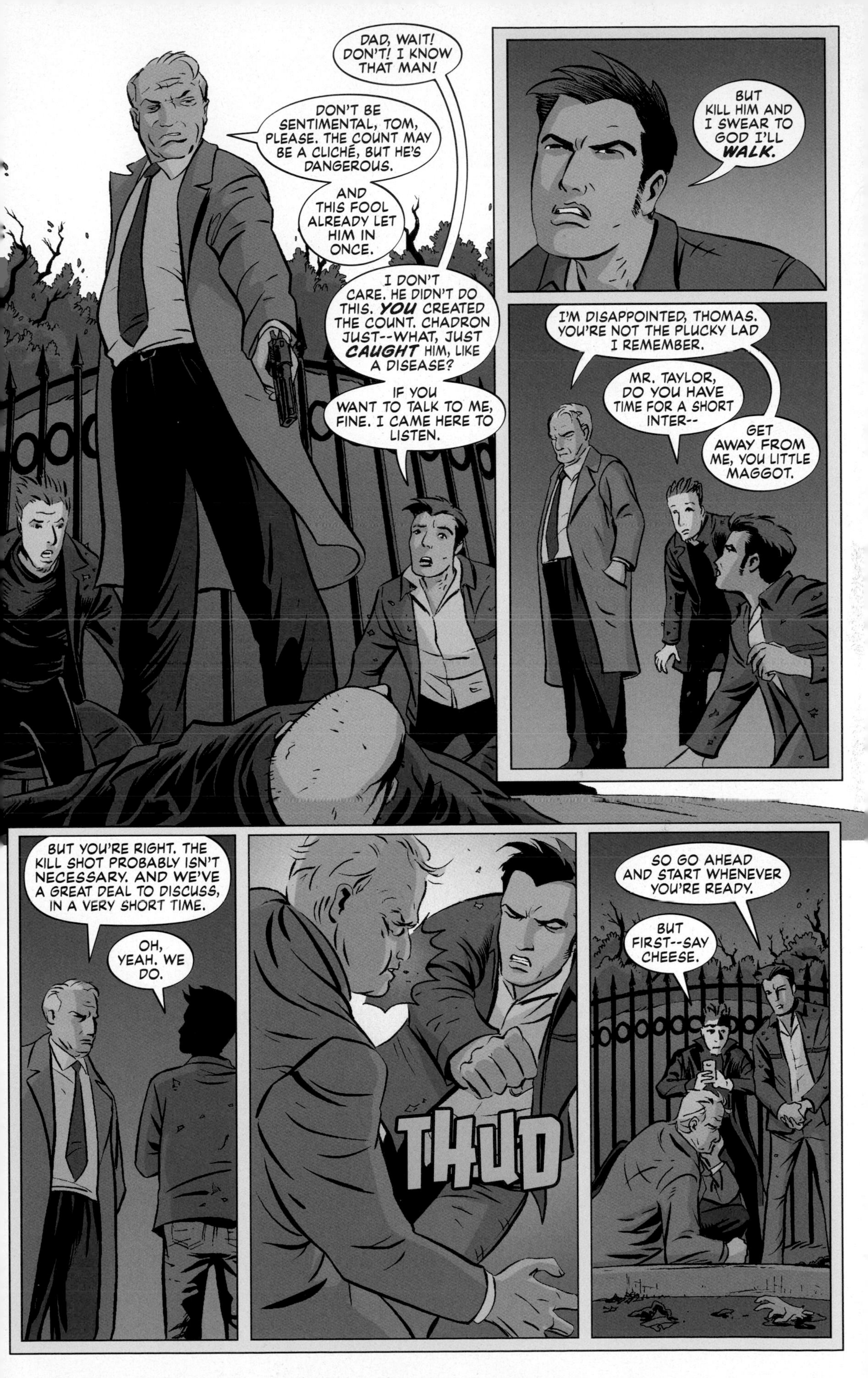
DAD, WAIT! DON'T! I KNOW THAT MAN!
DON'T BE SENTIMENTAL, TOM, PLEASE. THE COUNT MAY BE A CLICHÉ, BUT HE'S DANGEROUS.
AND THIS FOOL ALREADY LET HIM IN ONCE.
I DON'T CARE. HE DIDN'T DO THIS. YOU CREATED THE COUNT. CHADRON JUST--WHAT, JUST CAUGHT HIM, LIKE A DISEASE?
IF YOU WANT TO TALK TO ME, FINE. I CAME HERE TO LISTEN.
BUT KILL HIM AND I SWEAR TO GOD I'LL WALK.
I'M DISAPPOINTED, THOMAS. YOU'RE NOT THE PLUCKY LAD I REMEMBER.
MR. TAYLOR, DO YOU HAVE TIME FOR A SHORT INTER--
GET AWAY FROM ME, YOU LITTLE MAGGOT.
BUT YOU'RE RIGHT. THE KILL SHOT PROBABLY ISN'T NECESSARY. AND WE'VE A GREAT DEAL TO DISCUSS, IN A VERY SHORT TIME.
OH, YEAH. WE DO.
THUD
SO GO AHEAD AND START WHENEVER YOU'RE READY.
BUT FIRST--SAY CHEESE.

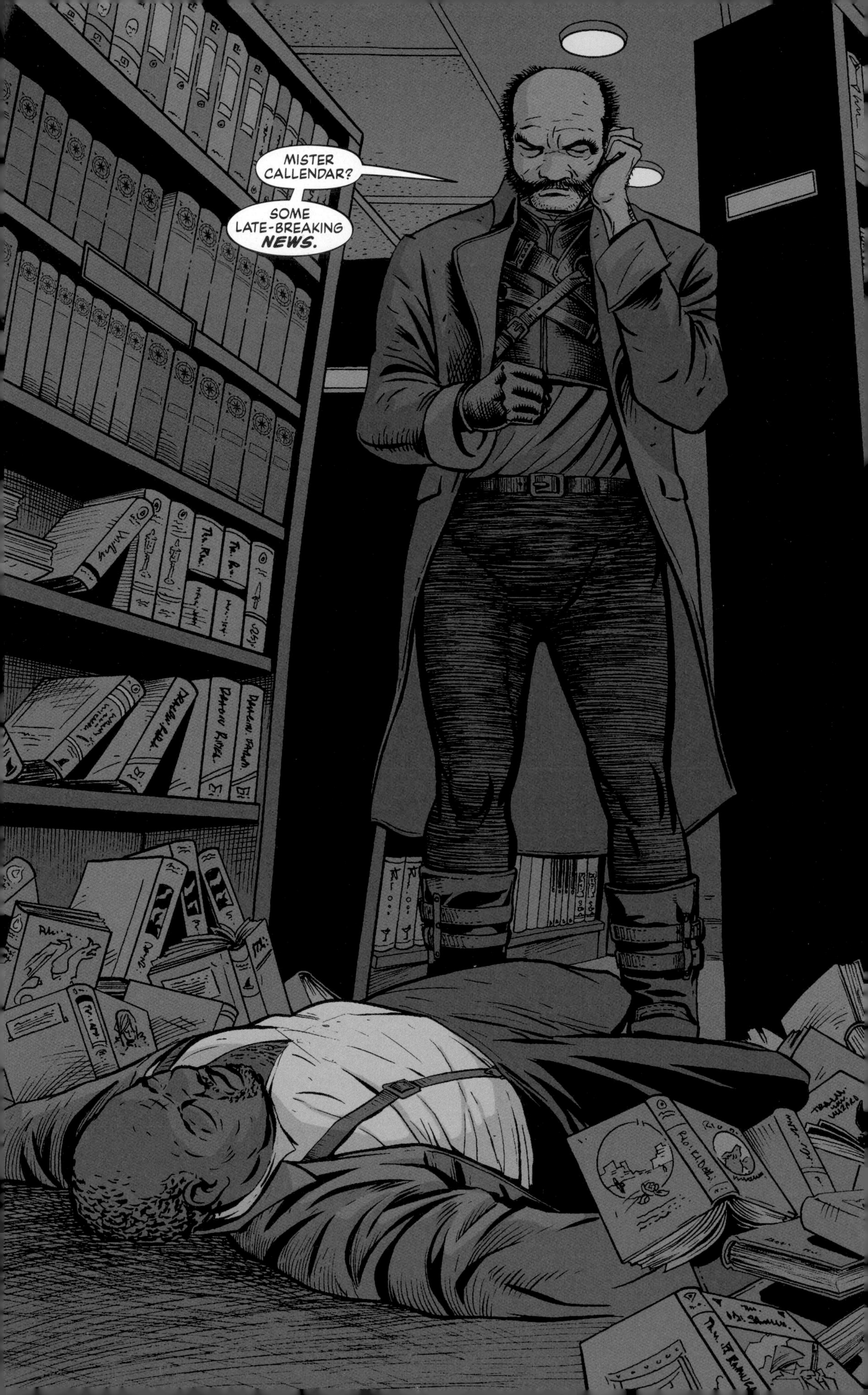
MISTER CALLENDAR?
SOME LATE-BREAKING NEWS.

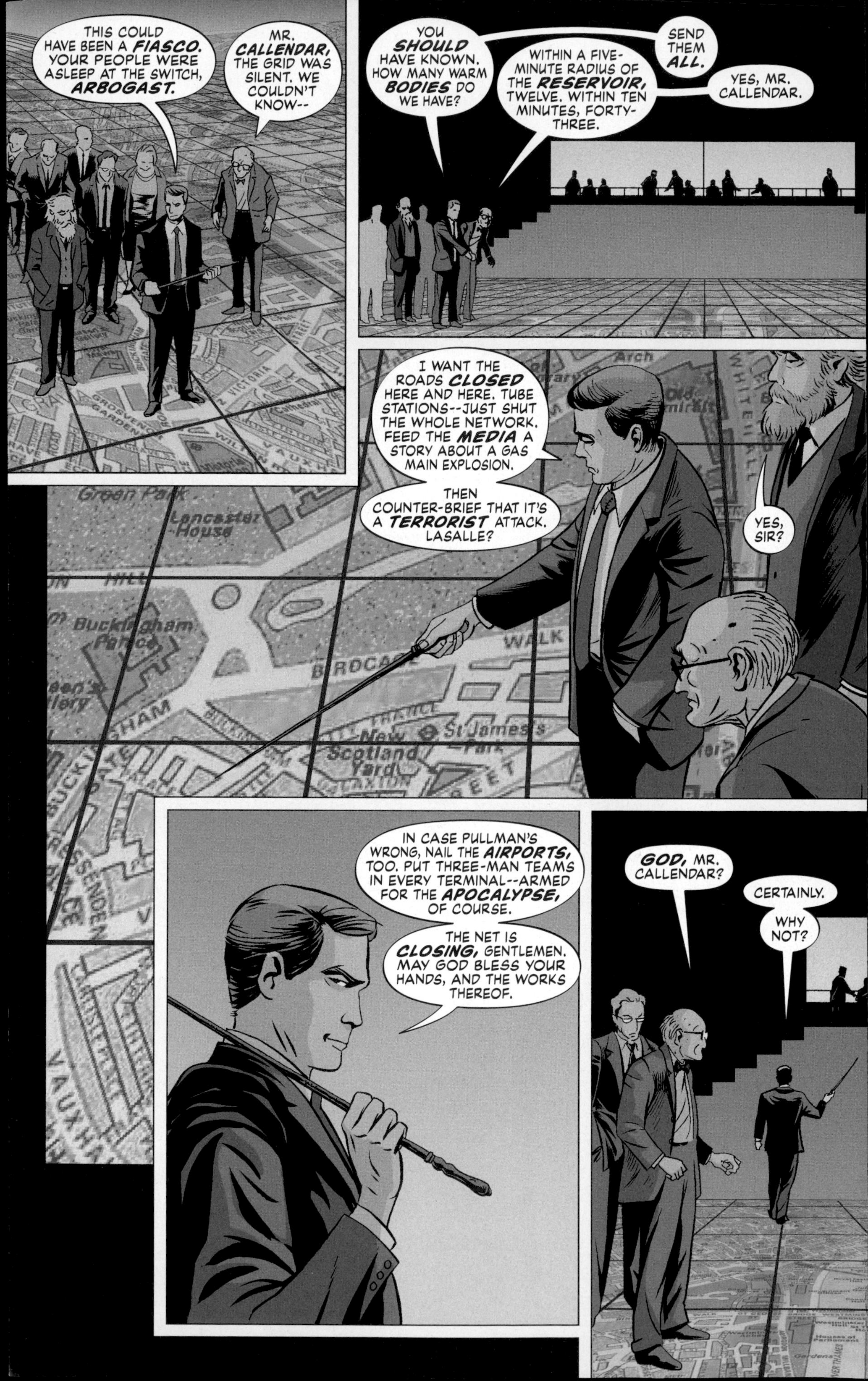

THIS COULD HAVE BEEN A FIASCO. YOUR PEOPLE WERE ASLEEP AT THE SWITCH, ARBOGAST.
MR. CALLENDAR, THE GRID WAS SILENT. WE COULDN'T KNOW--
YOU SHOULD HAVE KNOWN. HOW MANY WARM BODIES DO WE HAVE?
WITHIN A FIVE-MINUTE RADIUS OF THE RESERVOIR, TWELVE. WITHIN TEN MINUTES, FORTY-THREE.
SEND THEM ALL.
YES, MR. CALLENDAR.
I WANT THE ROADS CLOSED HERE AND HERE. TUBE STATIONS--JUST SHUT THE WHOLE NETWORK. FEED THE MEDIA A STORY ABOUT A GAS MAIN EXPLOSION.
THEN COUNTER-BRIEF THAT IT'S A TERRORIST ATTACK. LASALLE?
YES, SIR?
IN CASE PULLMAN'S WRONG, NAIL THE AIRPORTS, TOO. PUT THREE-MAN TEAMS IN EVERY TERMINAL--ARMED FOR THE APOCALYPSE, OF COURSE.
THE NET IS CLOSING, GENTLEMEN. MAY GOD BLESS YOUR HANDS, AND THE WORKS THEREOF.
GOD, MR. CALLENDAR?
CERTAINLY.
WHY NOT?

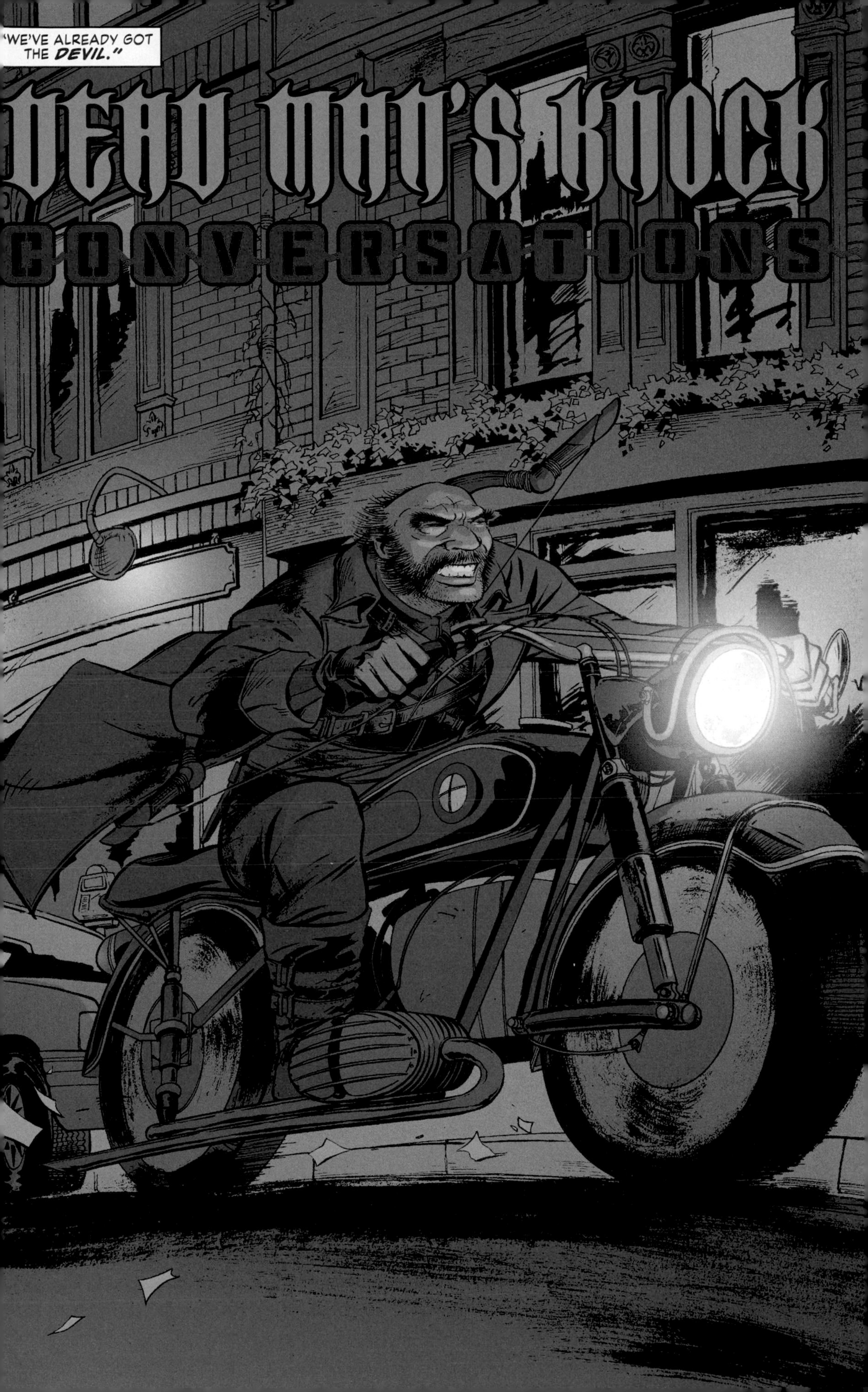
"WE'VE ALREADY GOT THE DEVIL."
DEAD MAN'S KNOCK
CONVERSATIONS

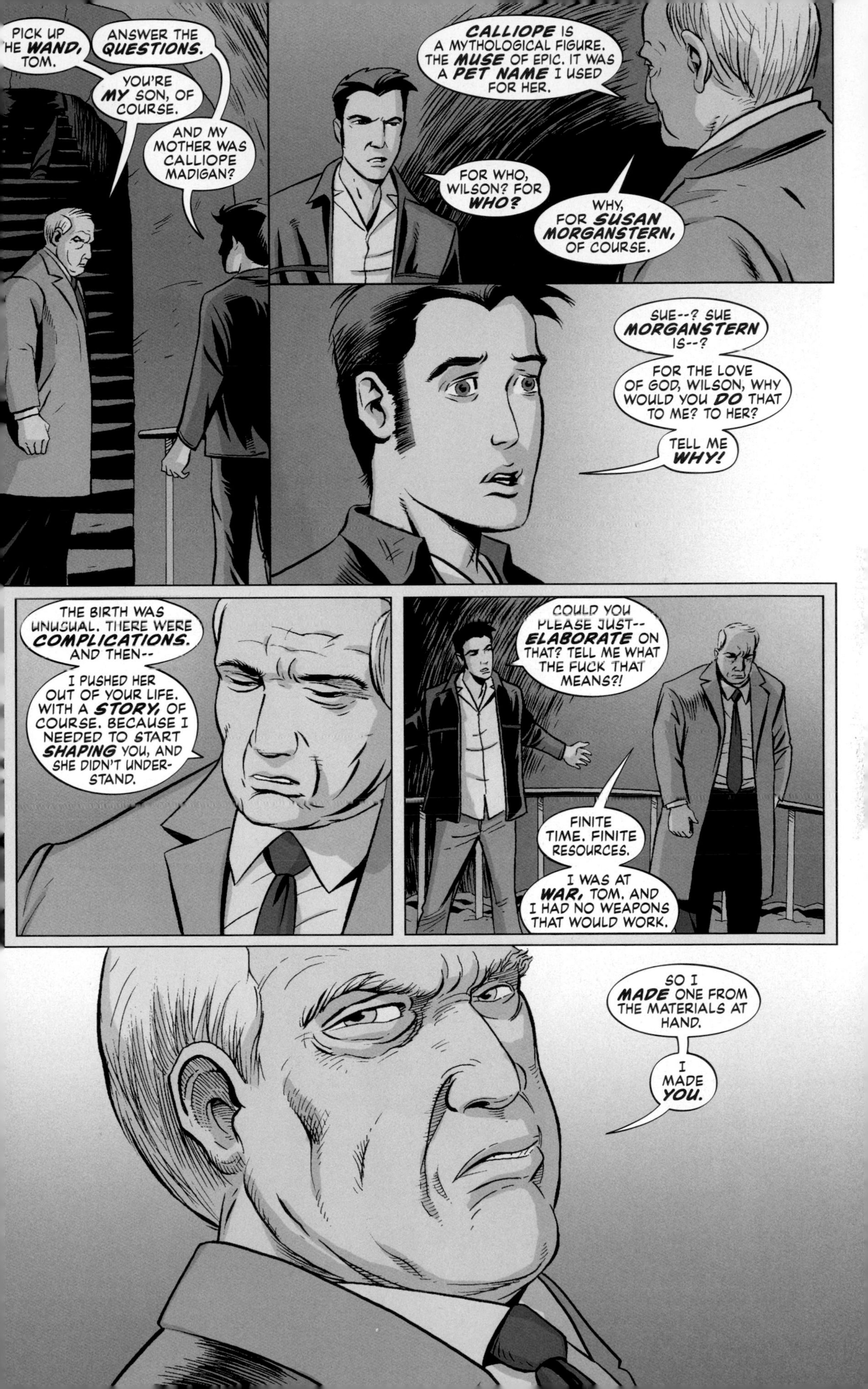
PICK UP THE WAND, TOM.
ANSWER THE QUESTIONS.
YOU'RE MY SON, OF COURSE.
AND MY MOTHER WAS CALLIOPE MADIGAN?
CALLIOPE IS A MYTHOLOGICAL FIGURE. THE MUSE OF EPIC. IT WAS A PET NAME I USED FOR HER.
FOR WHO, WILSON? FOR WHO?
WHY, FOR SUSAN MORGANSTERN, OF COURSE.
SUE--? SUE MORGANSTERN IS--?
FOR THE LOVE OF GOD, WILSON, WHY WOULD YOU DO THAT TO ME? TO HER?
TELL ME WHY!
THE BIRTH WAS UNUSUAL. THERE WERE COMPLICATIONS. AND THEN--
I PUSHED HER OUT OF YOUR LIFE. WITH A STORY, OF COURSE. BECAUSE I NEEDED TO START SHAPING YOU, AND SHE DIDN'T UNDERSTAND.
COULD YOU PLEASE JUST--ELABORATE ON THAT? TELL ME WHAT THE FUCK THAT MEANS?!
FINITE TIME. FINITE RESOURCES.
I WAS AT WAR, TOM. AND I HAD NO WEAPONS THAT WOULD WORK.
SO I MADE ONE FROM THE MATERIALS AT HAND.
I MADE YOU.

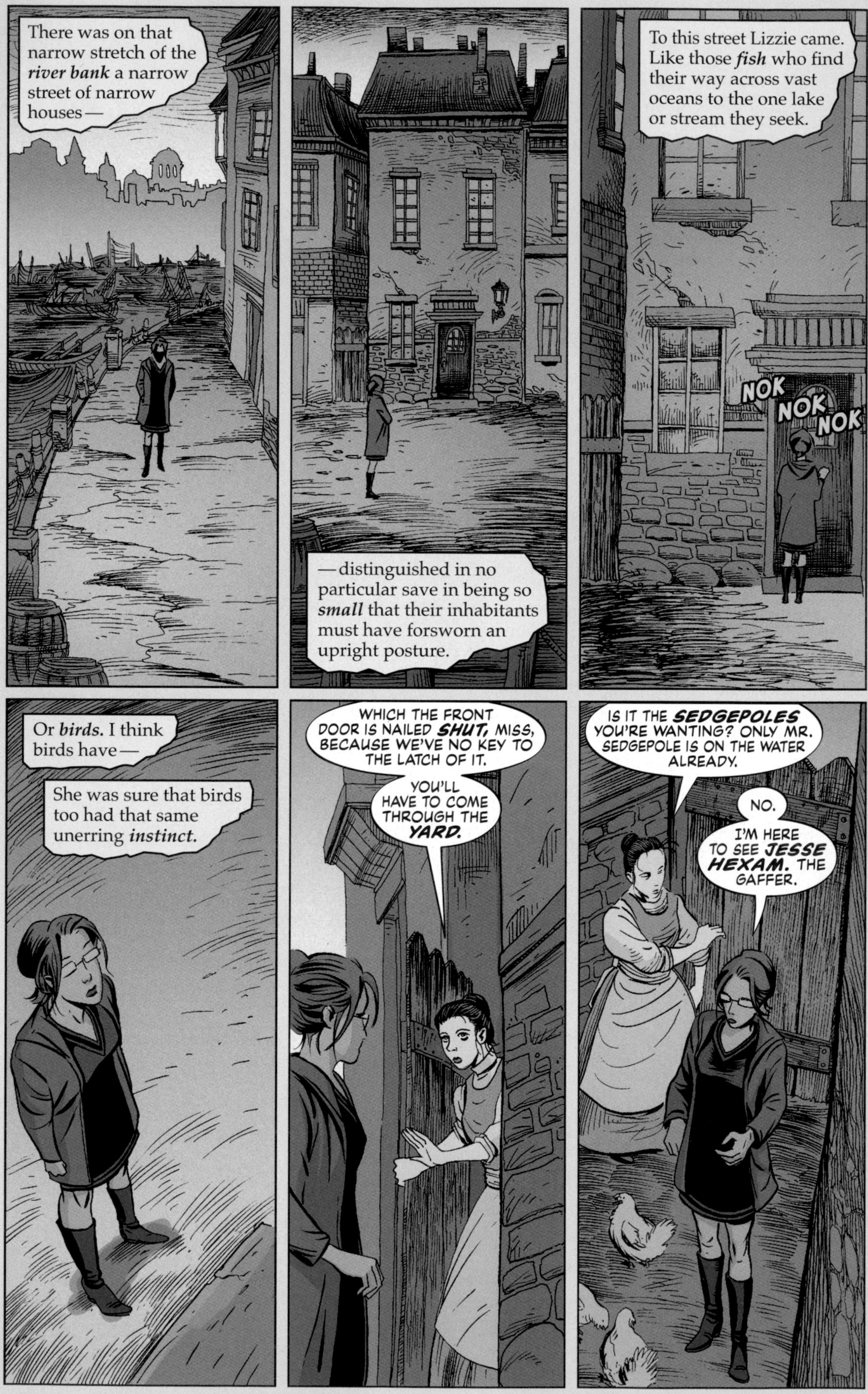
There was on that narrow stretch of the *river bank* a narrow street of narrow houses—
—distinguished in no particular save in being so *small* that their inhabitants must have forsworn an upright posture.
To this street Lizzie came. Like those *fish* who find their way across vast oceans to the one lake or stream they seek.
NOK
NOK
NOK
Or *birds*. I think birds have—
She was sure that birds too had that same unerring *instinct*.
WHICH THE FRONT DOOR IS NAILED ***SHUT,*** MISS, BECAUSE WE'VE NO KEY TO THE LATCH OF IT.
YOU'LL HAVE TO COME THROUGH THE ***YARD.***
IS IT THE ***SEDGEPOLES*** YOU'RE WANTING? ONLY MR. SEDGEPOLE IS ON THE WATER ALREADY.
NO.
I'M HERE TO SEE ***JESSE HEXAM.*** THE GAFFER.

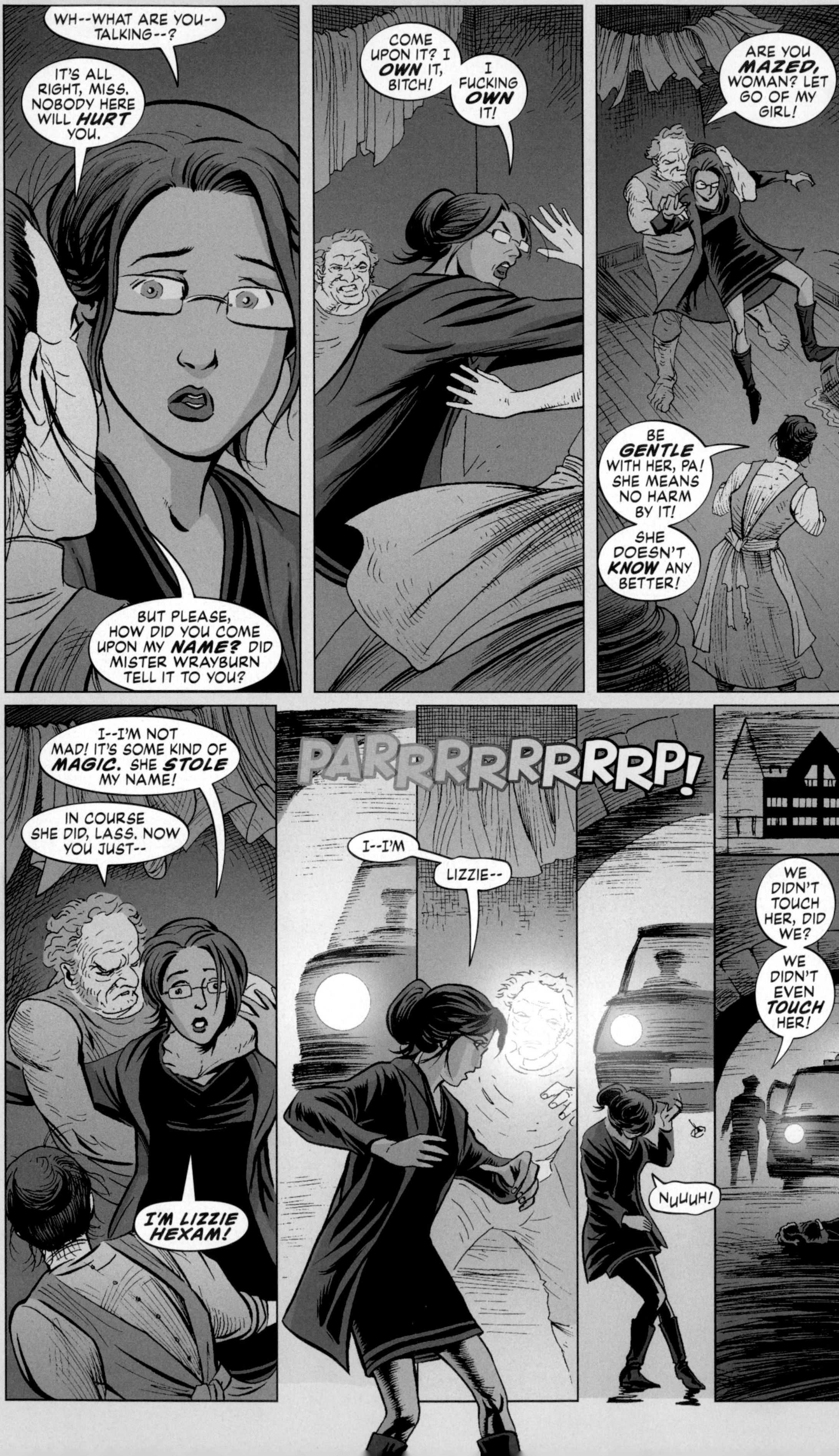
WH--WHAT ARE YOU--TALKING--?
IT'S ALL RIGHT, MISS. NOBODY HERE WILL HURT YOU.
BUT PLEASE, HOW DID YOU COME UPON MY NAME? DID MISTER WRAYBURN TELL IT TO YOU?
COME UPON IT? I OWN IT, BITCH!
I FUCKING OWN IT!
ARE YOU MAZED, WOMAN? LET GO OF MY GIRL!
BE GENTLE WITH HER, PA! SHE MEANS NO HARM BY IT!
SHE DOESN'T KNOW ANY BETTER!
I--I'M NOT MAD! IT'S SOME KIND OF MAGIC. SHE STOLE MY NAME!
IN COURSE SHE DID, LASS. NOW YOU JUST--
I'M LIZZIE HEXAM!
PARRRRRRRRRP!
I--I'M
LIZZIE--
NUUUH!
WE DIDN'T TOUCH HER, DID WE?
WE DIDN'T EVEN TOUCH HER!

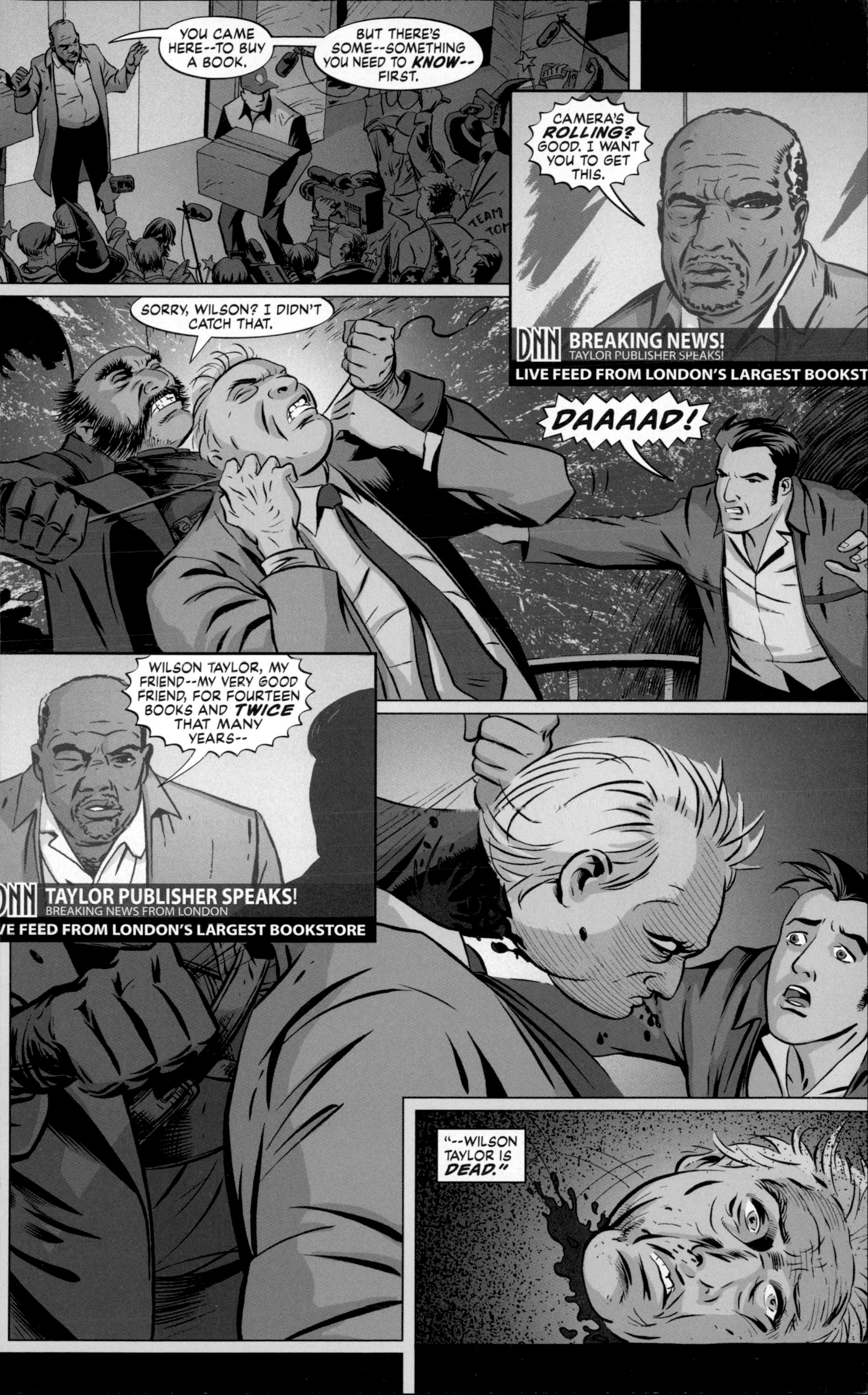
YOU CAME HERE--TO BUY A BOOK.
BUT THERE'S SOME--SOMETHING YOU NEED TO KNOW-- FIRST.
TEAM TOM
CAMERA'S ROLLING? GOOD. I WANT YOU TO GET THIS.
DNN BREAKING NEWS!
TAYLOR PUBLISHER SPEAKS!
LIVE FEED FROM LONDON'S LARGEST BOOKST
SORRY, WILSON? I DIDN'T CATCH THAT.
DAAAAD!
WILSON TAYLOR, MY FRIEND--MY VERY GOOD FRIEND, FOR FOURTEEN BOOKS AND TWICE THAT MANY YEARS--
DNN TAYLOR PUBLISHER SPEAKS!
BREAKING NEWS FROM LONDON
VE FEED FROM LONDON'S LARGEST BOOKSTORE
"--WILSON TAYLOR IS DEAD."

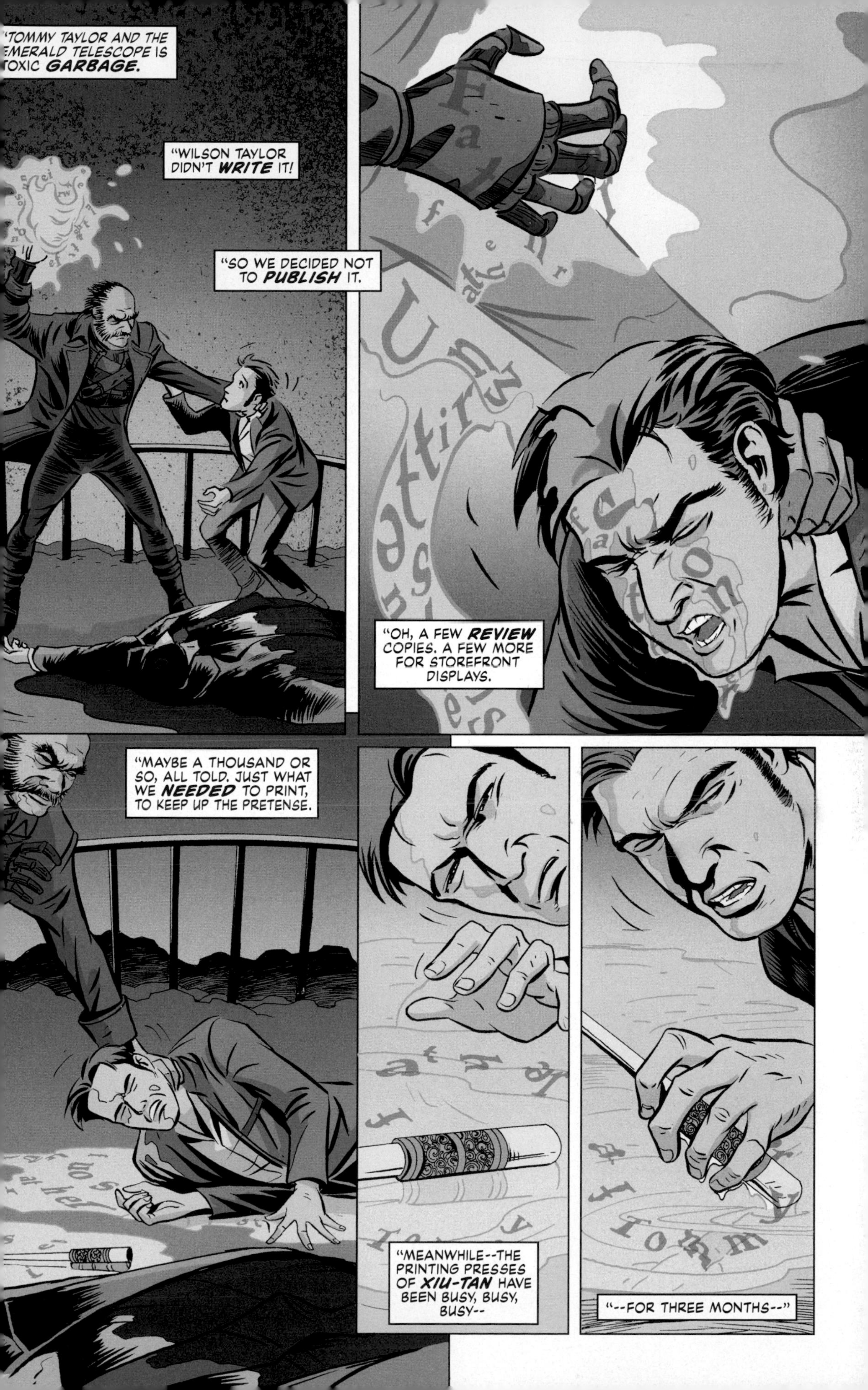
"TOMMY TAYLOR AND THE EMERALD TELESCOPE IS TOXIC GARBAGE.
"WILSON TAYLOR DIDN'T WRITE IT!
"SO WE DECIDED NOT TO PUBLISH IT.
"OH, A FEW REVIEW COPIES. A FEW MORE FOR STOREFRONT DISPLAYS.
"MAYBE A THOUSAND OR SO, ALL TOLD. JUST WHAT WE NEEDED TO PRINT, TO KEEP UP THE PRETENSE.
"MEANWHILE--THE PRINTING PRESSES OF XIU-TAN HAVE BEEN BUSY, BUSY, BUSY--
"--FOR THREE MONTHS--"

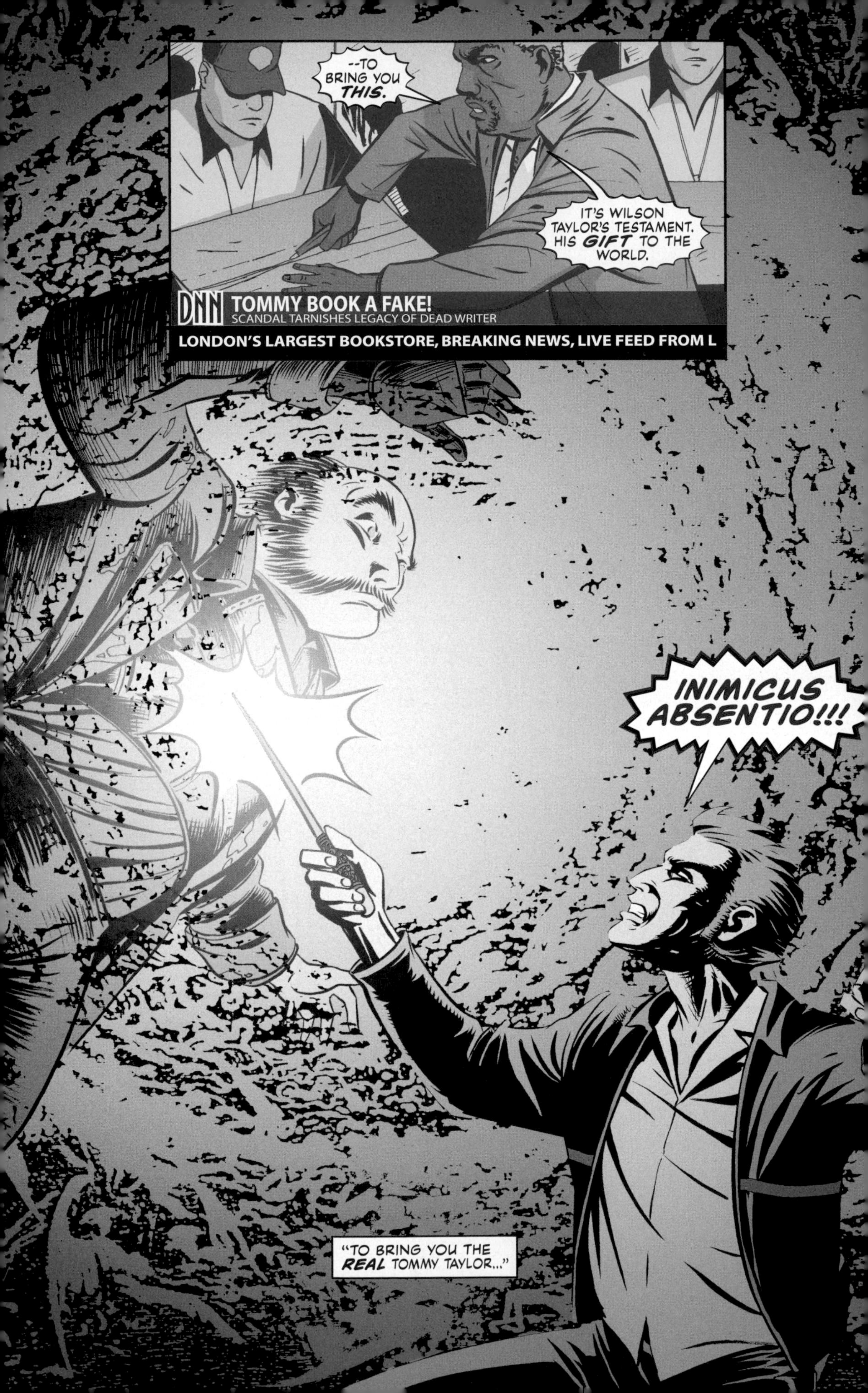
--TO BRING YOU *THIS.*
IT'S WILSON TAYLOR'S TESTAMENT. HIS *GIFT* TO THE WORLD.
DNN TOMMY BOOK A FAKE!
SCANDAL TARNISHES LEGACY OF DEAD WRITER
LONDON'S LARGEST BOOKSTORE, BREAKING NEWS, LIVE FEED FROM L
INIMICUS ABSENTIO!!!
"TO BRING YOU THE *REAL* TOMMY TAYLOR..."

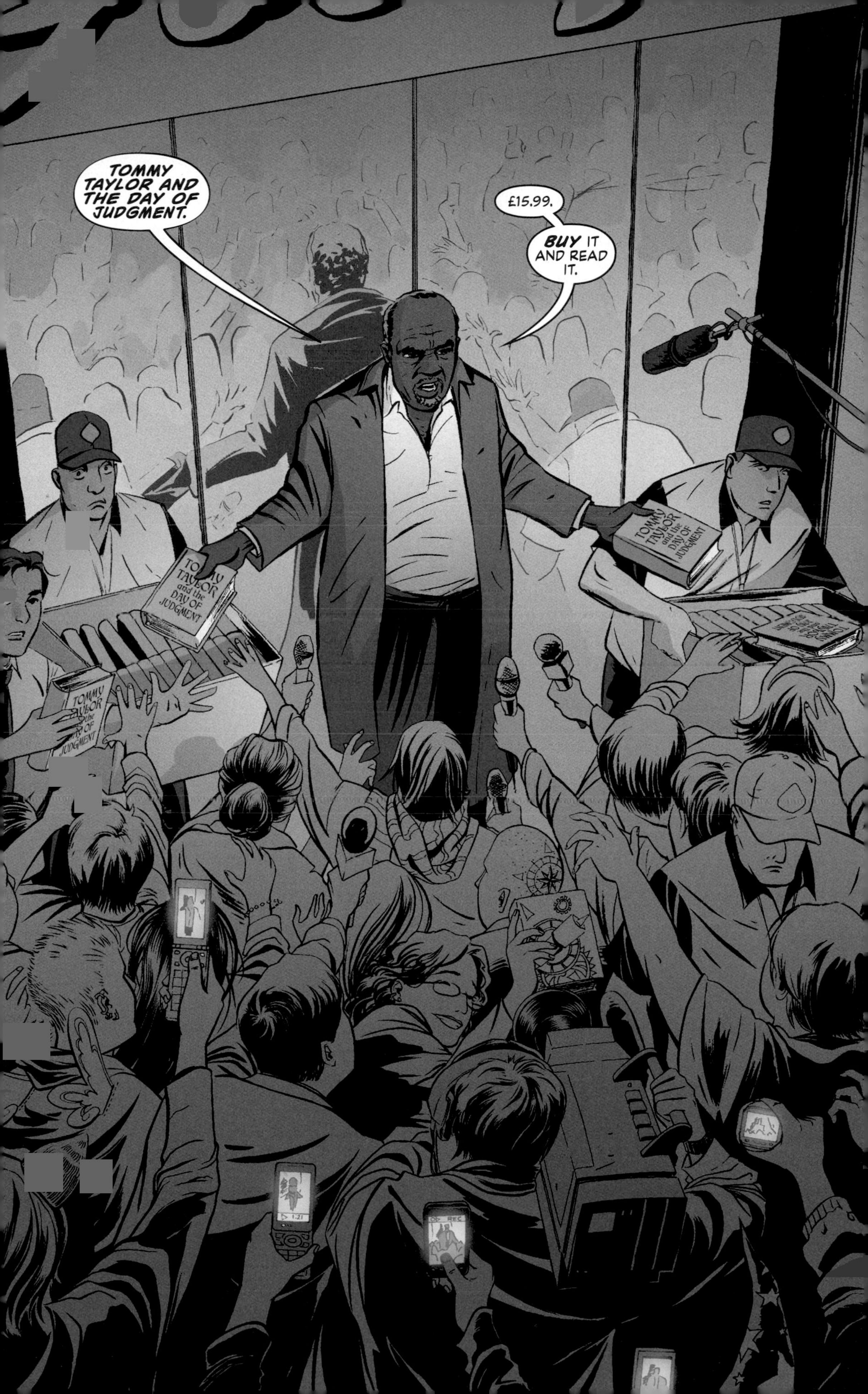
TOMMY TAYLOR AND THE DAY OF JUDGMENT.
£15.99.
BUY IT AND READ IT.
TOMMY TAYLOR and the DAY OF JUDGMENT

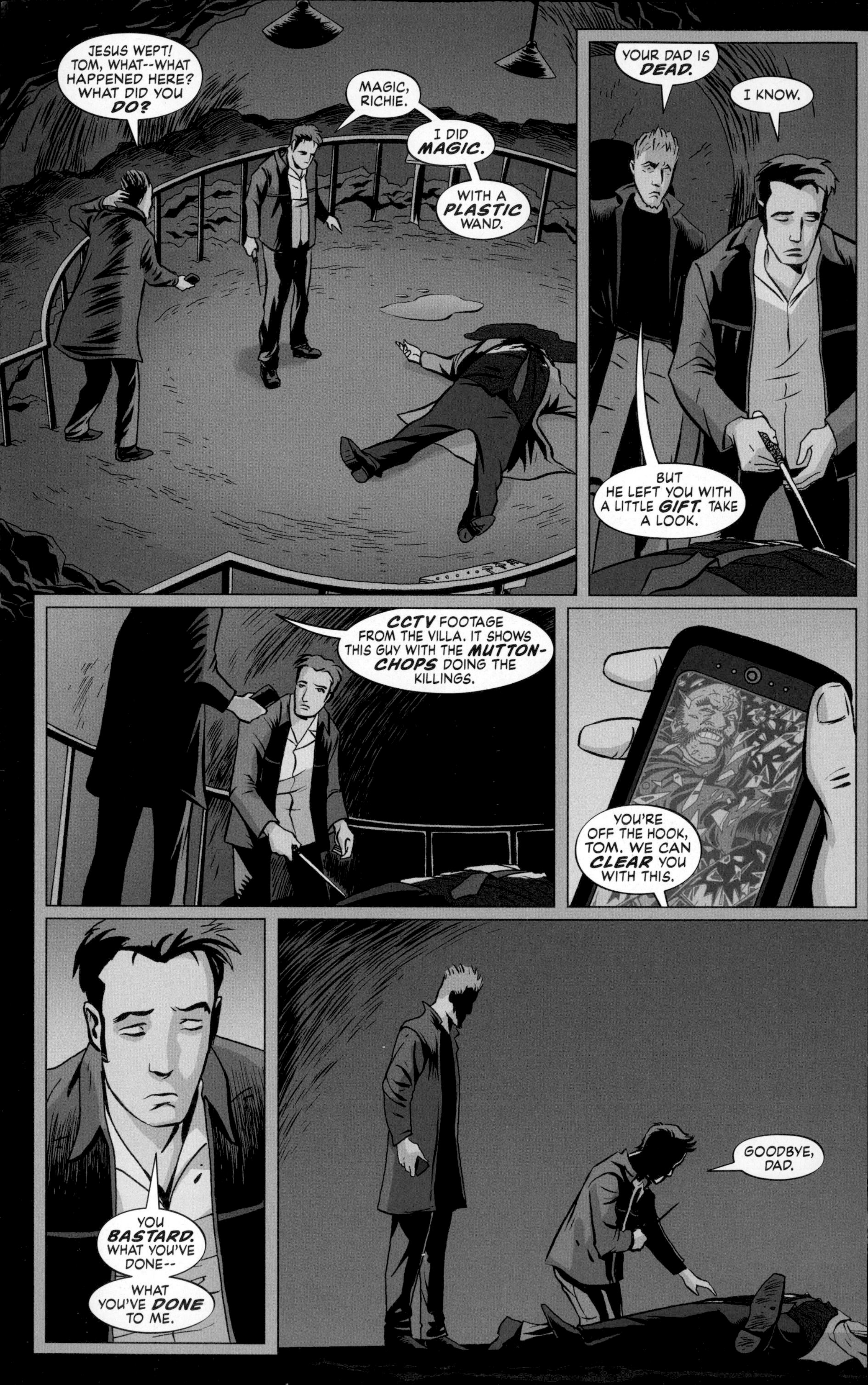
JESUS WEPT! TOM, WHAT--WHAT HAPPENED HERE? WHAT DID YOU DO?
MAGIC, RICHIE.
I DID MAGIC.
WITH A PLASTIC WAND.
YOUR DAD IS DEAD.
I KNOW.
BUT HE LEFT YOU WITH A LITTLE GIFT. TAKE A LOOK.
CCTV FOOTAGE FROM THE VILLA. IT SHOWS THIS GUY WITH THE MUTTON-CHOPS DOING THE KILLINGS.
YOU'RE OFF THE HOOK, TOM. WE CAN CLEAR YOU WITH THIS.
YOU BASTARD. WHAT YOU'VE DONE--
WHAT YOU'VE DONE TO ME.
GOODBYE, DAD.

All the news that's fit to post.

Home | News | Sports | Weather | Lifestyle | Arts

14TH TOMMY "A REVELATION"

After the violent death of its author, and the extraordinary maneuvering of publishers Queensberry in passing off a fake Tommy Taylor book on reviewers, then revealing a different book on the actual day of the launch, it would perhaps not be surprising if the book itself failed to live up to the real-life drama of its genesis.

Nothing could be further from the truth. Critics and fans alike are hailing this as Wilson Taylor's definitive masterpiece – a poignant and powerful reflection on truth, eternity and the value of human striving.

Casting his wizard hero as a savior bringing a new gospel to a troubled world, Taylor might have lapsed into pretension and grandiloquence. But in powerful and simple speeches, Tommy addresses us as his contemporaries, his countrymen, and we respond.

We respond with

CULT OF TOMMY EXPLODES

by: Barb L.G.

The fringe cults hailing Tom Taylor, namesake of the boy wizard hero of his father's best-selling books, as a potential savior of humankind fell into eclipse after Taylor was arrested on multiple counts of murder after the Villa Diodati slayings. Taylor's death in the Donostia fire of last December was mourned by few.

But now that new evidence has led to a posthumous dropping of all charges, the cult of Tommy has found a new lease on life. Fueled by the messianic tone of the new novel, Tommy Taylor and the Day of Judgment, the pseudo-religion of Tommyism has now moved out of the fringe into the mainstream.

With 700,000 adherents in the US alone, the cult is starting to cause alarm in some circles. "It can't be healthy for so many people to be looking to a fallible human being to change their lives and their world," said Cardinal Desmond Connell, of the Irish Catholic Church. "That's a recipe for

---

http://www.figmentsandfantasias/forum/.

Author	Message
pycat	Posted: 1:03 am — Tommy is still out there. They never found his body after that fire.
k Moreland	Posted: 1:10 am — You mean Tom. Tom Taylor is still out there.
rdsman55	Posted: 1:12 am — Haven't you read the book? "He put on new clothes, new flesh. He went out to meet them."
pycat	Posted: 1:20 am — Don't stop there, S55! "When they saw him, they didn't know him at first. He looked like someone they'd always known and never really seen until now."
e	Posted: 1:38 pm — So what do we do?
nky Robot	Posted: 1:43 pm — We wait. We wait for him to tell us what he wants.

---

http://www.TheNewsTimes.com/world/TommyGoesDarkbutFindstheLight/.

HOMEPAGE | TODAY'S PAPER | VIDEO | MOST POPULAR | TIMES TOPICS

The News Times

WORLD | U.S. | N.Y. / REGION | BUSINESS | TECHNOLOGY | SCIENCE | HEALTH | SPORTS | OPINION

Tommy Goes Dark – but Finds the Light

Readers across the world have waited patiently for years to read the conclusion of Wilson Taylor's fictional epic. But critics were left bemused at the shift in tone as the fourteenth and purportedly final novel, Tommy Taylor and the Day of Judgment, went on sale across the world yesterday.

The bizarre expedient of trailing a different book for review purposes – allegedly to minimize the risk of piracy and illegal downloads – had already created widespread controversy. But that discussion was washed away in an instant by the broader debate about the book itself.

In some ways darker and more mature in tone than the rest of Taylor's beloved fantasies, Day of Judgment is also unashamedly messianic and utopian. Returned from the dead, boy wizard Tommy Taylor has become a holy figure, a soothsayer, a spokesman for eternal values.

But while the strange gear-change baffled some, others – in numbers that can only be called vast – have embraced and welcomed it. "The change in the Tommy books reflects our changing status quo," said media guru Edward Lutyens. "These books are like a kaleidoscope through which we see the zeitgeist: in dark times, of course they become dark."

Lucas Filby, president of one of the many Tommy Taylor fan clubs, was even more categorical. "The darkness you see is in your own eye. Trust in Tommy, and he'll take you into the light. How many times do you need to be told?"

Around the world, spontaneous "Tommy-fests" involving tens of thousands of fans have been

---

http://thePOSTnation.com/video

New Mingus breed to show at CFA... New species of pelican discovered extinct in oil
"Plato Code" finally cracked in Manches... Homeopath found in self-medicated overdos

The POST nation
When all else fails, read everything.

HOME | BREAKING NEWS | POLITICS | BUSINESS | WORLD | MEDIA | TECHNOLOGY | ENTERTAIN
ARTS | LIVING | STYLE | VIDEO | BLOGS | LINKS

Death of a Great Master

Filed by: Margaret Guttmann

When the Thane of Cawdor dies, in the Shakespeare play Macbeth, even those who have fought against him have to admit that "Nothing in his life became him like the leaving it."

The opposite appears to be the case for author Wilson Taylor. In his lifetime he brought joy to uncountable millions through his best-selling Tommy Taylor novels. His death, by contrast, is a bleak, hole-in-corner affair dogged by anomalies and unanswered questions.

DNA evidence has confirmed beyond doubt that the headless body found at the Merlin's Cave tourist attraction in Islington, London, was that of the author, who had not made any public appearances during the last decade of his life. But police have still failed to find his head, or the weapon that was used to sever it, or any substantial clues to the identity of his murderer.

An early rumor that Taylor's estranged son, Tom, might have been present at the killing and indeed involved with it, has foundered both on a lack of physical evidence and on the CCTV footage from the Villa Diodati which appears to show that Tom Taylor has already been the victim of one miscarriage of justice. Officially, Tom remains missing, presumed dead after the fire at Donostia jail which

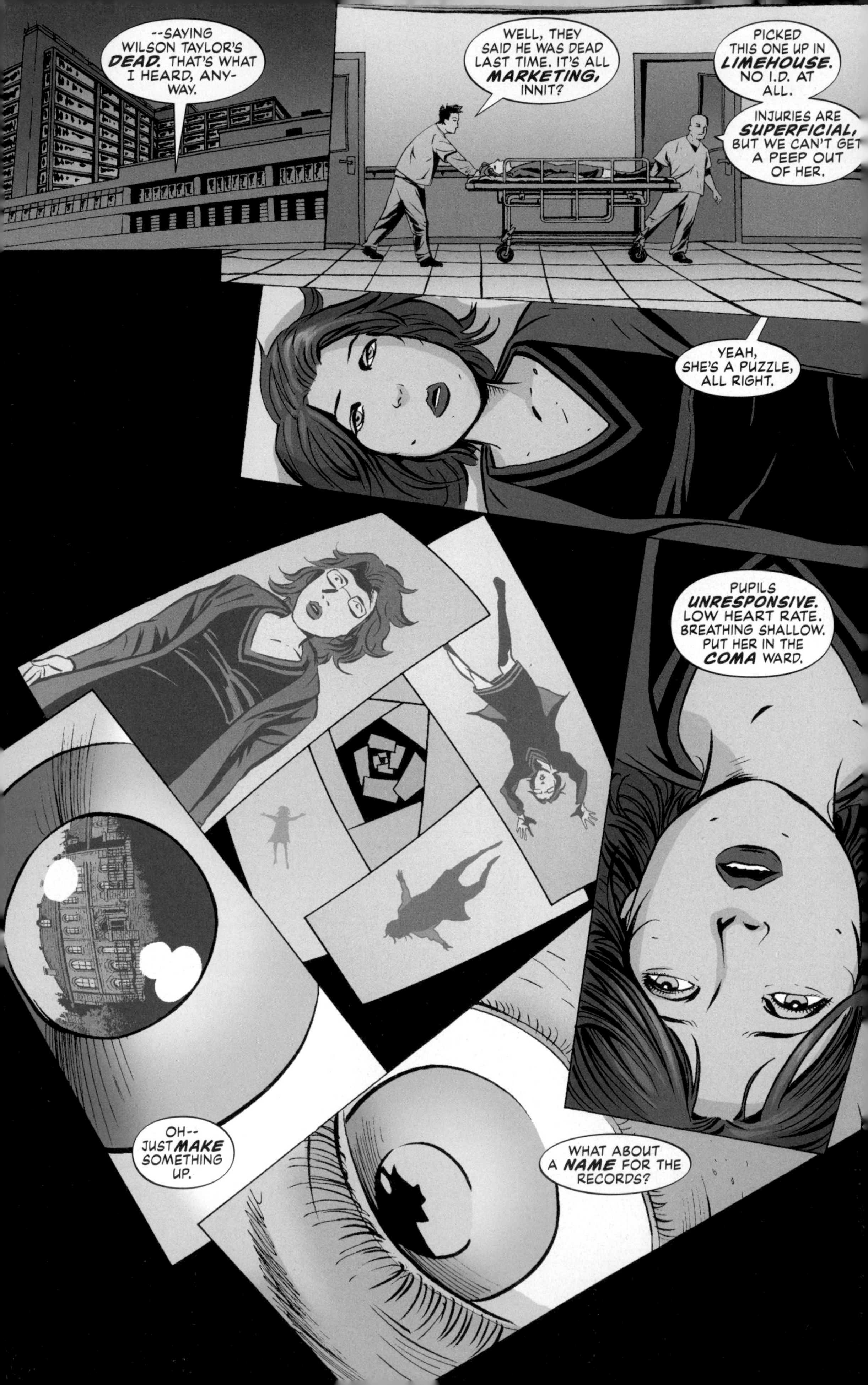
--SAYING WILSON TAYLOR'S DEAD. THAT'S WHAT I HEARD, ANYWAY.
WELL, THEY SAID HE WAS DEAD LAST TIME. IT'S ALL MARKETING, INNIT?
PICKED THIS ONE UP IN LIMEHOUSE. NO I.D. AT ALL.
INJURIES ARE SUPERFICIAL, BUT WE CAN'T GET A PEEP OUT OF HER.
YEAH, SHE'S A PUZZLE, ALL RIGHT.
PUPILS UNRESPONSIVE. LOW HEART RATE. BREATHING SHALLOW. PUT HER IN THE COMA WARD.
WHAT ABOUT A NAME FOR THE RECORDS?
OH-- JUST MAKE SOMETHING UP.

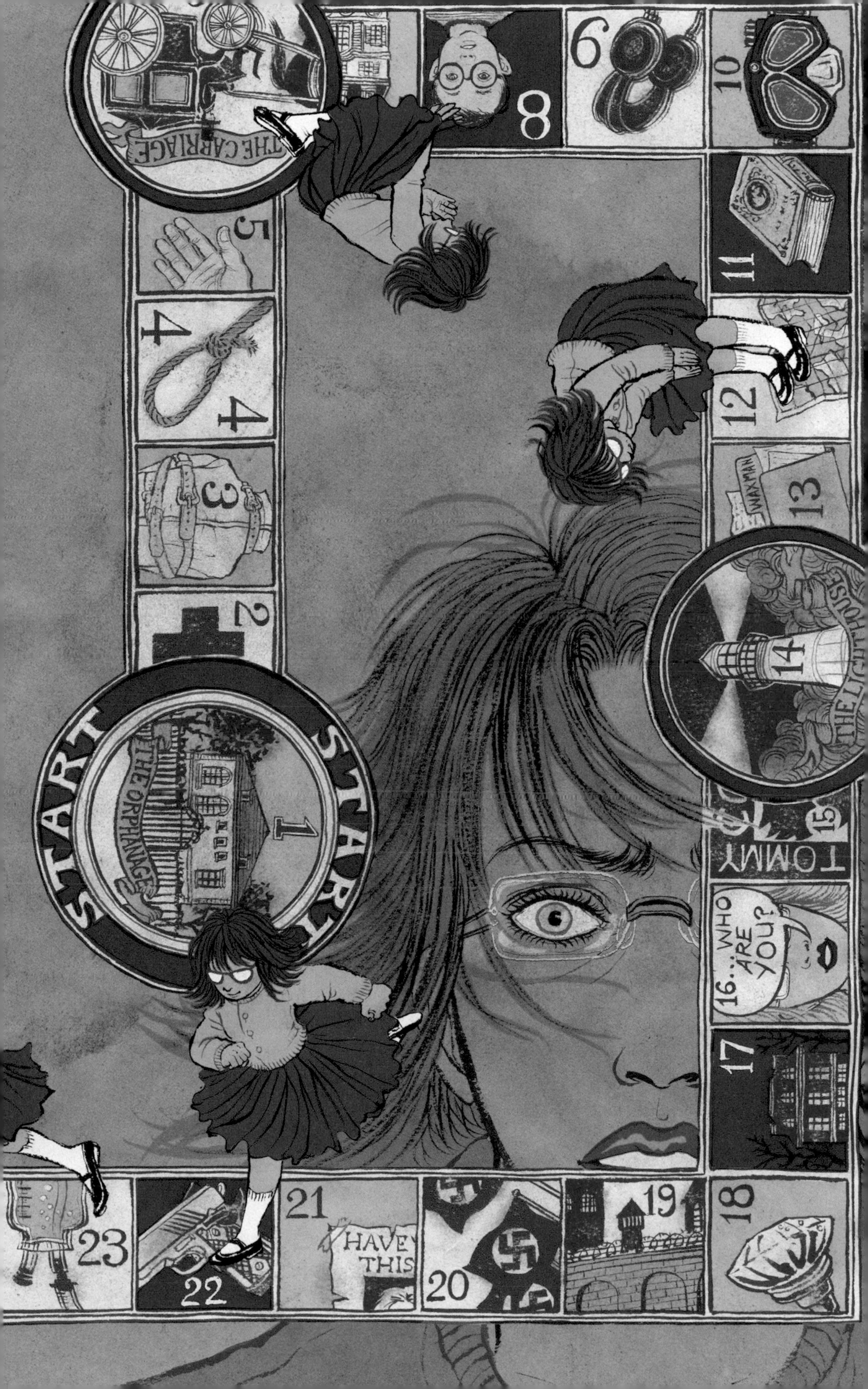
START
START
THE ORPHANAGE
1
2
3
4
4
5
THE CARRIAGE
8
9
10
11
12
WAXMAN
13
THE LIGHTHOUSE
14
15
TOMMY
16... WHO ARE YOU?
17
18
19
20
21
HAVE THIS
22
23

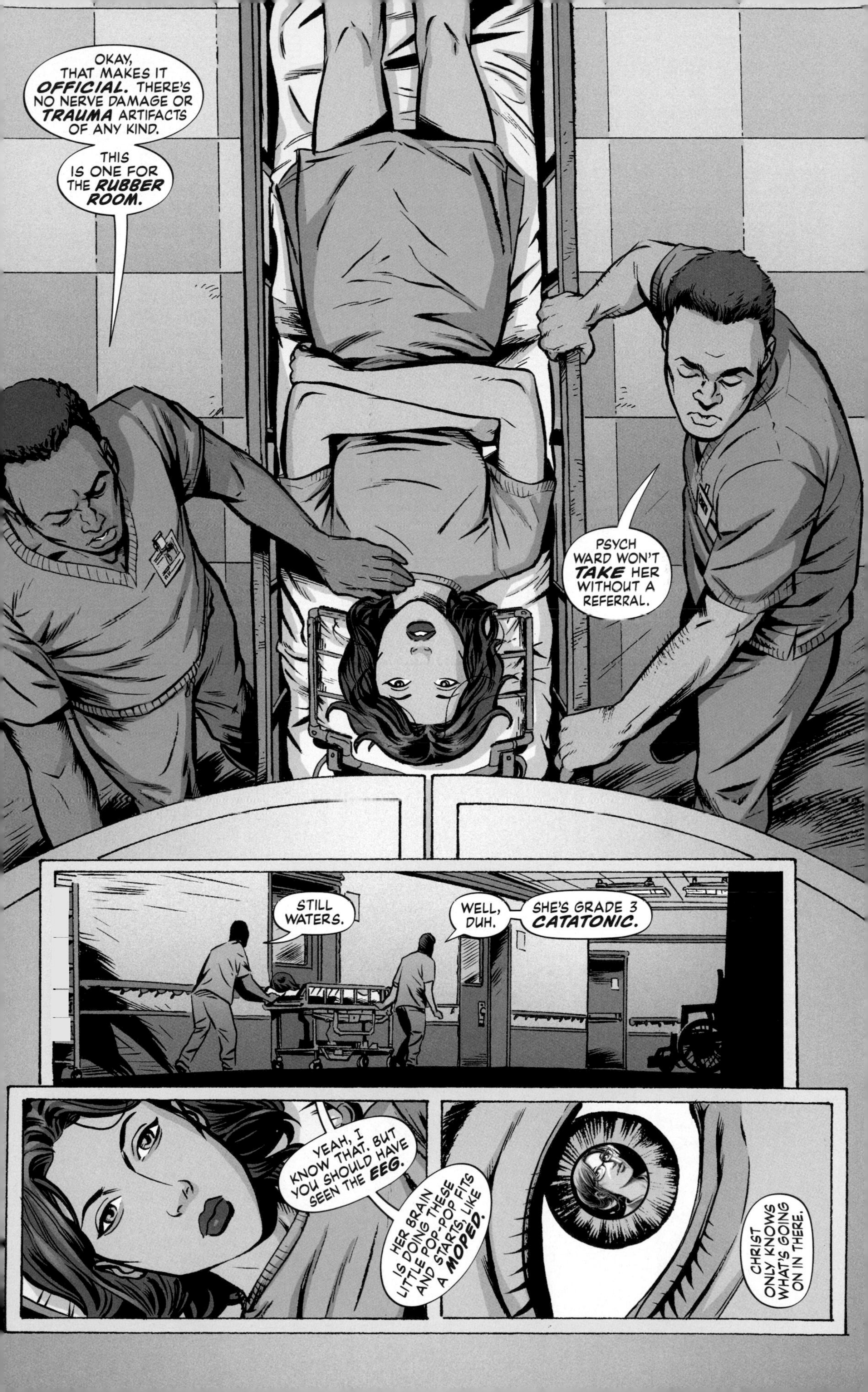
OKAY, THAT MAKES IT OFFICIAL. THERE'S NO NERVE DAMAGE OR TRAUMA ARTIFACTS OF ANY KIND.
THIS IS ONE FOR THE RUBBER ROOM.
PSYCH WARD WON'T TAKE HER WITHOUT A REFERRAL.
STILL WATERS.
WELL, DUH.
SHE'S GRADE 3 CATATONIC.
YEAH, I KNOW THAT. BUT YOU SHOULD HAVE SEEN THE EEG.
HER BRAIN IS DOING THESE LITTLE POP-POP FITS AND STARTS, LIKE A MOPED.
CHRIST ONLY KNOWS WHAT'S GOING ON IN THERE.

The MANY LIVES of LIZZIE HEXAM

Lizzie Hexam is a girl with a strange destiny — and it's up to *you* to choose it!

Tom Taylor's life has been thrown into turmoil, and Lizzie Hexam has to help him survive. But Lizzie has secrets of her own. Where does she come from? What is her link to mysterious recluse Wilson Taylor? Is Lizzie even her real name?

Shape Lizzie's life! Bring her to the fateful moment when she meets Tom Taylor! Uncover the mysteries that lie in her past, and launch her into a new future! Or fail, and see her fall. The power, and the choice, lie with you...

– INSTRUCTIONS –

When you read a Pick-a-Story® book, you steer the characters through a unique adventure that takes its shape as you make your choices. It's easy and fun, so long as you follow these simple instructions:

DON'T read the pages in numerical order. Follow the numbers at the bottom of each page to find your way through the story.

A GREEN number means **GO TO THIS PAGE!**

RED numbers mean **CHOOSE ONE OF THESE OPTIONS!**

If you get to the words **THE END,** the story's over – but if you don't like the ending, you can just begin again at page 1!

Time to get started. Choose wisely, and live well...

By Lizzie Hexam
A Pick-a-Story® Book!

Tommy Taylor and The Ship that Sank Twice

The Tulkinghorn had five hundred students and more. In this hive of ceaseless activity the big boy Tommy led a numerical childhood. He had a dozen mothers and fathers, half a hundred brothers and sisters.

His playground was ... no longer ... remembered or visited by its current inhabitants.

The students were another breed, ... stant and aloof. The masters, ... even more so. Tommy's friends ... ere the children of the other ...

Our Mutual Friend

... a step outside that caught ... was a soft knock at the ... and there her handle within her reach, ... pulling at a pleased laugh: 'Now here, ... her ... with a grown-up that's my particu- ... door said, is a Lizzie Hexam in a black ... she instance,' and ... for friend!' and ... ir entered the room.

'Charley! You!'

... e saw no one ...

'There, there, there, Liz, all right my dear. See! Here's Mr. Headstone come with me.'

Her eyes met those of the schoolmaster, who had evidently expected to see a very different sort of person, and a murmured word or two of salutation passed between

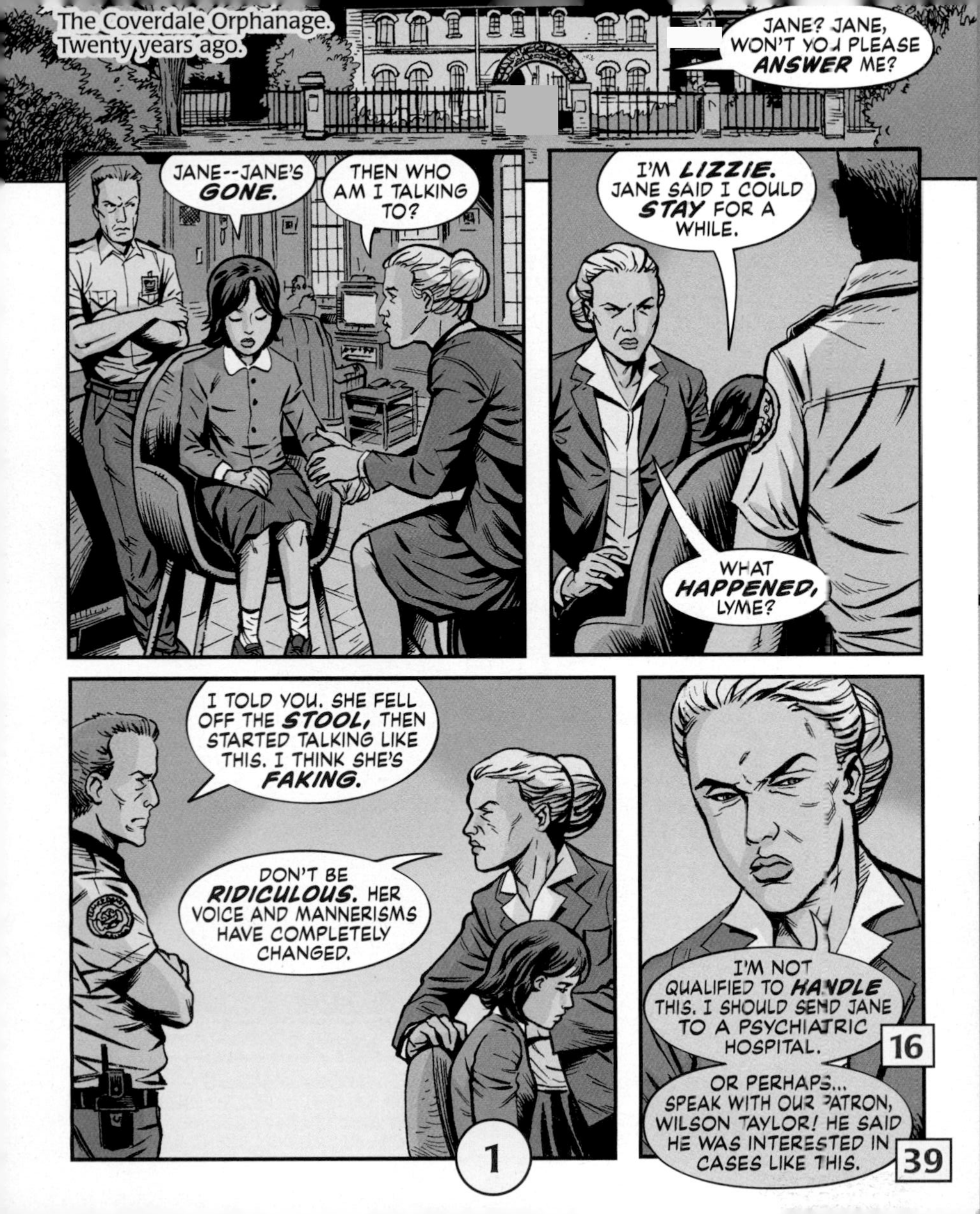
The Coverdale Orphanage.
Twenty years ago.
JANE? JANE, WON'T YOU PLEASE ANSWER ME?
JANE--JANE'S GONE.
THEN WHO AM I TALKING TO?
I'M LIZZIE. JANE SAID I COULD STAY FOR A WHILE.
WHAT HAPPENED, LYME?
I TOLD YOU. SHE FELL OFF THE STOOL, THEN STARTED TALKING LIKE THIS. I THINK SHE'S FAKING.
DON'T BE RIDICULOUS. HER VOICE AND MANNERISMS HAVE COMPLETELY CHANGED.
I'M NOT QUALIFIED TO HANDLE THIS. I SHOULD SEND JANE TO A PSYCHIATRIC HOSPITAL.
16
OR PERHAPS... SPEAK WITH OUR PATRON, WILSON TAYLOR! HE SAID HE WAS INTERESTED IN CASES LIKE THIS.
39
1

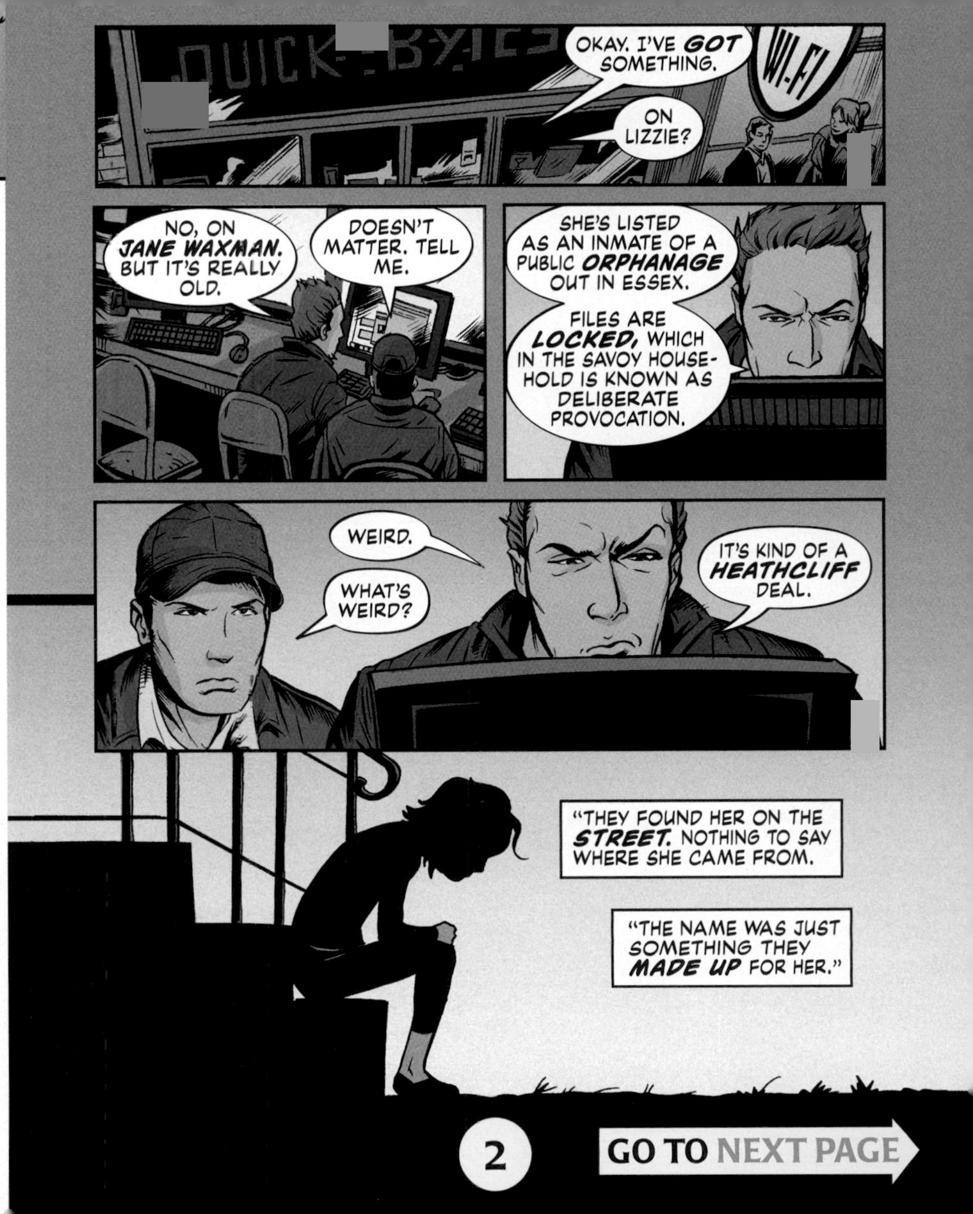
QUICK-BYTES
WI-FI
OKAY. I'VE GOT SOMETHING.
ON LIZZIE?
NO, ON JANE WAXMAN. BUT IT'S REALLY OLD.
DOESN'T MATTER. TELL ME.
SHE'S LISTED AS AN INMATE OF A PUBLIC ORPHANAGE OUT IN ESSEX.
FILES ARE LOCKED, WHICH IN THE SAVOY HOUSEHOLD IS KNOWN AS DELIBERATE PROVOCATION.
WEIRD.
WHAT'S WEIRD?
IT'S KIND OF A HEATHCLIFF DEAL.
"THEY FOUND HER ON THE STREET. NOTHING TO SAY WHERE SHE CAME FROM.
"THE NAME WAS JUST SOMETHING THEY MADE UP FOR HER."
2
GO TO NEXT PAGE

GO TO PAGE 18

(4)

GO TO NEXT PAGE

(3)

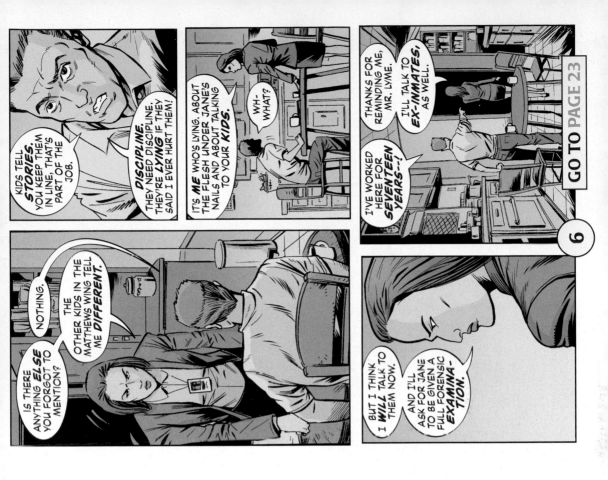

GO TO PAGE 23

6

GO TO NEXT PAGE

5

IT'S SO *GRAND*, SIR!

THIS IS THE *VILLA DIODATI*, LIZZIE, YOUR NEW HOME.

NOW I'M GOING TO TELL YOU A *STORY* LIZZIE, AND YOU HAVE TO LISTEN VERY ATTENTIVELY.

I WILL, SIR. I *PROMISE* I WILL.

GOODNIGHT, CHILD. I'LL READ YOU SOME *MORE* TOMORROW.

"In these times of ours, though concerning the exact year there is no need to be *precise*, a boat of dirty and disreputable appearance, with two figures in it, floated on the *Thames*, between Southwark Bridge which is of iron, and London Bridge which is of stone, as an autumn evening was closing in."

HER MIND IS SO *FRACTURED*, IT'S INFINITELY PLIABLE.

I CAN MAKE HER INTO THE EXACT TOOL THAT TOM WILL *NEED*, WHEN HIS TIME COMES.

8

GO TO
PAGE 35

SO, DO YOU *LIKE* TOM, LIZZIE?

YES, VERY, VERY MUCH. HE LETS ME BE *BOLDINAX* SOMETIMES.

ONE DAY, TOM WILL BE LIKE BOLDINAX, A *HERO* WHO WILL DECIDE THE FATE OF THE WORLD.

YOU CAN *HELP* HIM, IF YOU LIKE.

I SHOULD LIKE THAT *VERY* MUCH.

I *THOUGHT* YOU'D SAY THAT. YOU'RE A *BRAVE* AND NOBLE GIRL.

BUT WHAT I'M GOING TO ASK OF YOU REQUIRES RIGOROUS *TRAINING*. WE'LL BEGIN TOMORROW.

WORLD'S GREATEST DAD

7

What does Wilson have in mind?

A phantasmagorical excursion into a world where magic is real?

31

Or the sleazy and ruthless brainwashing of a vulnerable child?

26

GO TO NEXT PAGE

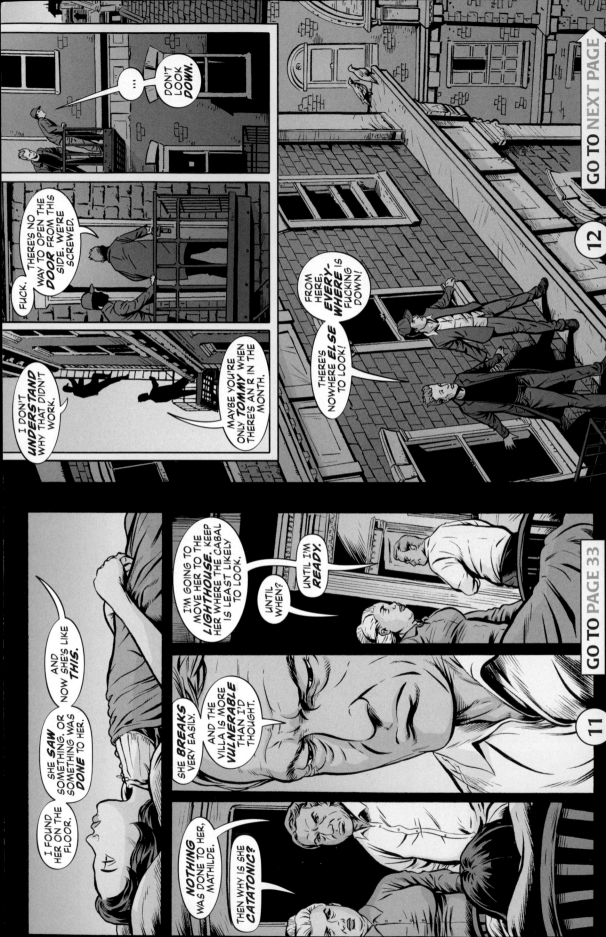

GO TO NEXT PAGE

GO TO PAGE 33

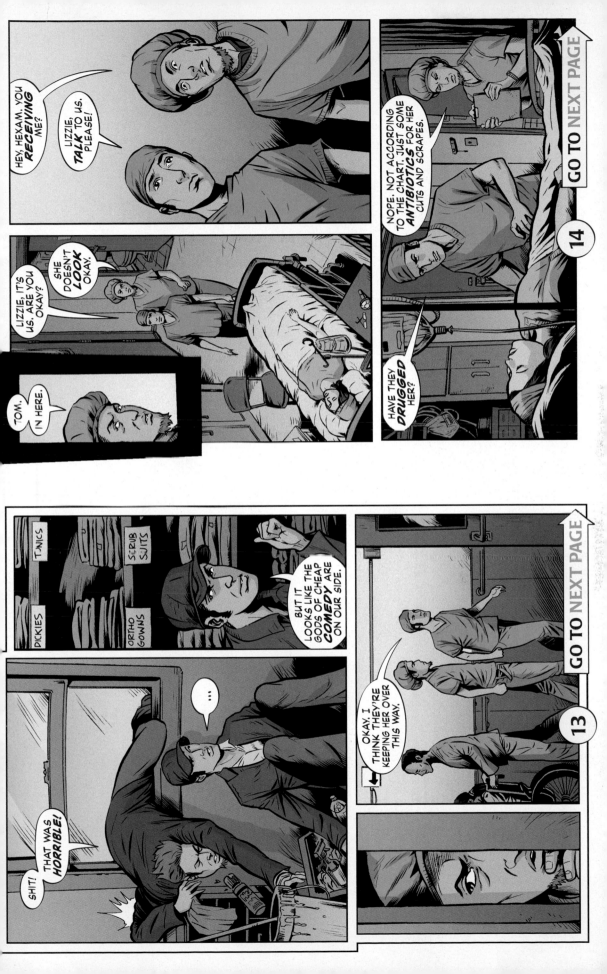

GO TO NEXT PAGE

GO TO NEXT PAGE

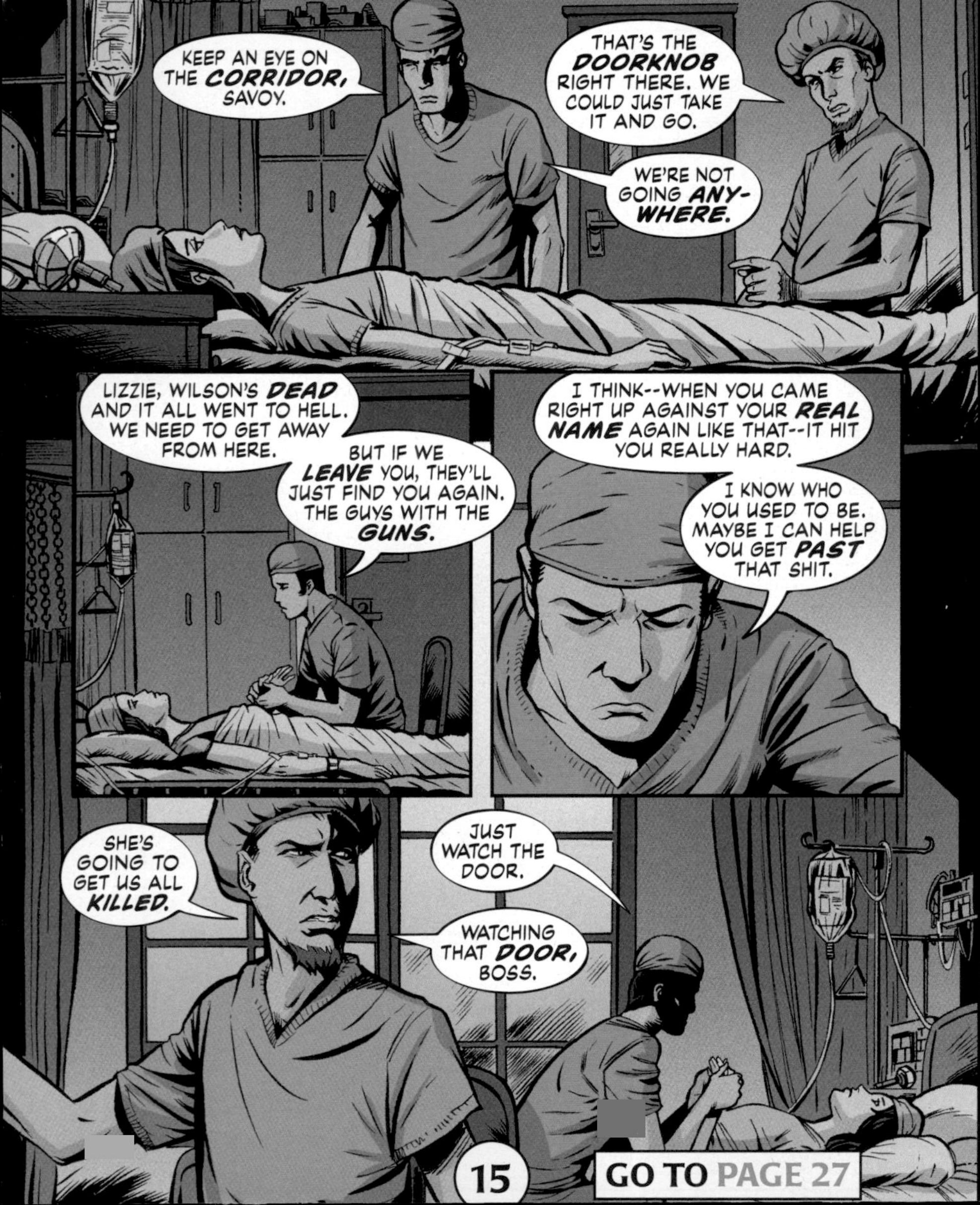
KEEP AN EYE ON THE CORRIDOR, SAVOY.
THAT'S THE DOORKNOB RIGHT THERE. WE COULD JUST TAKE IT AND GO.
WE'RE NOT GOING ANY-WHERE.
LIZZIE, WILSON'S DEAD AND IT ALL WENT TO HELL. WE NEED TO GET AWAY FROM HERE.
BUT IF WE LEAVE YOU, THEY'LL JUST FIND YOU AGAIN. THE GUYS WITH THE GUNS.
I THINK--WHEN YOU CAME RIGHT UP AGAINST YOUR REAL NAME AGAIN LIKE THAT--IT HIT YOU REALLY HARD.
I KNOW WHO YOU USED TO BE. MAYBE I CAN HELP YOU GET PAST THAT SHIT.
SHE'S GOING TO GET US ALL KILLED.
JUST WATCH THE DOOR.
WATCHING THAT DOOR, BOSS.

GO TO PAGE 27

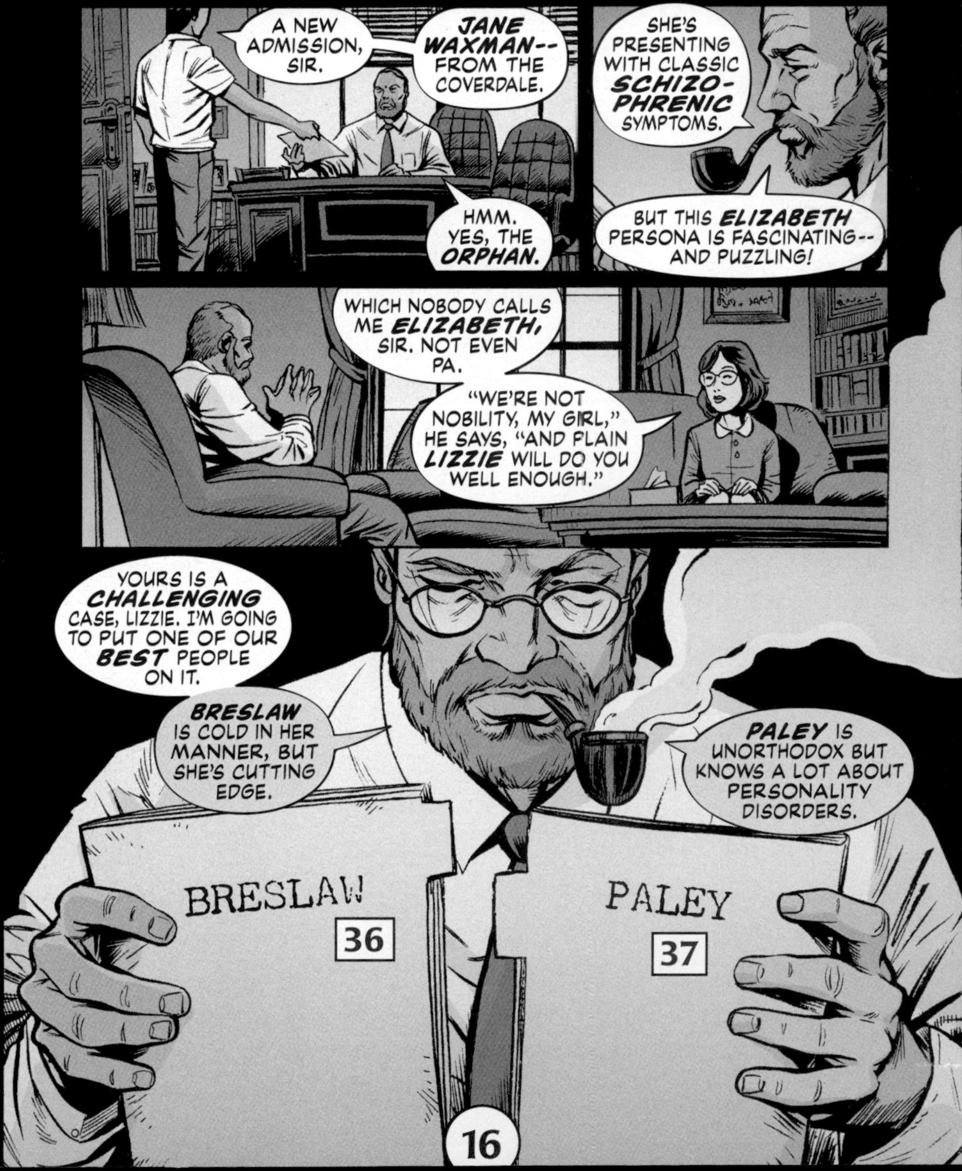
A NEW ADMISSION, SIR.
JANE WAXMAN--FROM THE COVERDALE.
HMM. YES, THE ORPHAN.
SHE'S PRESENTING WITH CLASSIC SCHIZO-PHRENIC SYMPTOMS.
BUT THIS ELIZABETH PERSONA IS FASCINATING--AND PUZZLING!
WHICH NOBODY CALLS ME ELIZABETH, SIR. NOT EVEN PA.
"WE'RE NOT NOBILITY, MY GIRL," HE SAYS, "AND PLAIN LIZZIE WILL DO YOU WELL ENOUGH."
YOURS IS A CHALLENGING CASE, LIZZIE. I'M GOING TO PUT ONE OF OUR BEST PEOPLE ON IT.
BRESLAW IS COLD IN HER MANNER, BUT SHE'S CUTTING EDGE.
PALEY IS UNORTHODOX BUT KNOWS A LOT ABOUT PERSONALITY DISORDERS.
BRESLAW
36
PALEY
37

GO TO NEXT PAGE

GO TO NEXT PAGE

20

RIGHT. I'M NOT.

TOM, YOU'RE NOT EVEN *LISTENING* TO ME.

WAIT!

IT'S NOT ABOUT THE FUCKING DOOR-KNOB. SOMEHOW THIS IS MY *FATHER'S* FAULT.

LOOK, I *GET* THAT WE NEED THE DOORKNOB, BUT WE CAN--

I'M NOT *LEAVING* HER, SAVOY.

THE POLICE REPORT SAYS SHE'S *COMATOSE.* AND THE LAST TIME WE SAW HER, SHE PULLED A *GUN* ON YOU.

YOU'VE GOT NO *IDEA* WHAT YOU'RE WALKING INTO.

SO IT'S DOWN TO *ME.*

I DON'T KNOW WHAT HE *DID* TO HER, BUT IT MESSED HER UP. AND NOW HE'S DEAD.

TOMMY LIVES

TOMMY DIED FOR OUR SINS!

GO TO NEXT PAGE

19

OH NO. OH NO.

... was dead, Lizzie. I'm dead, Lizzie. I was murdered seven hours ago...

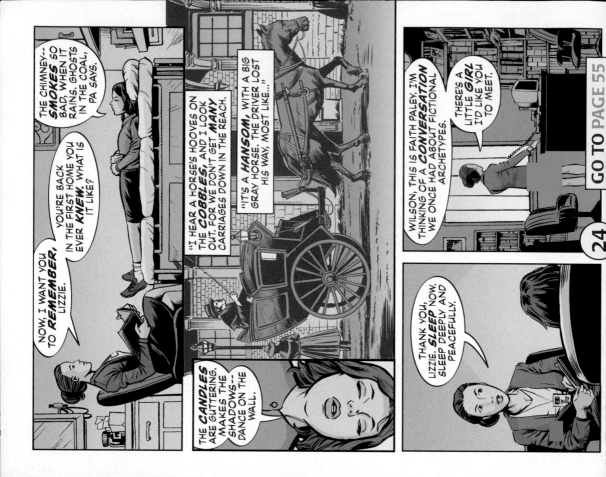

GO TO PAGE 55

GO TO PAGE 32

GO TO PAGE 56

GO TO PAGE 48

30

EITHER WAY, I THINK I KNOW SOME OF WHAT YOU'VE BEEN THROUGH. WHERE YOU ARE NOW.

AND IF YOU WANT TO BE *LIZZIE* AGAIN, I'LL TAKE A SHOT AT BEING *TOMMY,* JUST FOR YOU.

FUCK.

HOW DO I GET *THROUGH* TO HER?

SO MAYBE-- IN A CRAZY WAY-- WHAT WILSON DID ACTUALLY *HELPED* YOU.

OR MAYBE IT *HURT* YOU WORSE THAN YOU WERE HURT ALREADY.

MAYBE THEY CAN *HELP* HER.

SHE'S BEEN IN PLACES LIKE THIS *BEFORE,* RICHIE. AND THEY *DIDN'T.*

AND I THINK, MAYBE... THERE WAS A TIME WHEN YOU REALLY DIDN'T WANT TO BE *JANE.*

WHEN YOU NEEDED TO *ESCAPE* FROM YOUR WHOLE LIFE.

NOTHING, NOT A FLICKER.

THEN MAYBE SHE'S IN THE RIGHT PLACE. DID YOU THINK OF THAT?

29

I NEVER *WANTED* TO BE TOMMY.

I *HATED* TOMMY. HE WAS SOMETHING MY DAD THREW INTO MY LIFE LIKE A *HAND GRENADE.*

WARD ROUNDS, WE'RE RUNNING OUT OF *TIME,* TOM. HOW ARE YOU DOING?

GO TO PAGE 38
GO TO NEXT PAGE

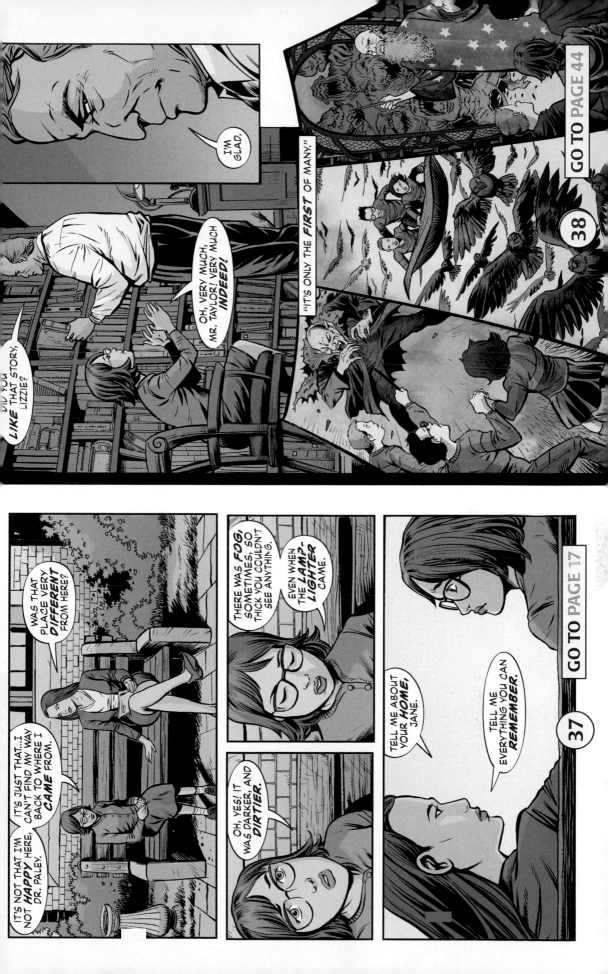

GO TO PAGE 44

GO TO PAGE 17

GO TO NEXT PAGE

GO TO PAGE 55

40

39

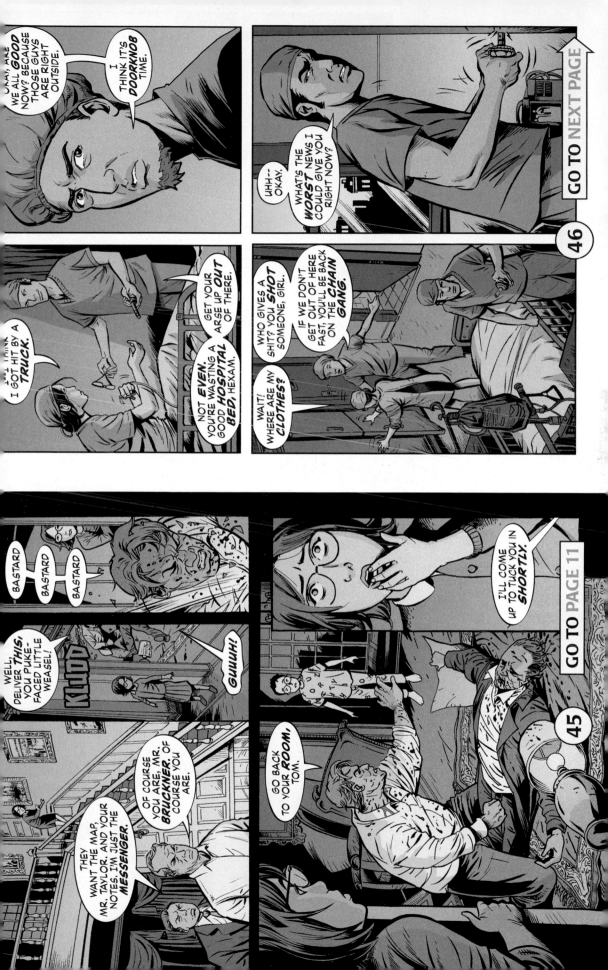

GO TO NEXT PAGE

GO TO PAGE 11

GO TO NEXT PAGE

GO TO PAGE 57

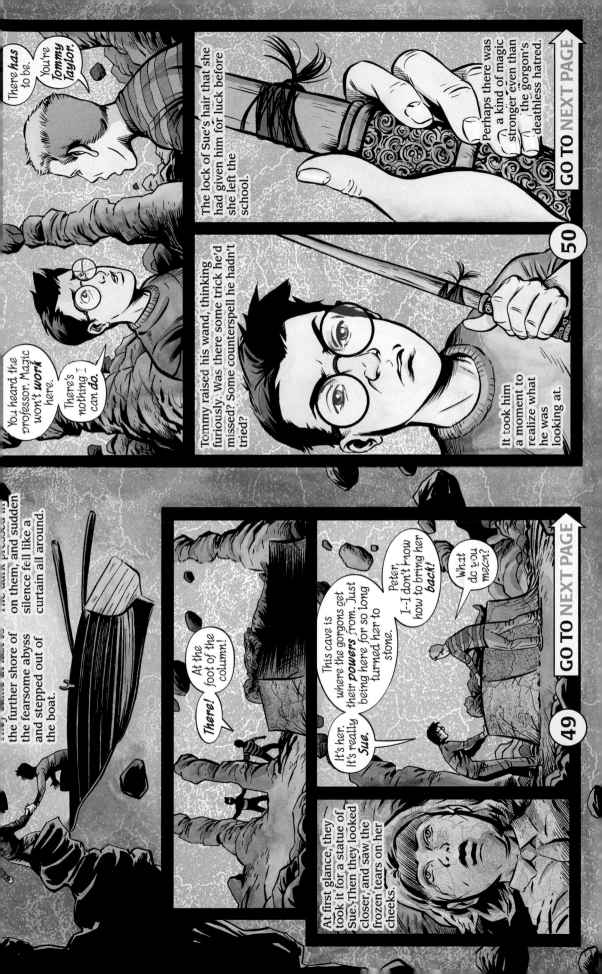

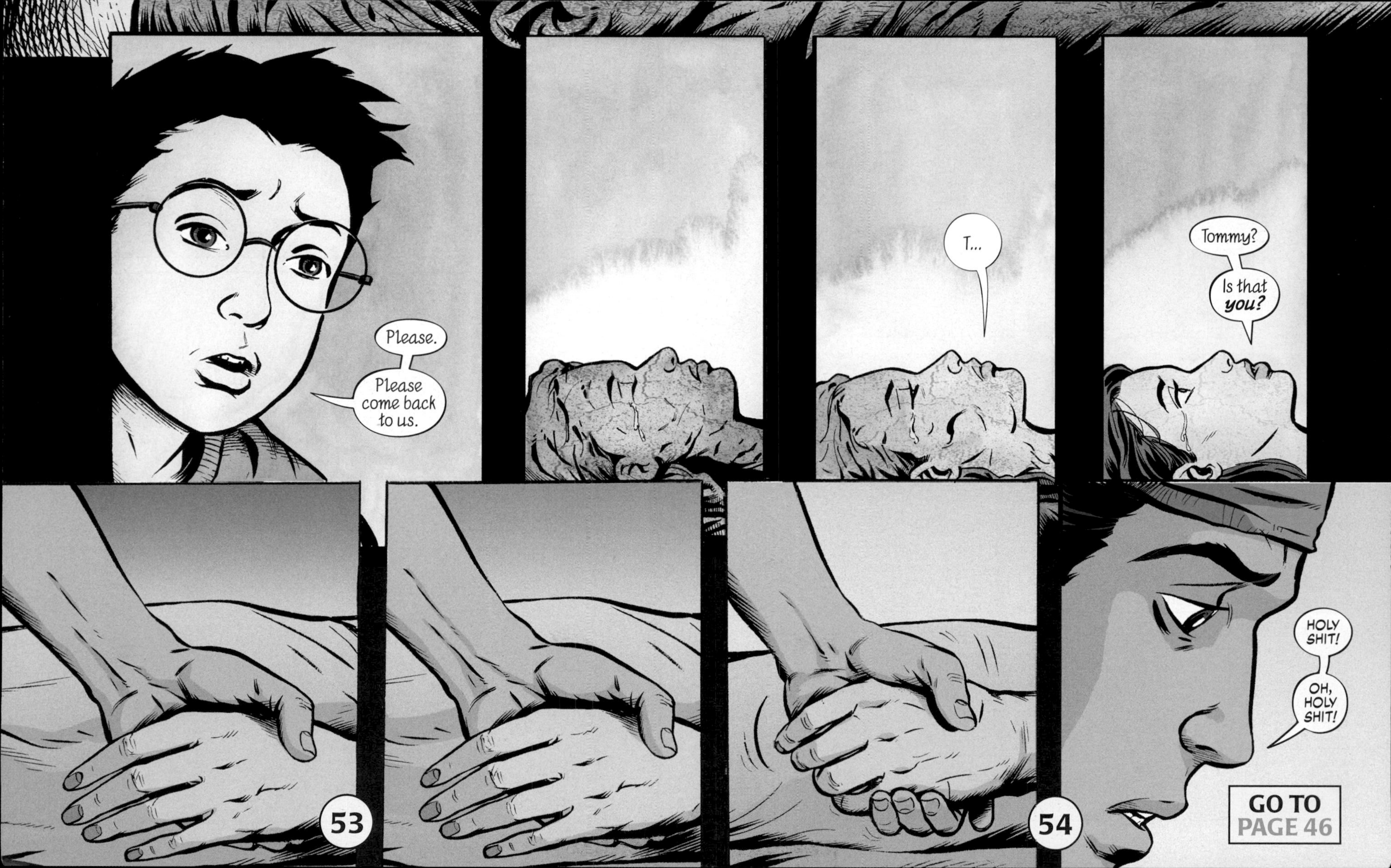
Please.
Please come back to us.
T...
Tommy?
Is that *you?*
53
54
HOLY SHIT!
OH, HOLY SHIT!

GO TO PAGE 46

GO TO NEXT PAGE

58

57

GO TO NEXT PAGE

GO TO NEXT PAGE

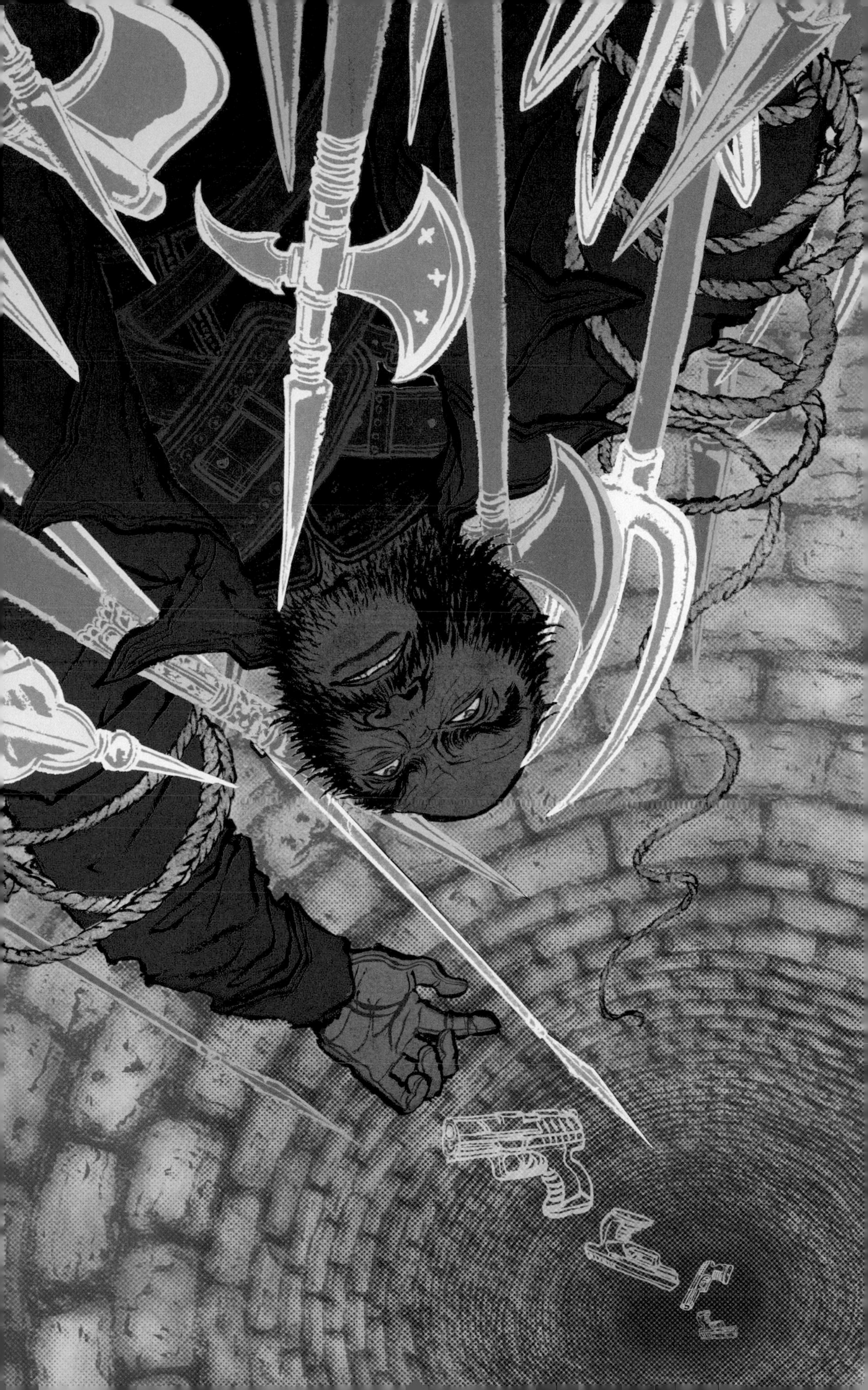

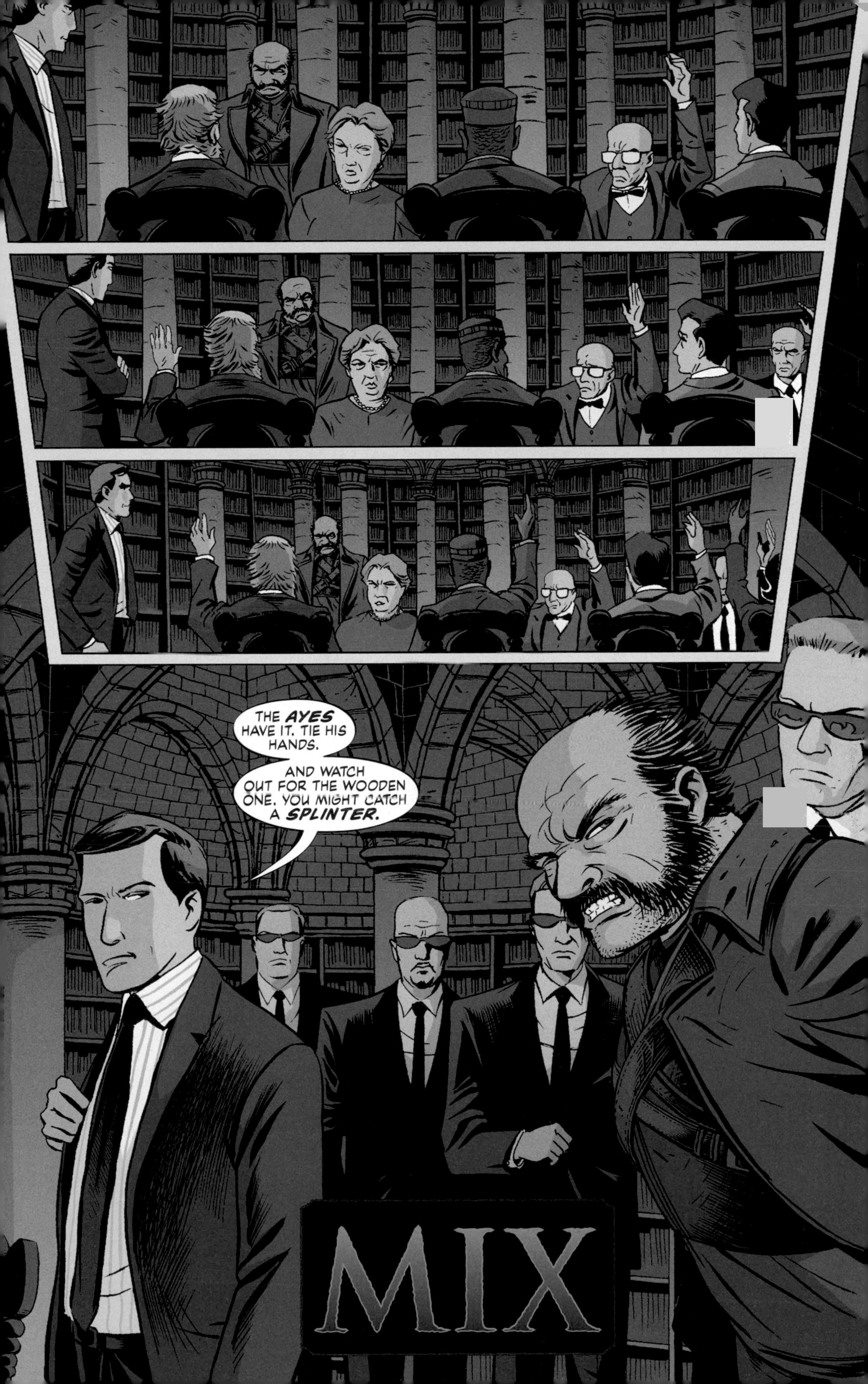
THE AYES HAVE IT. TIE HIS HANDS.
AND WATCH OUT FOR THE WOODEN ONE. YOU MIGHT CATCH A SPLINTER.
MIX

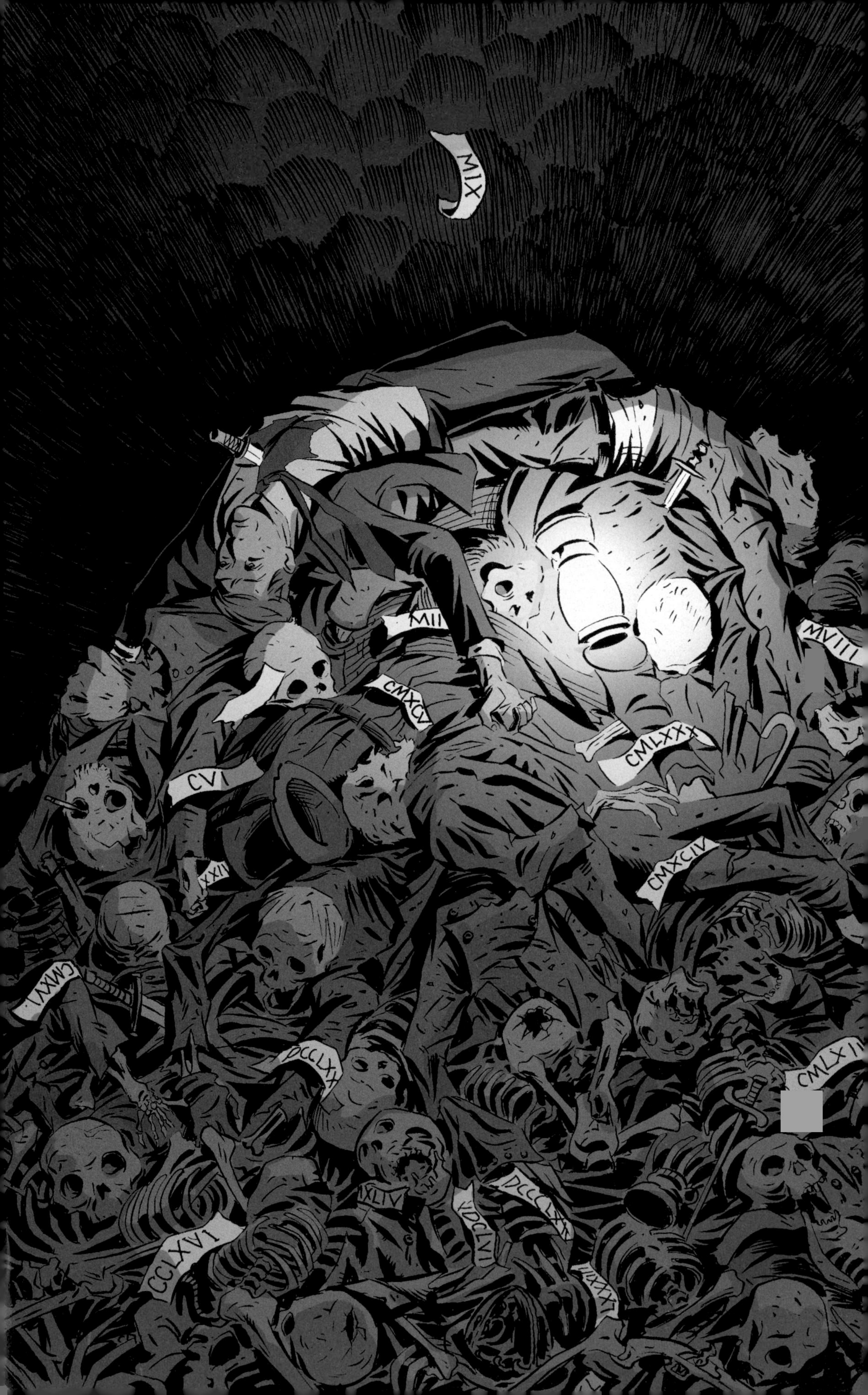
MIX
MII
MVIII
CMXCV
CMLXXX
CVI
CMXCIV
DCCLXX
CCLXVI

"FABLES is an excellent series in the tradition of SANDMAN, one that rewards careful attention and loyalty." – ENTERTAINMENT WEEKLY

BILL WILLINGHAM

"[A] wonderfully twisted concept... features fairy tale characters banished to the noirish world of present-day New York."
–THE WASHINGTON POST

WINNER OF
EISNER AWARDS

VOL. 1: LEGENDS IN EXILE
VOL. 2: ANIMAL FARM
VOL. 3: STORYBOOK LOVE
VOL. 4: MARCH OF THE WOODEN SOLDIERS
VOL. 5: THE MEAN SEASONS
VOL. 6: HOMELANDS
VOL. 7: ARABIAN NIGHTS (AND DAYS)
VOL. 8: WOLVES
VOL. 9: SONS OF EMPIRE
VOL. 10: THE GOOD PRINCE
VOL. 11: WAR AND PIECES
VOL. 12: THE DARK AGES
VOL. 13: THE GREAT FABLES CROSSOVER
1001 NIGHTS OF SNOWFALL

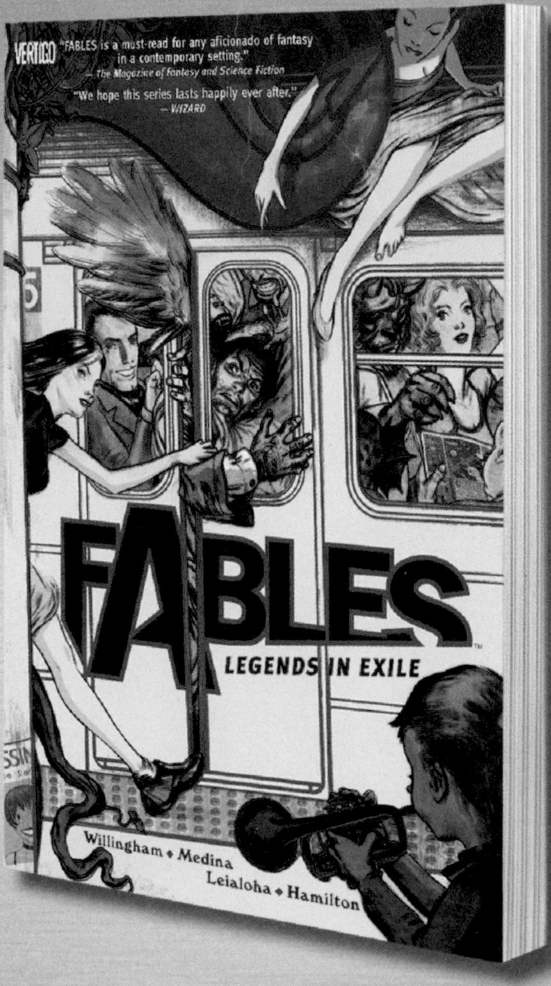
VERTIGO
"FABLES is a must-read for any aficionado of fantasy in a contemporary setting."
— The Magazine of Fantasy and Science Fiction
"We hope this series lasts happily ever after."
— WIZARD
FABLES
LEGENDS IN EXILE
Willingham • Medina
Leialoha • Hamilton

FABLES VOL. 3:
STORYBOOK LOVE

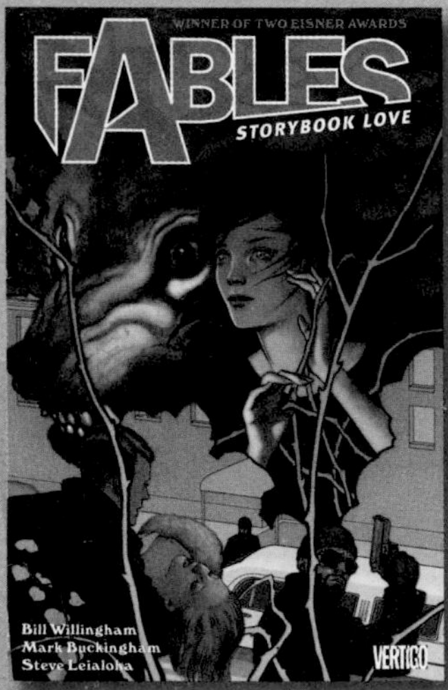
WINNER OF TWO EISNER AWARDS
FABLES
STORYBOOK LOVE
Bill Willingham
Mark Buckingham
Steve Leialoha
VERTIGO

FABLES VOL. 6:
HOMELANDS

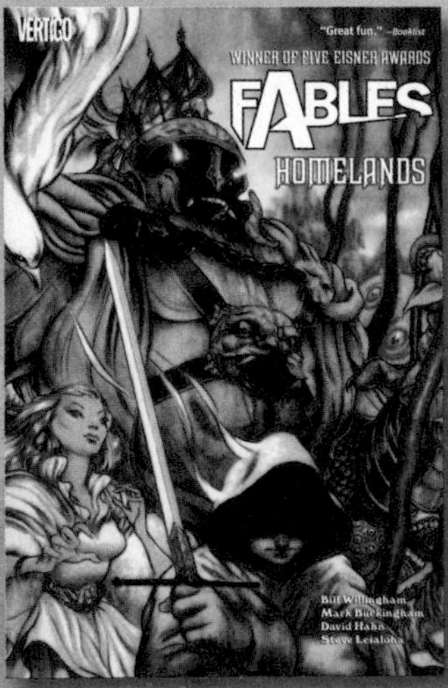
VERTIGO
"Great fun." —Booklist
WINNER OF FIVE EISNER AWARDS
FABLES
HOMELANDS
Bill Willingham
Mark Buckingham
David Hahn
Steve Leialoha

FABLES:
1001 NIGHTS OF SNOWFALL

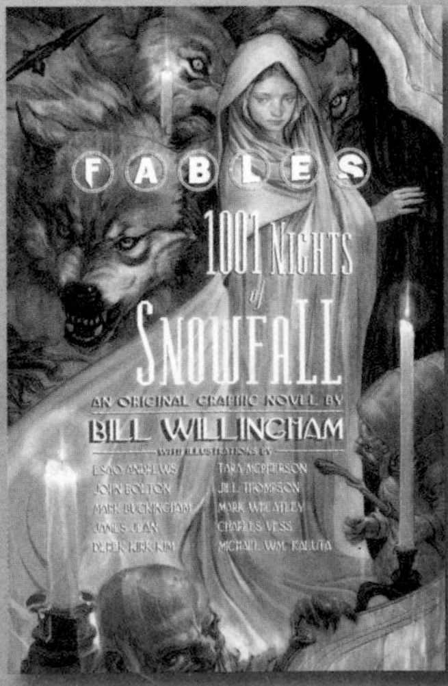
FABLES
1001 NIGHTS OF SNOWFALL
AN ORIGINAL GRAPHIC NOVEL BY
BILL WILLINGHAM

GO TO
...OBO...
FOR ... RST ISSUES OF OUR GRAPHIC NOVELS
...ed for Mature Readers